The Sarcastic Mother's Holiday Diary

Anne E. Thompson

The Cobweb Press

Copyright © Anne E. Thompson 2018
The right of Anne E Thompson to be identified as the author of this work has been asserted in accordance with sections 77 and 78 of the Copyright Designs and Patents Act 1988.

Condition of Sale
This book is sold subject to the condition that it shall not, by way of trade or otherwise, be lent, re-sold, hired out or otherwise circulated in any form of binding or cover other than that in which it is published and without similar condition including this condition being imposed on the subsequent purchaser.

Published by The Cobweb Press
www.thecobwebpress.com
thecobwebpress@gmail.com

Contents

Packing
1997 France
1999 St Croix
1999 Philadelphia
2000 Florida
2001 Devon
2001 France
2005 Italy
2007 Sicily
2007 Zambia
2008 Palma del Rio
2009 Verona
20009 Milan
2009 Lake Como
2011 Rome
2012 Sorrento
2012 Puglia
2012 Dubai
2013 Bitez, Turkey
2013 China
2014 Lake Garda
2015 New York
2015 Brazil
2015 Malta and Gozo
2015 Bangkok and Singapore
2016 Sri Lanka
2016 Argentina
2016 Uruguay
2016 Krakow
2016 Delhi
2016 Cyprus
2017 Mumbai
2017 Austria
2017 Slovenia
2017 Croatia
2018 Tokyo
2018 Camber Sands, UK
2018 Portugal and Gibraltar

Packing

Today will be stressful – packing for the family holiday. If you're a mother, you will know what I mean.

There is oceans of washing to do. It seems a bad idea to leave dirty clothes to fester in the laundry basket, plus there is all the bedding. I don't like the idea of returning after two weeks away to sheets that have been slept/sweated/dribbled in for a week and then locked into a room to ferment. Obviously I cannot wash it all the day we leave, but it feels better if it's washed the day before – so just *one* night of body fluids sweated into them.

Then there is the animal stuff. Dog and grumpy-cat taken to kennels, their bedding and towels left here.

I can leave them – and be welcomed home by the thick odour *a la dog*, or I can wash them before I go. Thank goodness for washing machines and please can mine not break today.

Of course, not everyone has this problem. I have known people (not female) who quite cheerfully shove dirty clothes into a bag before a holiday, and then return with the same bag of dirty clothes at the end. I am not entirely sure if they were worn, or washed, in between, because I didn't like to ask.

I have to pack. Always stressful. You assemble everything you need, the case is full, and you haven't even thought about clothes yet. There's the stuff in case someone cuts themselves, or has a headache, or is sick. The shampoo you'll never find abroad, the sun hat, sun lotion, sandals, plus hygiene stuff, a book, rechargers (because these magically disappear and people always need to borrow them) swimming goggles (which I never wear, but again, they disappear into the black hole of "I wasn't the last person to have them..."), etc. And even supposing you find room for clothes, which ones do you take? Will the food be good and the weather lazy, so you need clothes you can expand into? Or will you spend the time enjoying the hotel gym and pool and eating salads, so you can pack the slightly-too-tight-but-fitted-last-year clothes?

Then Husband weighs the case – why? Why do men do this? It can wait until check-in and be sorted out then if necessary – followed by ever so slightly tense conversation about the necessity of carrying certain items.

At least now I don't have to pack for the children. That was always a nightmare.

I had things sorted when we lived in the US, travelling back and forth with a 2, 4 and 6 year old, often on my own. Each child carried a small back-pack containing a complete set of their own clothes and an empty ice-cream container. You only ever carry a vomit-covered child off a plane once, before you plan things a bit better.

Of course, sometimes it went wrong. Like the time Jay couldn't decide what to pack and proudly tipped up his bag on holiday to empty out one of each piece of toy/puzzle/game that he owned. Just one piece. Or the year Emm packed his football. Just his football. And every year, although not having room for clothes, there does seem to be a disturbing number of inflatable animals in the pool with us.

Then there is the house. Sinks need to be bleached or they stink when you get home. But some oink always tips their unfinished coffee into the sink just before you leave. And surfaces need to be wiped and crockery washed and bins emptied. And always, after you have done that, someone will use something and make them all dirty again. Of course, you can't do it too early, because the family has to eat. They expect, amidst all this frenzy of cleaning, for a meal to appear. Which creates another whole lot of mess to be cleaned up.

So, you feel like you are stuck in a loop of cleaning, washing, wiping while everyone else is going round making it all dirty again. And no one cares, they cannot understand why it makes a difference to return home to a clean house, not a dirty stinky one, when within minutes of arriving it will get messed up again. But it does. If you are female you will know this – having a pristine house while no one is in it, is extremely important. Otherwise burglars might think you are tardy.

I haven't even started on the outside animals yet. Buying copious amounts of food so they can be fed in my absence, cleaning them out so kind pet-feeding person doesn't think I'm slack for not keeping them properly clean. Clearing up all the stuff I ignore when I'm there, but looks unsightly when I notice it. Ensuring fences are secure and bedding has fresh hay. It all takes time.

So, I had better stop writing and make a start. I will let you know how we get on, but I'm sure it will be wonderful. I shall do nothing but follow round Husband-with-a-plan, while laughing at my family's jokes and writing rude things about them in my diary.

I will start with my earliest holiday diaries (because they're less sarcastic than the later ones – I shall break you in gently). What you are about to read, are my actual holiday diaries, written at the time. Although I have edited them slightly, and removed anything people might find embarrassing or offensive, they are pretty much as written. I have removed or changed the names of people. I hope you enjoy reading them as much as I enjoyed writing them.

France 1997
(Children aged 1, 3 and 5 years)

Friday 23rd May

Got up at 5:30am (I didn't make these travel plans). Got dressed. Dressed everyone else (except Husband – he managed to dress himself). Gave everyone breakfast, then drove to Newhaven.

Jay was sick in the car. Super. Rest of journey scented with *Eau de Vomit*. I cleaned him up, and we all worried we'd miss the ferry to Newhaven. As soon as things were reasonably clean, we repacked the car, bundled Bea and Emm back inside (they hardly made any fuss at all about the smell) and zoomed off to try and catch the ferry.

Arrived Newhaven. Ferry delayed by 2 hours.

Rest of journey uneventful. Bea and Emm loved the ferry, and Jay toddled round on the deck. There was a little shop, and I managed to find some wristbands which stop travel sickness. Bought some for Jay, let's hope they work.

Drove to Alençon. Looked for a hotel (a bit scary, in case we didn't find one and had to all sleep in the car). Found a really nice one with vacancies. It's new and clean, with an ensuite shower and loo, and a balcony with beds for Bea and Emm. Hoping to sleep well.

Saturday 24th May

Had a nice breakfast, then drove for a couple of hours. Stopped in a park for snacks and loo. The loo was more like a cattle-shed. It didn't even have doors. Or toilets. This caused rather a lot of discussion from my children.

Drove for ages to a motorway service area and had lunch. Jay was very fed up, and cried when we put him back in the car. His vote was definitely to holiday at the service station! As I fastened his seatbelt, to stop him leaving, I noticed that one wristband was missing (you remember – those clever ones which magically stop travel-sickness?) One has totally disappeared. I've looked everywhere, but it's gone. Emm looked at me, with his cheeky round face, and told me, perfectly seriously, that he ate it. I am not entirely sure what I should do with this information.

Stopped mid afternoon for tea. Weather was lovely and warm, so we all changed into shorts.

Husband asked me to read out directions to cottage. Few moments of panic, as I had no idea where we were, nor where we were going. (I felt I should have had more warning about this.) Stopped in a town and bought a map.

Arrived at cottage about 7pm. Unpacked. Put everyone to bed. I have enjoyed driving through the French countryside, and apart from Jay at the end, the children were marvellous with such a long journey. I'm tired now, but it's been a happy day. (Still haven't found that wristband.)

Sunday 25th May
The best thing about the cottage is that it has shutters instead of curtains. They cut out every speck of light, so Bea and Emm didn't wake until 8am. Wow! My first lie-in for 5 years. (Thought everyone must be dead when I woke and saw the time!)

No food for breakfast except for breadsticks and orange juice. Husband hardly commented on this at all. Went to Lalinde and found a supermarket open (phew) and a bakers. Everyone we met was very friendly, laughed at our appalling French, but seemed pleased that we were trying. Bought French stick loaves. Felt very French as we walked through the sunny village, carrying our bread.

Back at cottage, swam in the pool. It was *freezing*.

Cooked tinned stew for lunch. It was as awful as it sounds. A lot like eating dog food.

Walk and ice-cream in Lalinde.

Fresh bread and cheese for tea, then played in the garden. It's a lovely garden, with miniature trees (or they might just have not grown yet).

Monday 26th May
Up late again (8am). Croissant and coffee – nicer than Sainsbury's. (And breadsticks and juice, but we won't talk about that.)

Walked to village in sunshine, then swam before lunch.

2:15pm I have just cooked *the* most revolting lunch! Luckily everyone was starving, so it all went. Fresh cherries for pudding.

I am now sitting under the shade of a vine, sipping sangria, listening to crickets sing and watching lizards play on the patio. Perfect.

***

Went for a drive through some pretty villages to Chateaux Languais. It had dogs, and looked expensive, so we didn't go in.

Found a supermarket (not very 'ethnic' but it made Husband happy).

Cottage boiling hot. Kids refused to go to sleep.

Tuesday 27th May
Brioche and coffee breakfast.

Drove to Gouffre de Proumeyssac (this spelling might be wrong). Saw some caves – really beautiful, and I don't even like caves. There were sparkling rocks, and inside was huge, like a cathedral, so it didn't feel like a cave. Ate ice-creams.

Steak for lunch, then strawberries.

I later found Bea's steak in the toilet. Am guessing she doesn't like steak. Naughty girl! Now I don't know whether to try and flush away said steak, and risk blocking French plumbing; or whether to put my arm into toilet and fish out the spat-out steak. Ah, the wonderful choices involved with having children...

Played in garden and swam.

Drove to bakers, and had bread and cheese picnic.

We're all getting a tan, even the children who I am regularly smothering in suncream. It's about 28°, though it is meant to get cooler tomorrow. I like it hot, but I worry a bit about the children.

Wednesday 28th May
We had a boat ride at Baynac and walked up to a Chateaux. It was a sort of French equivalent of Clovelly, but without all the tourists.

Friday 29th May
We had a tour of nearby villages. Found St Avir Senvia ruin, and a huge church (Cadouin). The atmosphere in these places is marvellous, you can *feel* the history. I wish I could paint it all, I will never manage to capture the essence of them in a photo.

We also went to a children's *animal farm and rides* place. The kids enjoyed it, so it was fun.

Saturday 30th May
We tried to find a strawberry market. It was shut.

Drove to Lot. Looked around a brilliant castle (Bonaguil). It was fabulous, half a ruin, but with secret passages underneath that you could walk through. You could imagine there were ghosts, knights in armour, damsels in distress, poor prisoners in the dungeons below.

We walked around, and then posed for a photograph on the steps. The photograph took almost as long as viewing the castle. (Just saying.)

Drove back through Monpazier - a quaint Bastide town. Ate ice-creams in the village square.

Sunday 1st June
Drove to a viewpoint overlooking the Dordogne valley and attempted to do a D.I.Y church (because I just could *not* face taking the boys to a French speaking church). It didn't go very

well, no one was at all interested, but I tried. It's hard to make Sunday special when you don't go to church.

Had lunch in a nice village restaurant. Very French. Drank too much wine.

Drove to Bannes Chateaux and looked around. Felt a bit like a museum (and I don't like museums). Not much romance or story left in the house. Weather cool and raining.

We have seen so many lovely places. The children mainly love playing in the cottage garden. Bea and Emm love the swimming pool, and are getting quite confident in the water. But they are all a pain at night, and won't go to sleep, and then wake several times during the night. Plus, Jay cries *every* time we put him into the car – doesn't bode well for the journey home.

Monday 2nd June
Went to La Roque Gaguac - a village cut into the rock face. We walked up steep footpaths, and found derelict houses and caves. You could almost *see* the smugglers!

Then drove to Domme, but that was too touristy. Had some nice crepes in a street-side cafe. Drove home via the Intermarche.

Wednesday 4th June
So, everyone has been sick (not me and Husband). Maybe it's the French water or something. It's bit of a pain, but last week was so lovely; and I'd rather they were ill here, somewhere pretty, than being stuck at home on my own all day, with Husband at work. At least they can vomit in sunshine!

Thursday 5th June
Everyone is well. Everyone is cranky.

Went for a drive this morning (Jay so pleased!) Spent afternoon in the garden. Jay spent hours collecting rocks to go in the buggy, and then pushing them down the drive. Probably going to be a landscaper when he grows up. (Doubt he'll be a lorry driver!)

Emm and Bea played, and argued. We swam, and played 'football' in the pool (I nearly drowned a few times).

Everyone starving, so lots of snacks. After tea went for another drive, trying to see chateaus and monasteries and quaint villages. Another nice day.

Friday 6th June
Went to Les Eyzies and La Grande Roc in the morning.

After lunch we spent the afternoon packing. The Mercedes boot has jammed shut – must be due to the heat – can't beat a classy car! Husband had to load the boot via the back seat.

Went swimming.

Saturday 7th May
Left cottage 7am. Drove to Alençon and booked into a B&B. Had an early dinner in *Buffalo Bills*. Very relaxed, and nice food, I enjoyed it a lot (mainly because I hadn't cooked it). Jay liked tottering along the balcony (it has a fence, so it's safe).

Husband and I spent the evening sitting on the balcony outside the room, chatting and watching a thunder storm, while the children *didn't* sleep.

Sunday 8th May
Drove to Dieppe. Bread rolls for lunch. Thunder storm. Ferry home. What a wonderful holiday.

St Croix 1999 Family Diary
While we were living in New Jersey.
(Children aged 3, 5 and 7 years)

Sunday March 28th:
I made pancakes for tea. After their baths, the children went to bed in their travelling clothes. They were so excited!

Monday:
Woke 3:30, left house at 4:00 am. Drove to Newark and parked in long term parking.

Monorail to airport. Checked in 5:30.

Boarded plane, all going well. Taxied to runway, then returned to gate because pilot felt sick. Super, as if I don't have enough problems with my family and vomit on holidays...

Delayed 3 hours. Husband phoned and sorted out connecting flight.

Finally flew to San Juan. Airport felt dirty and I was worried about eating anything there.

Got a tiny plane to St Croix. When we arrived, there were no bags. All our luggage must have been on a different plane. Husband left me and children in a nearby Pizza Hut while he went to find our cases.

As I sat there, surrounded by pizzas and a pitcher of cola, I was suddenly aware that I was on my own, in a strange country, with no money (left purse in car) or phone, or place to stay (Husband has all the condo details). All I had were three small children, and a food bill. Hoped Husband hadn't done a runner!

Husband returned and we drove to Colony Cove (800-828-0746) Our condo is nice. It has tiled floors (good for sweeping up sand), three bedrooms and two bathrooms, a sitting area and a little kitchen. You open the curtains and there is the beach — right there — sand and sea and palm trees, with the constant whisper of wind. It is breath-takingly beautiful.

Tuesday:
Shopped in local town and had breakfast.
 Walked along beach, found a *huge* pink conch shell.
 Swam in pool and played on beach.
 In the evening, when the children were in bed, there was a strange scratching in the kitchen. I went to investigate and found one of the shells that Bea had collected earlier was walking along the floor!

Wednesday:
Swam in pool.
 Drove along NW coast road looking at views. Walked through palm trees, banana trees and tropical flowers to a beach. Everywhere is so beautiful, I feel like I am soaking in the views, trying to remember forever.
 Went to Christiansted, and bought trinkets.
 Husband snorkelled. We walked on the beach, watching him and pretending he was James Bond. Afterwards, he said it was odd snorkelling, he felt like he was trespassing on fish territory. I was mainly just glad he didn't get eaten by a shark. He wanted to go to an aquarium so he could name what he had seen in the wild.
 In the evening we walked along the beach. We suddenly realised the sand was moving — it was completely full of hermit crabs.

Thursday:
Swam in pool.
 Went to Christiansted aquarium.
 Walked along boardwalk. Pretty.
 Drove around a rainforest.
 Walked in St George's Botanical Gardens. I loved the warm moist air. Lots of amazing plants and no snakes, so I was happy.

Jay fell over, so had to patch him up. We had no watches on so didn't know the time and were there for hours.

Played games in the evening.

Friday:
Swam. Breakfast.

Drove to Sandy Point. It was hard to find, as was along an unmarked dirt track. Beach was deserted and full of wonderful shells, sea sponges, coral (and washed up litter). It was really, really, hot and there was no shade, so we couldn't stay long in case the children burnt.

Saw a cotton bush (I'd never seen one before).

Drove back to condo via Fredericksted. Saw a liner out in the bay. It looked so big and out of place compared to the rest of the island, a big white plastic thing spoiling the view (I know it isn't really plastic, but that's what it looked like, very ugly). I guess when you are on one you are not looking at it, so don't care.

Drove through the rainforest again. I put down the windows so we could feel the humidity, smell the flowers, and hear the birds as we drove. We saw a banana tree with a flower. It was growing in a man's garden and when he saw us looking, he invited us in to take photos. The people here all seemed very relaxed and friendly, and speak to us as if they know us.

Lunch in restaurant of hotel next door to condo. Nice food. Walked in garden. Bea found a fallen coconut.

It is always breezy here, warm but not hot. We have to be careful to not burn. I spend hours on the little patio, watching the palm trees blow in the breeze and the little fishing boats bobbing on the sea. I saw herons and pelicans flying around, and the children collected orchids to go in the kitchen.

In the afternoon, Husband smashed up the coconut so the children could see inside. It was old and dry and we had another one which wasn't ripe; so we couldn't eat them, but it was interesting. We rubbed the milk on our skin (sure I'd read somewhere it was good for you).

We drove along the south coast. It was very barren, no palm trees, lots of cactus and rocks. Went all the way to the easternmost tip of the U.S., then walked down to the beach and played in the sand.

Saturday.
Swam, walked, shopped, breakfast.

Went on a boat to the coral reef. Husband snorkelled, I stayed in the boat with the children. It had a glass bottom, so we could see the fish. We saw a barracuda and lots of blue 'paraffin' fish and needle noses. The boat was hot and uncomfortable and smelt of petrol, and watching fish is quite boring, even when they're swimming wild in the sea, so I was glad the adults didn't swim for too long.

Then we went to Buck Island. The beach was fantastic, I had never seen such soft sand or such clear water. Husband swam, but the rest of us didn't have swim suits with us (because we knew the kids weren't allowed to swim off the boat, and the island was unexpected). Suddenly, while I was walking along the beach enjoying the view, Jay, fully dressed, ran into the water up to his chest to:

"Tell Daddy something."

So he swam too (momentary lapse in mummy concentration).

Pizza Hut tea.

Sunday:
Swam.

Breakfast, then went to a church. It was okay.

Spent afternoon on beach then packed. I didn't want to go home...

Philadelphia September 1999

We went to Philadelphia for the weekend. It was fun.

Arrived midday on Saturday and ate Philly cheesesteaks for lunch (seemed appropriate).

Walked around the historical park, and saw the tomb of the unknown soldier (I think he was called Terry) and liberty bell (which was big, but really, just a bell).

We walked around a market, and ate some ice-cream the Amish people were selling. The Amish people were more interesting than the ice-cream.

Got on a trolley bus, and had a tour of the city (with a very funny tour guide, who made fun of all the sculptures). We saw the graveyard which features in *The Sixth Sense* but this was probably not meant to be the highlight of Philadelphia.

Stayed at a Holiday Inn.

Sunday

We got a taxi to the science museum. I was really, really, bored. But the children liked it (clearly were switched at birth and not mine). We watched a demonstration about liquid nitrogen (bound to be useful).

Ate awful hot dogs. Really awful.

Walked up towards the art gallery and looked around the Rodin collection. Pretty cool. I took photos of *The Poet* and *The Gates to Hell*. I could have spent hours here, the sculptures were amazing. Rest of family bored (definitely not my genes).

Sat on a fountain (not literally) and ate some snacks (better than the hot dogs).

Drove home to NJ.

Florida May 2000

Saturday 19th May

Flew to Florida, drove to Disney. This was a big surprise for the children, who only knew that we were going to Florida, and whenever they mentioned Disney, I said it was way too expensive for us to visit.

Thursday 25th May

The children were *so* excited when we arrived at Disney.

The hotel was nice, and the children loved the pool, and feeding the ducks who visited every morning. Everything has the face of Mickey Mouse on it – even the coasters in the bathroom. (But not the ducks – obviously.)

There is a monorail train, so it's easy to get to all the different parks.

Day 1: Magic Kingdom.

We went on: Merry-go-round (a bit boring), Snow White (which was a bit scary), Peter Pan (my favourite), A Small World (also good), Lion King Show (a bit naff), Flying Dumbo (which had a 45 minute line-up).

We listened to Belle's story-time, then watched all the characters sing. It was hard to find a good space to stand.

Went on Goofy's rollercoaster and a train ride. I hate rollercoasters, I always have. Emm was sitting next to me, and he put out his hand to hold mine, and told me not to be scared. Very sweet.

Had lunch at the hotel. Swam in pool. Bea went on the water slide. She's very brave.

We went back to Magic Kingdom (on the monorail). Went on Jungle boat ride and the Swiss Family Treehouse.

Watched the fireworks, which were beautiful.

Day 2: Animal Kingdom

The children were tired (and cranky) so we hired a buggy for $13 and pushed them around. It was big enough for them to flop in it, and had a sunshade, so they weren't in the sun. Disney is expensive, but it seems to have thought of everything to make life easier.

We went on a Safari ride, which I thought was quite good, until Husband told me some of the animals were fake. You couldn't tell which were real, and which weren't.

Met Mickey and Minnie Mouse because Jay was keen to see them. It was a long wait.

Meanwhile, the others went white water rafting (they didn't want to wait for 23 hours to see Minnie...) Their faces were a picture, as they spun around in the water.

The children played in *The Boneyard* playground and got soaked.

Went on a dinosaur ride, which apparently was very scary, but I kept my eyes shut, so for me it was just uncomfortable.

The children danced while a band played.

We have given the children a single-use camera each. I have no idea *what* Jay's photos will be of – mainly his feet I fear.

Day 3: Epcot

The children managed to ride in the front of the monorail train (big excitement).

Watched 'Honey I Shrunk the Audience', which was very funny.

We had a *Spaceship Earth* ride, into the big dome.

Husband took Bea and Jay on *Test Track*.

We got a boat across a lake, then walked through scenes of different countries. It was very well done, but involved a lot of walking in the heat, and there wasn't anything for the children to do (and they weren't especially interested in different countries). We watched some bands, and some street theatre.

Went on a Mexican boat trip.

Watched the famous parade, which, to be honest, was a bit boring. The most interested people were the people in the parade, who were all super smiley and looked like they were high on drugs.

Day 4: Magic Kingdom (again)

We saw *Speedway Track*. These were little racing cars, on a track. Bea wanted to go in her own car, and she just made the height restriction, so we let her. Unfortunately, she had trouble pressing the accelerator peddle, so kept stopping. Which did rather ruin the ride for all the older kids behind her, who wanted to zoom around the track; they were stuck behind her car as it lurched, slowly, around the course. Then, as she approached the finish line, she finally got the hang of it, and put on a sudden burst of speed, crossed the finish line and started on a second lap. Which meant all the Disney workers had to chase after her, to make her stop and get out of the car.

You could see them thinking: "Oh no! She's going round again!"

I nearly wet myself laughing so much! When we collected her, she also couldn't stop giggling (which made me wonder if she'd done it on purpose – surely not).

We saw the *Carousel of Progress Show* – where we got to see that America is about 10 years ahead of the UK. I remember my mum using the '1950s washing machine' in the 1960s.

We went on the *Buzz Lightyear* ride (fun – we could shoot people with a laser gun).

Parade (excellent!)

***

We drove to our next hotel (which was loads cheaper than the Disney one, but near enough to still visit the parks as we had a car) then returned to MGM.

We went on the Backstreet Tour, which was really interesting.

Then we went to *The Little Mermaid Show* (Bea thought it was good).

***

The thing about Disney, is how well everything is done. Each park was beautifully presented, and everywhere looked freshly painted, with lovely flowers and sculptures. It was so well planned, with efficient queue control, all the facilities you could need, friendly staff. It's hard to think how they could do it better (other than lower the price). I don't really like rides and shows, but even I have to admit, Disney was wonderful.

Saturday 28th May
We drove through the Everglades. Saw alligators and lots of water birds. It was very interesting.

We tried to go for a walk through a mango swamp (sounded wonderfully tropical). We parked by the side of the road, and set off, through a tunnel of trees growing by the water. It was shady, and the path ran next to the swamp, so beside us we could see the gnarled trees standing in the water.

However, it rather showed our ignorance, as we had only gone a few yards when we realised we were dinner for about a million mosquitoes. We were all wearing insect repellent, but clearly not a strong enough one, because we were swarmed, you couldn't brush them away, they were everywhere.

We abandoned the walk, ran back to the car, and slammed the door shut. Then we spent a few minutes killing all the mosquitoes who had come into the car with us. All rather horrid, and me and Jay were horribly bitten (we must be the tasty ones in the family).

Sunday 27th May
We drove to Key Largo. Our hotel was pretty, with a lovely pool area, a band playing in a grass-roofed hut, and a little waterfall. The restaurant was okay.

We drove along the keys – lots of tiny islands connected by a long bridge with a motorway going over it. I didn't find them especially pretty – just houses and shops along a road, with sea on each side.

At one place you could pay to feed the fish. They told us to throw the bait into the water, but Husband decided to hold some just above the surface, to see what happened. He nearly got his hand bitten off! Fish can jump surprisingly high out of the water. We couldn't stop laughing.

Drove along a fantastic road (Route 75) through swamps to the East Coast, and onto Sanibel Island. We also have a new family motto: "Don't race the guy with the siren."

We're staying in an apartment on a complex. It is the prettiest apartment ever, and has been beautifully decorated.

The beach has the softest white sand and thousands of shells (even too many for the children to collect). We saw an armadillo walking across the beach. A man tried to catch it, and cornered it in a box – but it jumped right out and ran away. They don't look like they can jump, but they can. There was a pelican diving for fish, and lots of herons. The sea was full of stingrays, which had come to shallow water to mate. It was possible to go in the sea, you had to sort of shuffle walk in, so you didn't step on one and get stung. I wasn't sure this was as easy as it sounded, and I was too nervous to let the children paddle, so we all swam in the pool at the complex.

Monday 28th May

I am still suffering from mosquito bites, so didn't sleep very well.

We swam in the sea today, and it was lovely and calm, and then took the children into the pool.

The day passed very quickly, doing very little. I did some sketching, the family lived in the pool.

I lost the boys briefly, and found them at the air hose, where they'd inflated an armband to six times the size. They were delighted. It was quite funny, though would've been dangerous if it had burst, so I tried to not laugh.

Husband barbecued in the evening. I'm hoping charcoal is a healthy thing to eat.

Tuesday 29th May

Went to Bowmans Beach. Lovely big waves and thousands of shells. Husband lay under the sunshade, Bea read, Emm made sandcastles and Jay simply sat in the water, for hours, letting the waves crash over him.

On the way home we tried to find a nature reserve, but the map was hopeless – it marks all the places of interest but has no road names, and only major roads were marked.

I like Sanibel, it's not too touristy (no McDonalds) and has beautiful nature, very unspoilt. Shame about all the biting insects though. People had written in the visitor's book about them, calling them 'no-sees' because they're too small to see, yet leave a nasty bite.

After lunch Husband went back to the pool with the kids (because obviously they haven't been in water enough this holiday) and I walked along a sandbank in the sea. When I went to join them, Husband found he had been swimming with the car keys in his pocket, which I found more funny than he did. They still worked.

Had dinner at The Hungry Heron. I ate a very nice fish dish, and drank an extremely nice margarita. Drove to the end of the island and watched the sun going down. Beautiful. This is what holidays are meant to be like.

Wednesday 30th May
We all made a huge sandcastle village. My back got badly sunburned (to go with all the itchy bites).

Afternoon spent in the pool, Emm swam another width, and Bea learnt to dive for shells.

Barbecue tea.

Thursday 31st May
We hired bikes and cycled around the island. They had all kinds of bikes, so we hired a sort of pull-along-carriage for the boys to ride in, which kept them out of the sun, though was tough work for Husband to pull. It was lovely, cycling along flat paths,

whizzing past palm trees. We stopped at a lighthouse, and saw racoons fighting, a long black snake, and crested woodpeckers.

Went to Dairy Queen and ate ice-cream sundaes.

Afternoon in the pool again.

While we ate tea, I looked in the guidebook. I read that the nature reserve shut in five minutes, and wasn't open on Fridays. Abandoned tea and rushed out. Just made it to the nature reserve in time.

We saw mainly birds, and a man up to his thighs in mud photographing them. The man was the more interesting. Then we saw an alligator, right next to the road. When it saw us, it flashed into the river – so fast – you wouldn't stand a chance if it was chasing you.

Friday 1st June
Went to another beach. Collected shells. Saw a dolphin in the sea.

Packed, then had a last swim.

Saturday 2nd June
Got up at 6am. Right before we left, I went to the beach and saw a line of dolphins in the sea, leaping, just like in pictures. So wonderful.

Nice drive to Tampa. Returned car. Shuttle bus to airport, smooth flight home to New Jersey. Fabulous holiday. Now I just need to get those disposable cameras processed. Jay tended to point his at random objects while photographing us, so goodness knows what his will be of.

Florida has been a nice mix, from 'plastic Disney' to lots of wildlife on the islands. I like it, hope to visit again one day (though I might skip Disney next time).

Devon 2001
(Children aged 5, 7 and 9 years)

Palm Sunday, and we are staying in Devon on Robin Hill Farm. We are renting a nice little cottage, and there's a games room and a swimming pool.

Devon is always beautiful, but this year there's a tinge of sadness everywhere, as England is plagued with foot and mouth disease. Every time we enter a new farm, we have to drive through disinfectant, and we have to sterilise our boots if we walk anywhere.

Today was nice. We walked beside a stream on the farm (well, to be exact, Husband and the children walked *in* the stream). Then we went to a nice Baptist church in Westward Ho (stupid name for a town, wonder who came up with that one – suspect they were drunk at the time).

A man at church said he has lost all his cows to foot and mouth disease, and on Wednesday they have to be burnt. Horrid horrid horrid.

Had a nice meal at the Bell Pub, then went to a pottery, and the children could watch the potter working. Walked to Bucks Mills and had a cream tea – always good.

Monday
Went to Dartington Glass Factory, and the children painted coasters. I don't usually like factories, but this one wasn't too boring. They had a mill shop, and I bought some clothes.

Tuesday
Went to the market in Bideford, thinking it would be full of local produce. It was more like a church sale full of jumble. Went back

to Dartington instead, and the children made glass handprints. They are very distinctive – I would recognise their handprints anywhere.

Drove (for several miles) to a big beach. Flew the kite – which is always fun...for about the first 5 minutes. Then it gets rather tedious. On the way there, we had driven through a farm, and you could smell all the dead animals. Hard not to keep thinking about it.

Wednesday
Went on a fisherman's boat to Lundy Island. Sea was more choppy than I expected, especially when we were properly out to sea, but the island was lovely. The weather was bright and clear, and we had a windy walk along the cliff tops. Jay fell over in the mud several times. I think he was doing it on purpose by the end.

Lundy is full of wildlife, and even puffins. We, of course, didn't see a thing, because the children were way too noisy. I liked it there, it's the sort of place you run away to.

Thursday
We went to an amusement park. It was totally naff, but the children loved it.

Then we walked down a footpath (recently reopened) to Peppercomb Castle (which we never found) and a beach. Husband made up a funny story about a pirate called Jack, which made the children giggle, so it was all very nice.

Lovely cream tea in a pretty pub.

Friday
Collected the handprints from Dartington, then drove home.

France 2001

26th July 2001
We are in a motel in Bordeaux. I am writing this in a whisper. It is 10:10pm French time, the boys are asleep in one double bed, and Bea is reading on our bed. Husband and I have just eaten dinner on trays in the room. All going well so far...

28th July
Yesterday went to the beach at Archinon (might not be spelt like that). Cloudy but warm. Children paddled. Nice lunch in a French cafe – I had fish in Béarnaise sauce, and lemon tart. Drove back to hotel after Husband had found the car keys, which he had lost during a panic to feed the meter – which is probably against the law, so it's lucky we're not all in prison, but I didn't mention that. Sandwiches for tea (because we're British).

    This morning I woke up and my throat really hurt, like swallowing knives. Hurt all day.

    Breakfast was nice buffet in hotel. Drove to Touzac. Good drive, with a McDonald's lunch (in *France*. We ate *McDonalds* in France.)

    The cottage is very lovely. When we arrived we were shown around by an elderly French couple who spoke absolutely no English at all, but who chattered happily anyway. Unpacked and shopped. Then swam in pool before bread and cheese tea.

    Strolled around town. There's a wedding, and the church and town hall were strewn with flower petals.

29th July
Rough night. Jay kept waking with a croupy cough, which sounds like he's dying; and very tight breathing. Filling the bathroom with steam helped, but he kept waking and crying. Each time he

woke, I took him into the bathroom, turned on the shower and waited for the steam to ease his breathing so he could go back to sleep.

Jay woke this morning completely fine, we are exhausted. We ate breakfast outside in the sunshine. France has different sunshine to England, it's sort of more intense and less humid. Emm and Husband went shopping. They returned with *more* cheese. They told me they are going to write a cheese book. It stinks, so I hope they write it quickly.

Husband and children swam, then bread and cheese for lunch. We all played cards – trying to win 'The Family Cup'.

Saw Bonaguil Chateaux in guide book, and it looked really good, so we drove to see it. Then we realised it was the exact same one we visited 4 years ago. It is, however, an excellent castle, so I didn't mind at all. We tried to take the same photo on the castle steps, of me and the children. (It took almost as long to take as the first one.)

Swam, then pasta dinner. We all drank wine – the children had water with a drop added to flavour it, but they didn't like it.

30th July

Another rough night with Jay, and my throat is also no better. Drove to Fumel and bought some stuff in the chemist's. I am trying to not speak, as it hurts too much. This is not working very well – Bea just shouts louder until I answer, Emm completely ignores me, and Jay, for some weird reason, thinks he also mustn't speak and tries to point and act to explain things.

Played in the pool and had races. Quiche and sausage rolls for lunch.

Afternoon: went for a drive around countryside.

Husband cooked omelettes for dinner.

31st July

Incredibly hot, 36°. Shopped at Intermarche – fun buying new foods to try.

Had an incredibly good lunch at La Gringuette, near Gretzels. We had a 5 course meal for £10, and there were swings next to the river, so the children could play while Husband and I ate. In France, most restaurants serve the children's food first, so the parents can be more relaxed while they eat theirs.

Just played in the pool for the afternoon.

1st August
We had a pleasant day reading and swimming. Very hot all day, then very windy this evening. We thought there might be a storm, so locked everything away, but it never came.

2nd August
Another quiet day of swimming and cards. I am tired, lots of nights spent with ill children this holiday.

Today was a bit cooler. We are right next to the church, and the bells ring all day and all night, waking us up every hour. They do a double ring at midnight and 7am. I wonder who thought this was a good idea.

3rd August
Everyone well – yaay!

Drove to Cahors and wandered around the pretty old town. Interesting cathedral. Had a nice lunch upstairs in a semi-posh restaurant (the portions were small, but the food was tasty).

Sun came out after lunch so we walked some more. Emm bought some lego. I sat in the sun and drew, while Husband and Jay went to collect the car.

4th August
Shopped at Intermarche again. This time Husband bought a bag, last time he bought some plates. I have no idea why; we don't need these things.

Went to a creperie in Fumel. The owner thought Husband was American.

Drove south to Luzuerte. Nice drive. Looked at some Bastide towns for about 10 seconds each town, then Husband said, "Yep, that's nice, let's go." I don't feel we explored them very thoroughly. We also didn't go into the very lovely chateaux we saw.

We saw a peasant wedding party. The groom was dressed as a bull (so I don't know what that makes the bride...)

We couldn't find a restaurant open which looked nice, so drove home. Swam for 10 minutes (not worth getting wet for). Drove to La Gringuette again. Had another lovely meal, sitting outside, while the children played next to the River Lot. There were other families there, and the children all played together.

Drove to a deserted chateaux on a hill, then back to the cottage.

5th August

It's Sunday, so I tried to go to church, but the only one in the village is shut (it only has one service a month). France has great regard for lunch times (never disturb a French man eating lunch, it's a capital offence) and Mondays. Everything is closed on Mondays. But Sundays in France are pretty much the same as every other day. Shame.

Drove to Rocamador. Ate at McDonalds on the way there (my family is so cultured). The *Happy Meals* in France are sexist, with 'boys toys' in bags and 'girl toys' in boxes.

Rocamador was impressive, but had too many tourists to enjoy it properly.

It also had a severe lack of toilets. It did tempt you, with buildings masquerading as toilets, but when you went inside, they only had a hole in the ground – the actual *toilet* was absent. Bea now has very strong views about this.

Ate grilled rolls for tea. Saw a motorcycle accident. Booked a hotel for our last night. (Those sentences are unconnected.)

6th August

Up late, and played around the cottage. Played a family game of boule. Husband won, so the children pushed him, fully dressed, into the swimming pool. He pulled Emm in with him. All slightly shocked that they succeeded, but was very funny.

Went to a chateaux, and actually paid the £3 entrance fee so we could go inside. We were then taken into TWO ROOMS which were IN THE CELLAR! Very boring. Didn't have enough French to ask for a refund.

Drove to PuyLevec. Lovely walk around the old part of town, lots of narrow winding streets. Very beautiful (though not enhanced by the very strong smell of dog pee – better to visit after a heavy rainfall I think). Bought a selection of cakes from the local patisserie. Ate them all. Now feel slightly sick.

7th August
Went to *Wallibi Parc* – an amusement park.

We started with a log water ride, and I thought I was going to fall out. Everyone laughed at my funny face in the photo afterwards.

Bea loved all the scary rides, and Emm was slightly miffed because he was too short for them. The boys kept spotting "signs that Pirate Jack has been here" because Husband told them another pirate story in the car yesterday.

Jay walked very slowly, and refused to be hurried, saying he was: "too full of liquid."

They all went on a rollercoaster.

There was a nice fountain and music show.

My legs really ached by the time we left – too much walking in the hot sun carrying heavy boys. But it was a fun day.

8th August
Lazy day because everyone was tired. We all shopped at the Intermarche and had lunch at LaGringuette.

Bea and I went for a stroll, and were ambushed by the boys in the car with water squirters. We turned the hose on them when we got home.

Played cards and went for a drive.

9th August
Drove to Moissac. Nice drive, and the children were quiet because Husband told another Pirate Jack story.

Moissac was nice, with a beautiful church and interesting sculptures.

We found a nice restaurant, and were shown to a table. Jay announced he had a headache and felt sick. We left the restaurant. I sat in the car with Jay while he slept, the others went and found sandwiches for lunch.

Jay woke up, and said he felt better, so we had another walk around town.

Drove home. Jay was sick on the way, so not completely better after all...

I cooked pies for tea (Husband bought them in Moissac). Bea and Emm swam. I hope it's warmer tomorrow, we've had a lot of cool cloudy days.

Played boule with Husband. I slaughtered him. Very satisfying.

10th August
Drove to a farm at Bragnac, where they raise mohair goats. We all milked a goat. They were tethered on a raised platform, and while they ate, we stood next to them, and the farmer showed us how to milk them. It was amazing, so soft and warm. (Husband not keen, said it was too personal.) Then we made goat's cheese. The children could feed the kids with bottles, and play with them. It was really nice.

Drove to next village and had a nice lunch in a very French restaurant. No one was sick, and it wasn't a McDonalds. Perfect.

Swam and played cards in the sunshine, drinking *Orangina*.

Had tea, put everyone to bed, then packed (not my favourite thing).

11th August
Drove to the hotel we'd booked and left the cases. It wasn't really a hotel – more of a guesthouse with rooms in chalets round the garden. It has another one of those balconies for the children to sleep on, so I worried a bit about the stairs, and whether they might fall down them.

Drove to Penne St.Agnee. It was an interesting town and church, with caves. Had lunch. Drove to P sur Lot, looking for the market. We never found the market.

Went back to the hotel and swam in the pool. They cooked omelettes for the boys' tea, and then I put them to bed.

Bea stayed with the grown-ups; we all sat in the garden, around a big wooden table. They brought out a huge paella, and we all shared it and drank wine. Bea behaved really well, and tried all the food (at one point she whispered to me: "Mummy, I have been chewing this for 10 minutes, can I spit it out now?") It was a lovely evening, and a nice end to our holiday.

Italy, 2005
(Children aged 9, 11 and 13 years)

Venice

5am. Left home. Flew Gatwick to Venice. Flight was okay.

When we arrived in Venice, Husband took us round to where you could get a water taxi to the city. This was completely brilliant. We put our luggage on the boat, then watched as we left the airport behind and headed across the water towards Venice. The sight of the ancient city, getting closer and closer as you skim across the river is magical. A sight I will never forget.

We stayed in Hotel Kette. This was a pretty little hotel, with lots of Venetian decorations. The water taxi took us right there, which was fun. There is also a walking entrance, and we were very near St. Marks Square, so that is a nice stroll.

St. Marks Square was lovely. It was full of pigeons, which the boys chased (no idea why). There were lots of cafes, with tables spilling out into the square, and music playing, while people sipped coffee and watched the world go by. They must, I think, be very rich people sipping the coffee.

We ate lunch in a cafe, which was hideously expensive, but nice. I drank lots of wine.

Siesta (possibly related to the wine).

Bea slept, we walked, the boys chased pigeons. (I don't really understand the pigeon-chasing thing.)

We had dinner in a touristy, over-priced, cafe. There was not much food involved. I think Venice is going to be expensive. Went back to the hotel, and Emm pleaded to be allowed to go to bed as he was tired (too much pigeon-chasing).

***

The rest of our time in Venice passed very quickly. We wandered around, looking at the shops, though not buying much as it was all very expensive. We went to see a few touristy things, and Husband showed us all the things he'd seen when he went Inter-railing as a teenager.

If you come to Italy, bring all your best clothes because everyone is beautiful. Only Americans wear trainers/sneakers here, and I suspect that wearing wellies is a crime.

We loved the lack of roads in Venice – everyone travels by boat on the million canals, and the bridges are steep and pretty. Our hotel looked down on one of the rivers, and you could stand at the window, listening to the gondoliers, and imagining the age when people wore wigs and long dresses and masks. Visiting Venice is like stepping back in time (if you manage to avoid the tourists, and either have lots of money or don't plan to eat much).

One day we had a gondola ride, which was lovely. The children said they didn't like Venice, because all the buildings were old and broken.

Some friends, who were camping nearby, came and visited one afternoon. I was nervous about Tiny Child, who was quite small and active, in the hotel, but he didn't break anything. They too went on a gondola – complete with their pushchair.

I bought some masks, as they are everywhere and very pretty.

One day we sat at a cafe outside the Opera House, and two singers came out, and sang while we ate, which was lovely.

We went to a shop where a man was making little ornaments out of glass. Jay bought a cello player.

At the end of the trip, we caught the train to Florence.

***
Florence
In Florence, we stayed in Brunelleshi Hotel, which was a few minutes walk from Piazza Duomo, so was very central. The hotel has a tower – Piglazza Tower – and you could look down on the whole city from there.

We spent a few days wandering around, looking at various churches and bridges. The Duomo looked pretty, with its black and white walls. But there were always long queues waiting to go inside, and we couldn't quite face it with the children.

The same was true of the museum (Galleria dell'Accademia) so we looked at the statues outside, and listened to the street performers sing, and promised ourselves that one day we would return – without any children. There are several places I would like to revisit *without* children.

However, I loved Florence. The buildings were beautiful, and all the street cafes had singers or musicians, so as you wandered around the city you were usually accompanied by music. There were also ice-cream parlours everywhere, so it was possible to bribe the children to walk miles, by constantly restocking them with tiny scoops of delicious flavours.

One day we walked to Boboli Garden, which is full of statues, and fountains, and views of the city. It also had ice-creams, which was good for bribing tired boys who don't especially like statues, or fountains, or views of the city.

We walked there via Ponte Vecchio, which is an historical bridge, with shops on both sides, that sort of hangs across the river, looking like it will collapse. Before you go, it's worth reading up about this bridge, because then you can imagine how it was in the past, when it was full of butcher's shops, and all the effluence was dumped into the river. In 1593, the butchers were banned, because they wanted the bridge to be more classy, and the gold merchants moved in. (As a butcher's daughter, I have opinions about this.)

There was a fun market in Florence. I bought a leather jacket, and Bea bought a designer handbag (which might, if I'm honest, be fake). There were also lots of stalls selling leather-bound notebooks. I bought a couple, as they make great gifts. I wish I had bought lots, as they are for sale at home for about 6 times the price.

Florence is lovely, and definitely on my list for a return visit (without children). My memories are of warm evenings, sipping wine and listening to music wafting across the square.

We left Florence, and drove to Tuscany for the final leg of our holiday.

***

Tuscany

Saturday

We arrived in Tuscany. Fabio showed us the villa, then we shopped. The villa is huge, which is lucky, as we're sharing it with the Friends. There is an upstairs, but the staircase is locked. I am pretty sure it is haunted.

The villa has beautiful furniture and ornaments. It doesn't have air-conditioning, but due to the high ceilings and shuttered windows, it stays reasonably cool inside. It is also quite gloomy inside, which adds to the haunted atmosphere.

Sunday

Swam in pool. I read Jeffrey Deaver book.

Walked around the town in the evening.

Monday

The others decided to make a film. (No, they did not have any expertise or experience, they simply thought it would be a fun thing to do.) This involved quite a lot of shouting, and persuading Small Child to run in certain places. Tiny Child cried a lot. I read a lot – and looked after Tiny Child (but really, it lasted *all* day, and I didn't want to spend the *whole* day babysitting).

In the evening, we went to the town again and walked around. Shopped.

Tuesday

Another day filming. It felt like quite a long day. At one point, there was a wedding scene. Friend appeared wearing the net curtains from her room, and carrying the plastic flowers from the dining room. The people who live next to the villa appeared at the fence, trying to see who was getting married. It was very funny. I have absolutely no idea what they thought when she raised her 'wedding dress' and brought out two giant water-squirters to shoot people with!

In the evening, we went for a drive.

Wednesday
Swam in pool, and played badminton. If I'm honest, Small Child was not great at badminton, but it sure didn't stop him wanting to play.

We went for a walk in Borgo San Lorenzo. Bought ice-creams.

Thursday
We drove to a zoo. We had to drive through mountains to reach it, and the roads were very steep and twisty. The Friends were travel-sick. We could contact them via walky-talkies. Then they nearly ran out of petrol, so it was all a bit tense.

When we arrived at the zoo, we were about to get out and look around, when it started to hail. There were massive hail stones, like tennis balls. We rushed into the cars, and told the children to get down, then tried to cover them, in case the windows smashed. It was very exciting! Afterwards, we looked at the tops of the cars, and the ceilings were dented. Ours was a hire car, I guess the Friends will just have a weird memento of the holiday.

The zoo was a good one (though it was worth going, just for the hail storm!)

Friday
Swam in pool, and packed.

Taormina, Sicily August 2007
(Children aged 11, 13 and 15 years)

Saturday:
Arrived and picked up hire car at airport.

Drove to Hotel Excelsior Palace, which we booked through Citalia.

It was hard to find the car park, all got a bit stressy. Narrow roads, pedestrian walk ways, and lack of signposts did not help.

Our room had a view of Mount Etna. I wondered how far away it was compared to Pompeii and Mount Vesuvius. Husband convinced me that volcanoes that old never erupt unexpectedly.

Sunday:
Swam, walked in town, swam.

The best bit of the hotel is the pool. It is set in the gardens, below the hotel. You walk down through orange and almond trees, along flower lined pathways, to the pool area. The pool overlooks the coast on one side and on the other side, the cliff continues up behind the hotel, so you can lie in the water and look up at the mountain tops. It is beautiful.

Not entirely sure that two young boys and a large inflatable crocodile add very much to the atmosphere.

Monday:
Swam

Lunch in a pizzeria.

Walked through the town with Husband.

If you like very crowded walkways and lots of designer shops, you will love Taormina. Unfortunately, I hate shopping, especially for clothes, so it was rather wasted on me. Plus I got blisters from wearing pretty but uncomfortable shoes.

Tuesday:
Swam.

Bought lunch in a supermarket and ate it in the garden.

Dinner in hotel (nice.)

Jazz concert in a Greek theatre. This was excellent. We sat on chairs, listening to some really good jazz while watching the sun go down behind the Greek stage. Was very romantic (well, it would have been had we not had three quite vocal children with us).

Wednesday:
We decided to drive to Mount Etna.

I was very excited, having never been close to a volcano before and having rather a passion for bonfires and burning things in general. We set off after breakfast.

However, the hired car gearbox jammed up on one of the many extremely steep roads. We had no way to mend it, so phoned the hire company.

We waited in a very hot town (which had no public toilets) for a pick up truck, and then a taxi, to rescue us. It was hot and boring and uncomfortable.

Swam. Walked through town with Husband (it was still just a lot of shops and well designed women trotting around).

Had coffee in a square, which was nice.

Evening meal was by the pool. The hotel had set up tables with lots of candles and flowers. It was so pretty.

Thursday:
We got the hotel mini bus down to the beach. This was a mistake.

The hotel was up a cliff, so we couldn't walk back. We were deposited at the beach and told the mini bus would return in five hours. *Five hours.* The beach was full of beautiful people tanning themselves. The chairs were laid out practically next to each other, each with a small sunshade. Five hours is a long time. Even the sea was crowded!

No way you could go for a run, build a sandcastle or even swim properly. You just had to lie there, trying to read and sweating away, while beautiful people strolled elegantly between the loungers.

Returned to Taormina and bought ice creams.

The new hire car was delivered.

Walked through the town again. It is still just well-designed people in expensive clothes.

Friday:
The boys slept through breakfast so Husband smuggled hot chocolates to them in their room.

Husband announced he was going to eat only fruit, for the rest of the holiday (probably due to seeing all those beautiful people on the beach).

Swam.

Husband was seen eating bread rolls.

Drove to Etna. Lunch in a Deli in Gliaglosse. Husband ate a lot more than just fruit (that did not last very long at all).

Etna was brilliant. We walked over a recent eruption (that May). It was like being on the moon.
There was total silence, no birds or insects, nothing growing. Brilliant. Bea complained it was just a lot of black rock.

We saw some geologists with all their equipment.

Drove back early so we didn't miss the car park. Parking was a pain. The hotel didn't have a car park, and told us to use the main car park in Taormina. There was often a queue to get in, and it was sometimes hard to find spaces, especially if we got back late. I wonder if it is possible to just hire a car for occasional days when actually in Taormina, and not to bother actually having one for the whole holiday. It seemed more hassle than it was worth.

Swam.

Drank peach champagne cocktails and played cards in the bar.

Saturday, Sunday, Monday:
Days by the pool and strolling around town.

Tuesday:
Went on an excursion, booked through the hotel, to Stromboli. (After the excursion to the beach, I was slightly worried about this.)

We were picked up and taken to a little port by coach. We then were taken by boat to a small island. The children swam and we wandered around for a while. (Actually, the swim was a bit dodgy, as there were quite large ferries arriving.)

Had some lunch.

The boat then took us to Stromboli, which is an active volcano. About every twenty minutes, a plume of smoke could be seen coming from the top and flowing down the side, then steam rose up as it hit the sea.

We stopped on the island and could walk around the town. It was pretty, but I wouldn't want to buy a house there – not sure it would be a good long term investment.

Then the boat took us around the island. We were given a simple pasta dinner. As it got dark, you could see sparks and fire in the smoke as the volcano erupted. Excellent!

Wednesday to Friday:
More time swimming and relaxing.

Husband and I did another visit to Etna. Bea told us she had seen enough black rocks, but the boys came with us. We talked to a photographer who had been there at the last eruption. He said he had been climbing up while everyone else was rushing down! He said you could easily see the lava pathways, so it didn't feel dangerous and he took some really amazing photographs. I bought a couple.

We wandered around and found the roof of a building that had been completely engulfed by lava. It was so interesting. There was a clear line, one side everything was dead and covered in black lava, the other side, all was living, vibrant forest. Fascinating. It must be so exciting to actually be there when it erupts; so much power and energy, completely unrestrained. So much bigger than anything people do. I like things that remind me of how small I am.

I would have spent more days at Etna, but even Husband declared he was at saturation point for black rocks.

A brilliant holiday if you like either expensive shops or volcanoes. I realised I should have been a geologist. Bit late now.

Zambia 2007

October 2007, I sat on an aeroplane and flew to Lusaka, Zambia.

I was travelling with Husband and other members from the board of Tearfund. I was the 'tourist', sneaking along for the ride and to try and catch some of the vision that motivated these people. At the time, Husband was the Treasurer for Tearfund, and although most of this role was in the UK, checking numbers and trying to make wise decisions, the occasional trip was essential. It's almost impossible to make wise decisions about where to spend money, if you have never seen with your own eyes what the needs are, to understand the people you are trying to help. So, every so often, Husband would set off to a developing country, and I would stay at home and hope he didn't get eaten.

This time, I had decided to go with him. We paid all our own expenses, but Tearfund were organising the trip.

Before we left, we met the other team members and were given some training. The people we'd be staying with would have very few possessions, so arriving with a large suitcase containing more than they owned, would be tactless. We were given tips about how to dress – women should cover their legs at all times, though breasts were not considered rude. Husband whispered some suggestions for outfits I might like to consider, all of which I ignored.

The team were going to meet people who were HIV positive, to see if the money was reaching those who needed it. They were all travelling 'incognito', as the people in Zambia wouldn't be told that these were the people who ran Tearfund (otherwise they'd be treated like celebrities, and wouldn't get to meet real people).

We were told to visit Interhealth for medical advice and injections. There were a lot of injections. We were also given blood kits and antibiotics to take with us, in case of emergency. Receiving blood in Zambia was considered unsafe, due to the amount of AIDS in the country, so we were assured that in case of emergency, we would be taken to a safer country. I very much hoped we wouldn't have an emergency. We also bought some super-strength insect repellent, and some pop-up tent things which were a bed and mosquito net all in one.

Diary of Trip

Saturday 6th October:
Landed in Lusaka. Flight here very long.

Met Chris, who was going to drive us. He worked for a charity that Tearfund was linked to. He was small, black and laughed a lot – and seemed to find us very amusing

Dumped stuff in hotel, then went to a parade of shops. Everyone very black. I felt very white. We were stared at, which felt uncomfortable. I had never been anywhere so completely different to England, and I felt unsafe and vulnerable.

Bought some beautiful African print material for very little money.

My first impression of Lusaka was that it was like one huge motorway service station. It had the same transient feel to it, as if no one actually lived there or cared about it.

We visited a local church. One of Tearfund's aims is to work through local churches. Many people in developing countries live miles away from any health care or support network; but there are small churches *everywhere*. Every tiny village and hamlet and random home is within reach of a church. If Tearfund can mobilise them into action, then they can reach and help many more people. They can in effect, do the 'social work' that is necessary, and help people to improve their lives. We went to the church, and listened.

Everyone sat on hard chairs in a big circle, and I was bored. I was tired, hungry and uncomfortable. I'm inclined to daydream, and I failed to listen to the introductory speeches, and then had no idea what everyone was talking about. I began to doubt my ability to do 'mission trips', it was feeling a lot like a business meeting, or a physics lesson – something to be survived without actually engaging in.

We were introduced to the pastors from several churches. They were very black, and wore very white shirts. They were a serious lot, and spoke in accented English, while I tried to concentrate on what they were saying, and not the general heat and smell in the room. They talked a lot about AIDS, and their own attitude to it. AIDS is a massive problem in Zambia, and initially the pastors had been preaching about the evils of promiscuity, that AIDS was a punishment, sent from God, that people must repent.

However, they now realised (I suspect with a little help from Tearfund) that actually, most AIDS sufferers were children, or women who had always been faithful to their polygamous husbands; and if the church made AIDS a matter of sin, then people wouldn't come forward for testing, and the problem would never be solved. The church wasn't helping the very people who needed it most. So they changed, and began to encourage people to seek the health care they needed.

The men sat and talked to us.

But the women took us out.

We sat in the front of the truck, and they all piled into the back. There was lots of laughing and loud voices, and I would rather have sat in the back with them. I felt they were strong, brave women, who were fighting to change what they could. This was more how I had envisioned a 'mission trip' would be, and I had renewed enthusiasm.

We visited some of the people they were helping. First, we went to a white stone house that looked a lot like my garden shed. It was small, with concrete walls, concrete floor, unglazed windows. It was very dark, and very hot; though it was clean and didn't smell horrid. There was a television, which felt rather incongruous amidst so much poverty.

A woman lived here with her grandchildren. Four of her seven children had died of AIDS and their orphaned children now lived with her, despite her being HIV positive. One of the children was also HIV positive, the others had not been tested. In Zambia, this was normal – many orphaned children live with a relative, who is often ill themselves. You could see she was ill, she looked like her very bones were tired, and she sat wilting on the sofa, while we, big white foreigners, invaded her home. I could not imagine how she coped with seven energetic grandchildren, who looked to be aged from about twelve to a chubby baby of about a year. She twisted rags together to make rugs to sell. Often she did not have enough food, which is one of the ways the church ladies were helping her.

The children were great fun and found us hilarious. They were very keen to be photographed and then crowded around to see their image on the screen. As they laughed, and pushed to see, with their sparkling eyes and gappy smiles, you realised they were just kids. Like my kids.

The child who was ill, was taking ARV tablets. These don't cure AIDS, but they do help to stop some of the symptoms. The pills were very big, and they were hard for a child to swallow. Giving children medicine is always a delight, isn't it? I remember having a syringe, and being able to squirt medicine into the back of a struggling child's throat. In 2007, there was no syrup form available for ARVs, I have no idea if there is today, or if children are still gagging as they try to swallow life-saving medicine. Eventually, those pills will cause irreparable damage to the body, and the patient will die. But in the meantime, they are extending and improving life; giving parents a few more years to care for their children, enabling people to be strong enough to grow their crops.

The next home we visited was run by teenaged orphans. Their parents had died of AIDS, and they were living together in the family home. The church ladies checked regularly that they were eating properly, attending school, keeping clean. This is so much better for the children than being split up and sent away. We heard that there are many, many, orphans in Zambia due to AIDS.

My initial reaction was the same as one American charity we heard about. They raised lots of money, and built a beautiful orphanage, fully equipped and staffed. However, *Zambian people do not use orphanages* and the expensive building remained empty. I realised that my own reaction to Africa was not dissimilar to those white missionaries in ancient times, who taught everyone to speak English and wear hats. To really help, you have to understand the culture and provide aid that is *appropriate*, not necessarily what is nice to give. There is a tendency for gifts to sometimes benefit the *giver* – to do things that feel like Father Christmas giving out presents. Sometimes, the things that are needed are the boring, everyday things, things which are unique to a particular culture. We do not always know best. (Gosh – who'd have thought!)

In Zambia, when parents die, their children are usually sent to a relative. Then, when this relative also dies, they are sent to a more remote relative. Often people are left to look after many children, some of whom are quite distantly related, and the level of care is erratic. No one who cares about the child knows where they are. In the meantime, the family home is sold (I assume the money is taken by the first carers.) As the child is passed from relative to relative, they become increasingly isolated. Then, when they are old enough to care for themselves, they have nothing. Their home has been sold, and they have no entitlement.

However, if when they are first orphaned, they can stay in their family home, then that possession is always theirs. When they leave school, they have a home, often with a garden where they can grow food. This is one of Tearfund's initiatives. They hope to encourage local churches to enable orphans to remain in the family home, regularly helped and advised by church members. People pop in to check they're going to school, to show them how to cook, to nag them into being clean. But the children stay together, in their own home. They are not lost in a cycle of constantly moving from relative to relative to relative...

Sunday
We visited another home in Lusaka. There was a comfy sofa, a television and DVD player. But the house was very hot, with insects running up and down the walls and no storage cupboards, so all the possessions were heaped in corners. I could not come to terms with the disparity between poverty and ownership of electrical goods. It was hard to understand *why* someone who had so little would strive to own a television above other things. Maybe it is a way to escape.

The lady who lived here had suffered from depression when her husband died. The church ladies visited her, and persuaded her to be tested. She found she was HIV positive and began taking ARVs, so was much healthier and able to take care of herself and her son.

As we drove around Lusaka, we caught glimpses of what life was like. There were many tiny corner shops, which were really just a table, placed at the edge of someone's land, where they can sell excess produce. They were often manned by children who grinned widely when they saw us and posed for photographs with their friends.

Many children had toys they'd made themselves, from old tyres, or pieces of twisted metal. Many of the houses had a water hole in the garden. A bucket on a rope was used to haul the water up to ground height. It was used for washing and cooking and had to be boiled before it could be drunk.

There was litter everywhere – as in, everywhere. I couldn't get used to this. Everyone seemed to keep their own space clean and tidy but along the roadsides were empty cans, pieces of paper and cloth, all just discarded. When I think of Zambia, I think of litter, blowing in the trees.

As we drove from Lusaka to Choma we saw many things. You could not, even for a moment, forget you were in Africa. I have driven around many suburbs in the world – Singapore, Rome, Dubai, New York and they seem ubiquitous. You can almost imagine that you are anywhere, they seem interchangeable. Not so Lusaka. I did not see any major food chains or dress shops. Even the roads, full of pot holes and often just hard packed red mud, were different.

As we left the city we watched the scenery move past us. There were men sitting beside the road, bashing rocks with mallets to make shingle. Men selling bricks. Women smoking wood to produce charcoal for cooking. Trees that appeared to have roots that extend skyward and branches that sink into the earth. Red mud. Dried grass. Lines of people walking along the road, the women carrying plastic bowls of goods on their heads. Thatched-roofed mud huts, clustered into villages. A different world.

Monday
We arrived in Choma. We were staying in a guesthouse/hostel. It was very simple but clean and felt safe.

We went to meet the bishop, who was the main contact for the village where we would be staying. He was a large, tired looking black Zambian. We later learnt that he was suffering from malaria. We crowded into his little office and he sat behind his desk and gave us some advice about how to survive the next few days, when we were to be sent into separate villages.

He suggested that we should take some foam mattresses to sleep on and then leave them there, so our hosts could use them afterwards. We were told to take enough bottled water for the visit. There was some cell phone coverage but it was intermittent. However, there was no electricity, so we would be unable to recharge our phones until we returned to the town. If there was an emergency, we needn't worry, as every village had a bicycle. (I possibly found this less reassuring than was intended.)

We were told that only women carry objects on their heads, unless the load was extremely heavy. Women tend to be known as "mother of …" rather than an individual name. (I figure this would make you very careful when choosing names for your children.)

The bishop told us that they had heard there was a married couple in our group, and they had therefore changed the original arrangements, as they realised that the wife would want to stay in the same village as her husband, so she could take care of him. Husband was very pleased by this news.

We went back to the hostel to pack small bags with the clothes we would need at the villages, and then we set off. We soon left proper roads, and bounced along hard red mud roads, filled with ruts and holes.

Husband and I were driven to the pastor's house, as we are staying in his village – a few mud huts with straw roofs. I think that each 'village' is actually made up of family groups. When a child is too big to sleep in their parent's hut, they are given a hut of their own. There are also huts for cooking, and for washing, and for the toilet pit. The space between the huts is a living space, and is kept free of litter. The family and their animals all occupy this same space. We could not see any other 'villages' from the pastor's group of huts. In the pastor's hut was an area for sleeping, and another with a wooden table and chairs.

We were given our own hut to sleep in, the equivalent of a guest room I guess. It had a wooden bed inside, so we popped up our pop-up tents and it was fine. Best of all, it had a door, so we could shut out all the animals that were wandering around.

We were given chairs and cups of *tuwantu*. This looks like thin white emulsion paint with bits floating in it. It is actually made from a plant root and we were offered brown sugar to add to it. It tasted like watery yogurt. Tepid, watery, yogurt. Drinking it required some effort. I decided again that I wasn't very good at mission trips, as I felt an insane desire to laugh hysterically when faced with a mug of *tuwantu*. My whole body went into lockdown, no way I could swallow.

The house smelt of charcoal. There was a slight breeze wafting through the unglazed window but it was still very hot. There were lots of flies, and we sat and listened to hens and turkeys foraging outside.

By 6:30pm, it is pitch black. After dark, the women cooked. They spoke in low voices, laughed and sang, all while sitting around the fire and cooking. They had one fire, pulling the hot ash across onto other dishes to heat them. Two tree trunks fuelled the fire, and these smouldered together, the women kept pushing them together to maintain the heat. They frequently wash their hands and utensils, using water from large containers which they have carried to the village earlier. It seemed a special time, with lots of cooperation between the women.

A younger woman was feeding a baby, teenaged boys hung around, playing with a football. They teased me, telling me to watch carefully because tomorrow, I would be cooking. Actually, there was a limit to what I *could* watch, because as I said, it was pitch dark. In the end I got my torch. No idea how the boys were managing to kick a ball, but I guess if your eyes have never encountered electric lights, your night vision is excellent. I felt old.

The men ate while sitting at the table in the pastor's house. I did too, as a special guest from England, though I think the women had more fun, eating next to the fire, chatting and laughing.

There were chicken pieces in a sort of soup, rape (very like chopped cabbage) and *mapawpwee*, which is a maize cooked until it is thick. (I am making up these spellings.)

The women had prepared a bowl of warm water which they put into the 'bath house' for us to wash. This was another mud hut, with a drainage area and a curtain across the doorway. I also used the toilet hut (it is amazing how long one can avoid using a toilet for when necessary). This was a small mud hut with a straw roof, but *no door*. It faced a large termite hill away from the village, so there was some privacy. There was a broken cover over a small hole. When the cover was removed, swarms of flies escaped from the pit below.

Tuesday

I got up soon after dawn. The temperature was perfect: warm with a slight breeze. The women were busy sweeping the living area with brooms made from twigs. I asked if I could help, and was given a brush, but it kept falling apart in my hands.

There was lots of rubbish to sweep away – animal droppings, crumbs of food, a broken plastic pen case and an abandoned flip flop. One woman pounced on the flip flop and started to talk loudly. I didn't need to speak her dialect to understand her – I am a mother, I had teenagers, I knew exactly what she was complaining about.

We swept the rubbish to the perimeter of the village, where I guess it stayed until it was blown away. There wasn't any sort of rubbish collection or disposal, and as we used the wet wipes and water bottles we'd brought with us, we had to put them back into our bags, to take away with us.

There was already a fire burning and the women had heated water so we could wash. As I swept, I saw school children file past in their navy blue uniforms. They walked, one behind the other, carrying their books and bottles of white *tuwantu* for their lunch.

Schools were free, but children had to wear the uniform to attend. If a family was too poor to afford several uniforms, the children would share, with one sibling attending school in the morning, and then switching at lunch time with their brother or sister, who would change into the same clothes. I can just imagine the comments if I suggested my children might like to share clothes.

The animals wandered around freely. The turkeys and hens all roosted in the trees at night and they seemed quite content to share the ground with dogs, cats, kittens, pigs, goats and cows during the day. They were part of life here and wandered in and out of the huts. Probably not a bad life, unless there's disease. When there's disease, the animals are doomed. As are the people.

I found the people to be quiet and dignified. They greeted us with smiles and handshakes and a half curtsey. The women were beautiful, with dark skin and clean bright clothes. I still don't know how they managed to wear clothes that looked clean and ironed, when washing involved a bowl of water heated over a fire. The children were gorgeous. They smiled with wide mouths and delighted eyes, and loved to see themselves in photographs. The elderly and the sick moved slowly and carefully. They listened and nodded, but said little. Around them, life seemed harmonious.

It was hard to accept the impact of AIDS here. Both our hosts were HIV positive. In a quiet moment, the pastor's wife took me to one side, and showed me the green and orange bruising on her sides and arms. She drank medicine made from herbs each day. She didn't speak English, but her quiet manner and gentle movements had a sort of dignity about it, and I understood that she wanted to show me, she wanted me to be aware of her suffering. That was in 2007 – I doubt she is still alive today, which makes me sad.

Most people who we saw were younger than us. It was odd to be the eldest people we saw in a country when we were only in our forties. I knew that life expectancy in Zambia was 35, it was altogether different to actually experience that – to be the oldest person in a country when you're 42 is a bit weird.

I saw some cows being milked (this is the first job that I saw a man do – I was wondering what they did). They tied together the cow's back legs first, then milked it into a plastic bucket.

***

We were called into the house for breakfast. They poured very milky tea out of a teapot (it looked like milk, there was hardly any tea in it at all). We drank it with bread and scones. The scones were sweet and tasty. We ate with Chris, our driver. I didn't see the other people eat anything at all, though some were drinking *tuwantu* (I was very relieved not to be offered any.)

After breakfast, I washed up. This involved several bowls of water. One had detergent in for washing, then two others were for rinsing. It was all done on the floor with animals walking around. I had to keep pushing the pig away because he wanted to drink the dirty water.

Husband talked about football with the boys. They all supported English teams. He gave them a football and they played with it, doing tricks and laughing. One of them asked Husband if he could send him some football boots when we are back in England.

***

We visited a school. My impression of the school was not great. It was a large white building, with lots of blue-clad children milling around. The classroom we were shown was full of broken furniture, heaped at the back, and some children were sitting on the floor. These people were skilled at building their own houses, I couldn't understand why they had not moved, or repaired, the furniture. The children themselves were teenagers, and some of them looked big enough to help move the rubbish. I couldn't imagine teaching in that room – if I were the teacher, my first lesson would be to clean up the classroom.

I later wondered if the rubbish had been placed there for our benefit, to try and make the school look neglected, so we would give them some money. This was something I found very difficult in Zambia, (this, and the toilet facilities). I wasn't used to people asking me for money so blatantly, and it felt uncomfortable. How do you know who really needs it, and who is trying to scam you? What should the people do for themselves, and what do they need to be given? We saw a lot of aid-dependency in Zambia, people who had given up all motivation and were waiting for a 'charity' to do things for them, people who took no ownership over their own lives. This must be a danger with all aid work, and something which needs wisdom. Tearfund help people to help themselves, and this feels right to me, to enable people to be independent.

The children all walked to school. Some had to leave home at 4am to be there on time. They must have been exhausted before the day even began. They were taught Zambian literature, maths, science and English. All the lessons were conducted in English, the official language in Zambia. However, most of the children could not understand even quite simple phrases. This seemed such a waste. They had walked so far, in uniforms they could barely afford, to sit in a broken classroom, and hear words they could not understand. I found this immensely frustrating. Why were they not being taught food hygiene? How to avoid catching AIDS? Some basic science that could help them grow crops and conserve water? Zambian history? Some Physics? It made me very angry.

The government owned this school. They had a lot of policies. It was regularly inspected, but they weren't given any feedback. I decided that my own feedback was probably also inappropriate to share. I was meant to be watching, not giving advice.

***

We visited a family. The husband had died of AIDS, leaving both his wives widowed (polygamy is normal in Zambia), and several children. We sat in the shade, helping them to shell nuts. They talked about missing their husband, about every day remembering again that he had died, feeling the hurt as a raw pain. I found this to be very poignant.

Sometimes, when I watch people in developing countries on the television, it seems almost as if they have grown accustomed to death. When they have lost *so many* friends and family members, I feel that they must not feel the same agony that I feel. I so easily forget that their love is just as strong as my love, and their loss hurts as much as mine.

Our lunch was *tuwantu*. I just could not manage to swallow any, which was very embarrassing. It made me gag. There was nowhere to dispose of it, and a nearby chicken showed no interest at all when I offered it. I tried pouring some on the ground but it left a white puddle which our hosts would have noticed. I then got the giggles (feel I had failed at being an aid worker several times already). In the end, had to just leave the unfinished drink coagulating on the table.

We visited the Bishop's mother and when we left she gave us a chicken as a gift to thank us for visiting. Not a butchered one, wrapped in cellophane, but a living, squawking one. We gave it to the pastor, who assured us that it was a good gift. Husband named it after our team leader – not entirely sure she appreciated the gesture.

We were given scones and salad at tea time. The meal times came round with awful regularity. The scones were delicious and the salad looked good, but we daren't eat any because it would have been washed in local water. Had another attempt at feeding it to a chicken but a dog kept chasing it away.

I used the toilet. This was not a pleasant event. There were two footprint markings where you placed your feet and then you perched over a stinking hole swarming with flies. I was thus precariously poised when I heard a cough and footsteps coming nearer. There was no door to the hut and I quickly calculated how quickly I could cover my embarrassment (and everything else) when the footsteps arrived, and the pig stuck his head in the doorway. I nearly fell over with shock (which would have been very bad indeed).

In the afternoon, the women went fishing. A group of them had obtained permission from the head man and they all went together. They all stretch out across the river with their cone-shaped nets, walking upstream to catch the fish. I wanted to join them, but the pastor took us visiting again.

 I was interested by how well the people ate. Okay, so *I* found the food hard to eat, because it was very unlike English food; but if you looked at it dispassionately, they grew vegetables and fruit, they raised animals for meat. We often heard that people in these places exist on less than a dollar a day but that seemed a fairly meaningless statement. There was nothing there to spend a dollar on! People grew their own food, and made their own houses and furniture. If nothing went wrong, it was not a bad life style. It was different to life in England but I am not sure that it was worse. Yes, there were hard things, but there were lots of excellent things too.

The thing that threw everything off kilter was any kind of disaster. If people were ill (and many were, due to AIDS) or if there was a change in climate, then they had no back-up plan. There were no safety nets. (Apart from that bicycle, of course – every village had a bike.)

We visited a dam that Tearfund had sponsored. It looked like it was in the middle of a dried up field but they told me that during the rainy season it is on the river.

The women walked to a bore hole to collect water. It was about a ten minute walk from the village. They helped each other to lift the heavy plastic containers onto their heads, then walked back, laughing and chatting. I tried to help. Couldn't even lift the container up off the floor, never mind raising it to head height. Their necks must be incredibly strong. They told me that they walk in a line, one behind the other, so if anyone drops their load it does not fall on the next person. Sometimes the 14 year old boy would collect the water on his bike (but I have no idea how he manages that).

In the evening, I cooked the *mapawpwee*. I had lots of help. Every time I put down the spoon, I needed to turn on the torch so I could find it again. It was also quite an art to stir a pot over an open fire without getting burnt, while your skirt flaps towards the flames.

We ate the fish for supper. They were like sardines, small and fried whole. They were crunchy but not unpleasant. They were served with the *mapawpwee*, rape and tomatoes. I would have liked to eat outside with the women but I think that would have been odd, so ate at the table with the men again.

There was milky tea again, poured from the large pottery tea pot. The pastor's wife had made it, milk and tea and hot water, all put into the pot together.

We went to bed, completely exhausted. Outside we could hear everyone else sitting around the fire, talking and laughing.

In the morning, they told me that Chris had put on music from the car radio and danced with the children. It sounded like a party as we drifted off to sleep.

Wednesday
Got up 5:30 and helped sweep.

Then washed up the crockery and pans from last night's meal. The women showed me how to use sand from the ground to scour off the stuck on bits, then everything is washed in a bowl with detergent and rinsed twice. Would've been easier without the pig, who was still determined to drink the water.

Went into 'bathroom' (hut with a curtain across the door) and washed. The women use a pumice stone to rub dirt off skin, then rinse in water warmed over the fire. A chicken came in and watched me.

Chatted with Bertha while she fried fritters. It was interesting watching her cook. She had a place for everything: spoon gets stuck into the straw roof, uses a bunch of leaves to lift hot pans so she doesn't get burnt, and so on. It was very efficient. She was cooking 'inside' because it was windy. This hut had half walls and a thatched roof. Breakfast was bread and fritters. Very nice.

We drove to see a couple of dams, a new church that is being built and a new bore hole for water.

Went to church. Women sang – brilliant! It was nice to see lots of people who we recognised from our visits. I felt a real bond with the women. Our interaction had mainly been them trying to teach me Tonga and then laughing, but I realised that our day to day focus was very similar (childcare and meals) even if the mode was different.

Someone from Tearfund did a talk, which was translated, and then the school children sang (they looked very fed up – children are the same the world over). We were presented with a basket of groundnuts. Then we stood outside and everyone filed past and shook our hand. When they shake hands, the left hand holds your elbow, then they squeeze your hand, then link thumbs, then squeeze hands. If we wanted to show respect to an older person we also did a dipped curtsey.

One man said to me:

"When you go back to England, you may forget us. But never forget that we are part of the same church. Tell people at home, God has one church. The part in Zambia is part of you. We need your help."

We had chicken and rice for lunch. I got to hold a baby. I told the mother that when I was small, I had always wanted a black baby. She laughed and said she had always wanted a white one! We held our arms together and compared skin colour. She was so dark, I felt pasty beside her.

Then we left the village. Our few days there had been such an experience, so different to life in England. I think we were tense the whole time, looking for dangers and trying not to offend anyone with our ignorance. I was glad I had stayed there, but the relief when we left was immense.

Drove to Choma and went to a supermarket. Shopped in a Spar. It could have been an English supermarket except for the big sacks of maize down one side, and the security guards on the door.

We went back to the guest house. It now felt very luxurious. Flushing toilets and showers. Aaah.

Thursday

The 'work' bit of the trip was finished, and we all wanted to rush off to Livingstone for some sightseeing. But nothing happens quickly in Africa.

We went to say goodbye to the bishop. This took ages. More photos.

Then we went to *another* church. Met *more* people, who are all beginning to blur into one by this stage. Too much new stimuli. If I could've had a break, perhaps a day doing nothing, then I might have appreciated what I was seeing and hearing. But to be honest, I was finished, there was too much new stuff, and I had stopped processing it. However, we saw and heard lots, so I will try to explain it all to you. Some of it is important.

There were lots of rag rugs on the church floor, and the stained glass windows all depicted Bible scenes, but were set in Africa. It seemed odd seeing a black Jesus, but I guess is no more weird than the Italian one that tends to be in European churches. (He was Jewish – in case you have forgotten!)

We had to introduce ourselves again. When I introduced myself they always laughed; because I was very old, and only had three children.

We listened to a talk about HIV and what the church is doing to help – like taking people food supplements, and teaching them. They also lent them bicycles, so they could keep their hospital appointments and go to collect their medicine. The church women made tablecloths to sell, to raise money. It was very hard to hear, because there was lots of noise from outside, but I tried to listen.

People were becoming more open about AIDS which enabled them to get the correct treatment. They also visited witch doctors who make cuts in their arms to 'take away the bad magic'. It cost about 5 dollars to see a witch doctor, though some would barter and take a goat or something instead. They advertised in newspapers and were in both towns and rural communities. They tended to be rich and drive nice cars, and so they were respected. The churches were trying to teach that there was a better way, and to tell people about God, but it would be a slow process. (Note, witch doctors are different to traditional African medicine. The church was not teaching against that, and actually was encouraging people to continue growing their herbs to supplement the ARVs.)

The use of ARVs had improved health for many people but they did tend to see it as a cure, which it wasn't. They had done much to remove the fear of AIDS, which was good, but unfortunately that also meant people sometimes became careless. We heard that there was especially a problem amongst teenagers who were HIV positive, as they often contracted the disease from their parents, and then felt very resentful.

We visited a man called Peter. He was clearly dying and was too weak to even stand. He lived in a hovel, it was horrible, worse than my garden shed, and full of flies (though it wasn't particularly dirty). It was very dark inside, with a hard mud floor and broken furniture. He was worried that his house would fall down when the rains came and he was too ill to repair it. Four of his seven children and his wife had died already. What can you say to someone in that situation? We prayed with him. I will always remember him because he had the same name as my Dad.

We went to the home of a young single mother. Her previous baby had died of AIDS because no one had told her to boil her milk before feeding the baby. Would such a tiny detail have meant the baby would survive and not catch AIDS? I still don't know if that is true. However, her second baby was healthy and was not HIV positive, so maybe it is true. The girl's mother attended church and they had given her lots of advice, which she then passed on to her daughter. The house was hot and smelt of urine. It had lots of flies. She grew vegetables in her garden and sold the surplus on a table at the end of her garden.

We then visited a young girl who was HIV positive. She looked about seventeen. Her house was tiny but it had a television, a DVD player, a video player and a HiFi. I found that very strange, but maybe not so different to the things my teenagers would strive to own – I like to think they would buy food and clothes and education, but maybe they would prefer electrical products too.

We bought lunch at another Spar and drove to Livingstone. I was happy to leave Choma. The slums around the city were much harder to be in than the rural communities. People had left the countryside because they thought it would be better but I didn't think it was. In the villages they had routine and support, and they could grow their own food. The city just seemed hopeless to me.

We saw baboons fighting next to the road. We couldn't find the guesthouse so phoned and they sent a car for us to follow.

***

The guesthouse wasn't finished. Not as in: *they hadn't cleaned the rooms;* not finished as in: *they had not finished building it*!

There was no electricity. Our room had been painted, but they had left a space where the fitted wardrobe would go – when it was built. They had fitted mosquito nets, but not sealed them to the windows so there was a nice big gap for insects to fly through. There was a very plush en suite bathroom, but unfortunately no water. We had to ask for a bucket so we could flush the toilet. The ceiling leaked, so I hoped it wouldn't rain; and there were lots of holes for spiders to crawl through (there was a huge one on the wall. I am not good with spiders).

So, even though we were now in a 'proper' hotel, even though we were now on holiday, we slept in our pop-up tents.

We went to Victoria Falls. It was good, but you could tell it would be magnificent in the rainy season, when the whole river floods.

We went to a market and bought souvenirs. This was great fun, there were lots of interesting crafts. Chris bartered for us, though sometimes the prices were so cheap that we just paid.

Ate pizza for tea. Normal food was a novelty.

Friday

We got up early and drove to a game park. I loved this. We saw lots of animals and took lots of photos. In some ways, it was similar to a safari park in England, but something about being in Africa, knowing the animals belonged there, made it so much more exciting.

They had a rhino, which was guarded by wardens with rifles. They had lost one rhino to ivory poachers. Not sure how that happens when it has an armed guard. The rhino was resting when we arrived, and the warden let us leave our cars to photograph it. Which was probably completely stupid of us, but we survived (and death by rhino would be quite a cool way to die).

Saw hippos swimming in a river, and a herd of giraffe running through trees. Wonderful.

We drove to Lusaka via a white person's farm. They had lawns and flowers, which felt a bit surreal. They were trying to show how Westerners farm, in the hope that Africans will copy them. (This wasn't a Tearfund project, we just visited out of interest.) I was tired now, and wanted to just get to Lusaka and get the plane home. I was missing my children, and felt I had seen enough. But when you're on a trip with other people, you have to 'go with the flow' and fit in with what other people want to see. Because none of you might ever come to Africa again.

At one point, some men came with a snake. They asked if we wanted to see it and we all went outside. They tipped it out of a sack onto the grass. They assured us it was dead. I was not so sure, I have seen snakes my cats have caught, and I knew they could lie very still. It was a puff adder, so very poisonous. Suddenly its tongue flickered, we all jumped backwards very fast, the men grabbed a garden fork, and whisked it away. I think they planned to bash it on the head out of sight. I wasn't bored any more.

We continued on to Lusaka. The car was hot and dusty with very bad suspension, very uncomfortable. We arrived at the hotel to find they had misallocated our rooms (probably because there were two men with the same name in our party). They didn't seem to think this was a great problem, and were keen to remove the other man from the shower and make him move to the correct room. We told them not to, and took the smaller room.

This hotel had been completed, so the taps were plumbed in. Unfortunately they had not been secured to the sink, so they swivelled when you turned them.

We all had a meal together and a 'feed back' session. Everyone seemed positive about the trip, it had been good to see that Tearfund was managing to make a difference in the areas that most needed it.

Saturday

We got up early. My stomach was bad – not great for a 10 hour flight. Had Immodium and antibiotics for breakfast.

We went to the airport. I so wanted to go home now. My stomach was still bad (prayed lots). It began to improve. We checked-in our luggage, went through security, and had our visa cancelled, then sat playing cards in the departure lounge.

Then there was an announcement, saying our flight was slightly delayed. Husband looked out of the airport window, and saw a BA aeroplane in pieces on the tarmac. We hoped it wasn't our plane.

Half an hour later, we were told the flight would be very delayed, and were issued with lunch vouchers. I really did not fancy eating airport food. I so wanted to go home.

We were told that hydraulic fluid was leaking from the plane and we needed to wait in hotels for it to be mended. A lady with a clipboard ushered us round to collect our suitcases, and then onto buses. We sat on the bus for about an hour.

It did occur to me that no one had actually shown us any identification. We had all trustingly obeyed the lady with the clipboard. Our visas had been cancelled, all the paperwork showed we had left Zambia. I wondered if we were being kidnapped. Decided there wasn't much I could do about it.

We arrived at *Taj Pamodzi Hotel*. It was a nice hotel, very plush in comparison to where we had been staying. We had a nice buffet lunch and were given rooms. We were told the flight would leave at 9pm.

At 7pm, we were later told the flight would leave at 9pm tomorrow. We contacted people in England to try and rearrange work and checked my Mum was okay with the children for a bit longer.

The following day, we were told the flight would leave first thing, the *next* day. We settled into an odd limbo, where we had no control, and just had to absorb time. We had no visas, so could not leave the hotel.

Chatted with various people and looked online for possibility of flying home via Nairobi or Johannesburg. In Africa it seems to be cultural to always tell people what they *want to hear*, rather than the *truth*. So, although our plane was in pieces, with a part needing to be ordered from another country, they persisted in telling us the flight would leave in a few hours. Which made it rather difficult to know who to trust.

Eventually, *two days late*, caught a flight home via Johannesburg.

I was so incredibly happy to finally get home. It was so nice to see my children, have a long shower, eat familiar food and to use a proper toilet.

I am very glad that I went to Africa, and saw the country, and met the people who live there. I don't think I ever need to go again.

Palma del Rio 2008
(Children aged 12, 14 and 16 years)

A learning experience......
Saturday 2nd August (Please note the month. It matters...)
Flew to Malaga.

Waited over an hour for Hertz hire car to be ready.

Drove to Palma del Rio. The instructions, map and actual road numbers all completely different. Felt somewhat stressed.

Spent about an hour in Palma del Rio trying to find villa. In the end we phoned the owner and forced Bea to use her GCSE Spanish and get us directions. (She actually did rather well.) Met Pepe. Pepe took us to the villa, and showed us around. There was no way we would have found it using the directions we'd been sent, as many of the roads had no names.

Villa was pretty, with lots of dark wood and comfortable furniture. Rather smelly (of poo). Extremely hot, though all the rooms had ceiling fans.

This villa can still be booked. I notice that it now has air conditioning. If your husband ever tells you that ceiling fans are just as good as air conditioning, do not believe him.

Went to Supermarket in Palma del Rio. Everyone helped to find the stuff on my list, though it was quite hard to find stuff without speaking much Spanish. Bought food and cleaning materials.

Family swam, I cleaned villa.

Family had tea, I had aspirins. So hot. At 9pm it was 40°.

Sunday:
Fuse blew at 6am and everyone woke because the fans stopped working. Husband sorted it.

Late breakfast then swam, read, relaxed.

Evening, had dinner in Rio del Palma. Most restaurants have shut for August, because it is so hot that everyone who lives here goes somewhere else. This area is known as 'The Frying Pan' and I know why now.

Walked through a park and had an ice cream and some nice sangria.

Monday
Shopped, had pizza lunch then swam.

Went into Palma, but did not manage to find the Tourist Information Office.

Ate dinner in a restaurant that used to be a monastery. Menu was all in Spanish, but undeterred, we used our dictionary to translate. We settled on 'road kill', 'chatty aubergine' and 'gizzard'. Meals were pretty awful when they arrived (so maybe those were the correct translations after all).

Puddings were very nice, so was the sangria.

Way too hot.

Tuesday
We found the Tourist Info but they didn't speak any English. Did very little, too hot.

Too hot to sleep. Or read. Or move.

Wednesday
Had a very nice coffee in town and strolled around.

Drove to Cordoba.

Saw a Mosque-turned-Cathedral, with lots of arches. I found it more interesting than the boys did. Cordoba is very pretty, lots of narrow streets selling silver. I bought a silver necklace.

Had hot chocolate and *churros*. Cafe had a remarkably pretty washroom. Walked around a park. Found a nice tapas cafe.

Walked some more. My feet hurt (probably swelled up in the heat) so bought some leather sandals. Then got a whole new lot of blisters in different places.

Walked to a horrid square. Ate horrid ice creams.

Drove back to Palma. Passed a castle on a hill which was lit up so it looked exactly like it was floating in the sky. Magical.

Everyone got rather loud and giggly, and Husband managed to not kill the suicidal dog who ran in front of the car.

Thursday
Did nothing, too hot.

Dinner in Ecija, in a museum restaurant (was better than it sounds).

We were always the only customers in all the restaurants.

Friday
Swam and lazed. It was too hot.

Saturday
Went into town and managed to buy postage stamps without Bea helping.

Had lemonade and coffee. (Not in the same cup.) It is extremely good coffee, and we have found a little cafe, full of old men, where they serve very nice coffee in chipped old mugs. Feels Spanish.

Did nothing. I cooked pasta for lunch.

Drove to the castle (the floating one) and had a beer. I got locked in the toilet. For ages. Family didn't notice. Super.

Sunday
Bea traumatised as there was a lizard in her room. Emm not overly sympathetic. I tried to catch it and chased it behind the wardrobe, which didn't seem to reassure her.

Went into town for a coffee. (I cannot, if I'm honest, remember whether the lizard was still behind Bea's wardrobe at this point. I'm pretty sure, as a concerned mother, I would have sorted it first. But possibly not.) It's nice coffee but I'm sure the price went up a little every day. Husband tried to order coke instead, and the man asked if he wanted milk in it, so gave up on speaking Spanish and had coffee too.

Went back to villa to find a mouse swimming in the pool.

Went to Chinese restaurant in Palma. Nice, lots of food, really tasty.

Swam in pool.

Drove to Cordoba. Found *Salon de Té*. Very interesting, with Moroccan teapots and oil lamps.

We had drinks and tapas. Husband spilt his tea all over his bag. Not sure why.

Drove home via a really cool square—*Plaza Cappuchino*—full of low lights and candles.

12:30pm I cooked pizza for the boys and went to bed to not sleep. Too hot.

Monday
Drove to Seville.

Followed walk in guide book for a while but extremely hot, and children complaining. Gave up and went back to Palma for dinner.

We found a "pubby" restaurant in Palma, where locals had parked their trucks and horse and carriages outside. It was nicely relaxed, and had okay food.

Tuesday
Lazed around.

Started planning another trip to Seville tomorrow, will be better prepared this time.

I did some washing in the children's bathroom and noticed sewage bubbling up into the shower tray. This explains the unfortunate smells. Phoned Pepe.

Had lunch in Chinese restaurant.

Went to supermarket. Some of the brands are the same as in the UK, but most are not. It takes much longer to shop here – but at least the supermarket has air-conditioning.

Swam in pool. Husband and Jay extremely loud.

I did more washing. More sewage bubbled up into shower tray.

Wednesday
Men came and emptied the septic tank. Stinks.

Drove to Seville.

Left the children at an amusement park with a telephone and lots of instructions about staying together.

We got a taxi into town. I had worn comfortable shoes. Wandered around Seville, very pretty (though still hot).

Had coffee.

Had a horse and carriage ride around the city and park – much the best way to see the city without dying of heat exhaustion. Tried to buy a tea pot but all the shops were shut.

Seville is very pretty, with lots of pretty brick buildings, lots of history, lots of narrow streets to explore. But to be honest, I can tell you very little about it other than it is very, very hot. I would suggest you visit in the Winter.

Collected the children. They had all had fun, and were still alive, so that was good.

Drove back to stinky house.

Husband made cocktails then gambled with the children. (Sometimes not convinced we would get any parenting prizes.)

Thursday
Coffee in town.

Tried to order a bread and tomato dish that we have seen other people eating. Failed.

Tried to buy a tea pot. Failed.

Read swam, played cards, and gambled with matchsticks.

Went for a drive in search of tea pots. Failed.

Dinner in Palma, then watched a Jude Law film in Spanish. Was not great.

Friday
Had coffee at the ice cream parlour in Palma. Nice.

Husband had crushed tomatoes, olives and bread with oil and salt (which we'd tried to order the day before). He was happy. We ate sickly cakes. We were happy too.

Drove around, swam and lazed.

Dinner at a nice hotel in Ecija.

Packed. Husband appeared to be trying to pack the drawers but he assured us he was mending them.

Saturday
Home. Felt cold.

Verona, Italy, August 2009
(Children aged 13, 15 and 17)

Flew Gatwick to Verona.

Taxi to *Romeo and Guillietta Hotel*. Hotel was small, but a great location as it is in an alley right next to the opera arena.

Our room was okay but tiny – there was not even room to open the suitcase. However, the air conditioning was good and the shower was excellent. (It should perhaps be noted that in 2014, when we wanted to return to Verona to see an opera, we decided to stay here again. For position and price, it is fabulous.)

Lunch in an outside pizza place, *Canteena del Arena*. Pleasant.

Walked around. Had coffee and ice cream and a spritz. The spritz cost €19 each. Not checking prices first is an expensive mistake.

Found a supermarket. This is always the best place to buy bottles of water and snacks, and saves a lot of money.

Had dinner in the main square, right next to the Roman amphitheatre (which is where they stage the opera). It looks better preserved than the one in Rome but is smaller.

Spent the evening walking through pretty squares which the children complained were spooky.

Wednesday
A brilliant day—possibly my best day on a holiday ever.

I woke 6am and made Husband get up. The boys joined us and we borrowed bikes from the hotel and cycled round Verona. It was perfect. Lovely cool air, very few people or cars. We saw lots of pretty squares and ancient buildings.

Back to hotel for breakfast. Was impressed by how much food Emm ate.

Walked to Dante's Square and had coffee and ice cream. Looked around a market. Some nice 'touristy' stuff.

Saw the balcony from *'Romeo and Juliet'*. Though actually, as I believe that Shakespeare never visited Verona, I am unsure why everyone calls it "Juliet's balcony". I suspect some clever marketing has taken place. It is however, a pretty 13th century house, with a balcony, and there is a statue of Juliet in *Casa di Giulietta*—so perhaps I'm just an old cynic. It used to be possible to write a note for your lover, and stick it to the wall with chewing gum. But now everyone is worried about the effects of gum on the old building, so you are fined if you do. Which is perhaps less romantic.

At 8pm, we went to the opera (we had pre-booked our tickets when in England). We were shown up to the stone steps, where everyone sat, apart from a few people who had paid extra for chairs in the main arena. I think our view was better, though probably not so comfortable. (When we returned in 2014, we took garden chair cushions to sit on!)

They herded more and more people in and we kept squashing up until it was completely full. I loved it. It made you realise what it must have been like in Roman times: they sat on the same steps, looking at the same stage, being jostled on all sides by the rest of the audience.

The two girls next to Jay (who we didn't know) had a picnic. Somehow he managed to be invited to share it. He will go far in life. The rest of us sat there, slightly in awe, as he shared strawberries and cakes and champagne.

The opera was brilliant. We had told the children that they had to stay at least for the first act (it was Aida). The boys left during the first interval, and because the hotel was so near they could safely walk there on their own.

Bea and Husband both stayed until the end.

The Triumphant Entry scene was fantastic – there were 300 people on stage, including four white horses. (After that scene, everyone clapped and cheered and some people thought it was the end and left!)

It was probably not as good musically as *The Royal Opera House* in London, but without a doubt, it was the most impressive staging I have ever seen, and was a brilliant introduction to opera for anyone who has never seen one. There were soldiers with flaming torches, and horses, and hundreds of people singing – magnificent.

We sat on ancient stone steps and watched the moon rise in the warm sky, while listening to the music. It was magical.

It finished about 12:45. We collected the boys and had a pizza and red wine supper. Everywhere was open, it was as busy as daytime.

Went to bed 2am. Great day.

Thursday
Got up 8:30.

Breakfast in hotel. It is an okay breakfast, pleasant buffet and good coffee.

Walked to a Roman theatre next to the river. Woman giving out guide books at the entrance asked our nationality and Husband said, "German."

Why? We were then given all the information in German, which none of us can read. We wandered around the amphitheatre, not knowing what anything was.

Went back to hotel via market square and had iced drinks.

After dinner had hot chocolate in the square. It was very thick and dark, reminded me of blancmange, which my Mum used to make when I was young.

Went to bed early.

Friday
Walked to cathedral.

Bea had to wear a ghastly blue hooded cape over her shorts, as a sign of respect. None of us laughed at her. I found that all the churches in Italy have a very strict dress-code, and legs and shoulders must be covered, even by fairly young children.

Drank lemonade on a terrace next to the river.

Lunch in square. Boys had buckets (literally) of Fanta. They were happy.

Taxi to station, caught 4:30 train to Milan.

We discussed how noisy the Verona hotel had been. We all thought the sound-proofing was very bad. Except for the boys. They said they had not heard a thing. But the lady next door had been very rude and kept banging on their wall. Oh dear.

***

Milan 2009

Day 1

Train from Verona to Milan, 1½ hours.

Rather hot because the air conditioning broke.

Checked in to *Hotel De La Ville*.

Nice hotel with good facilities. Our rooms seemed huge after the Verona hotel.

Looked at pool (small), bar (pleasant) and fitness room (looked okay.) It should be noted that we always do this when we arrive at hotels. We then always use the pool, rarely visit the bar, and I don't think we have *ever* used the fitness room. But you never know...

Walked around Milan looking for somewhere suitable for a family to eat that did not involve taking out a mortgage. We walked for a very long time. Found a pub, which had a free buffet (which was not especially nice) with drinks. Plus you could order extra food. We had lasagna and pizzas.

Wandered around the cathedral, which was very pretty. Felt hungry.

There is a nice big square outside where the whole world hangs out. The outside of the cathedral is covered with some pretty cool gargoyles. Very gothic. It took over 600 years to build – which seems excessive until you see it. I expect it caused a few arguments at the time.

Strolled around some posh shops trying on perfumes.

Back at the hotel, Bea had to change rooms because her air-conditioning didn't work. The new room was further from our room, which worried me, but she said she was fine.

Day 2
Buffet breakfast.

We were quite late eating and it looked like it had been there for a while, though the selection was good. The best bit was a little news sheet that you could pick up as you went into breakfast (in various languages).

Walked around Milan. Found a Ferrari shop. Bought a Ferrari bag. Also bought a Ferrari hat for a friend's new baby (family felt he would have sufficient teddy bears and cute clothes).

Saw a few pretty squares and the Galleria Vittorio Emanuele II. Which sounds like another church but is actually a four-storied arcade of shops. I am not much interested by shops but the arcade was worth a visit.

I sat in the cathedral square and drank espresso while the family continued shopping. It was the most expensive coffee I have ever sipped, but I told myself I was paying for the atmosphere, not the coffee (or the dirty table). Watched the world go by.

Bought some Dolce & Gabbana perfume, and was somehow persuaded to buy the big bottle, as that came with a 'free' vanity bag and body lotion, which would be for Bea (not sure how she managed to persuade me into that one). When we paid, it was put into a regular shop carrier bag, so I asked for the assistant to go and find me a D&G carrier. No point in buying useless expensive things unless you can pose. We then wandered around with the D&G bag, pretending to be rich.

Sandwich/burger from a food hall (so clearly not very good at pretending to be rich).

Boys swam in pool on hotel roof.

We went to an art gallery. Saw some fantastic art (and some really bad art). There was one really cool picture, of a girl who looked like she was checking her phone, there was a chair where dirty clothes had been thrown; the floor was littered with letters and shoes and make-up. On the wall was a picture of Romeo and Juliette. It made you realise that teenagers are the same, whichever century they happen to be born into.

We wanted to see 'The Last Supper' at Santa Maria Delle Grazie. However, tickets need to be pre-booked a couple of months in advance, which we hadn't realised.

Went to hotel gym with boys. Unexpected detour from normal holiday routine. They went in the jacuzzi (which was broken). We used a few machines but all the best ones were broken or had pieces missing. Shame.

Ate in McDonalds. By far the poshest McDonalds I have ever been in.

Walked down to *Sforza Castle*. This is a fifteenth century castle and at night it is floodlit. There is a big fountain in front and it is very pretty. Had ice creams.

Husband and I had drinks in the hotel bar. Pleasant.

Day 3

I went to Mass in the cathedral (Duomo).

People were queuing to go inside but if you are attending Mass you can go straight in. You need to be appropriately dressed (covered shoulders and knees). I found it hard to follow the Italian, though there were some discernible words. I just liked being there.

Walked back to the castle. It was way too hot and felt a lot further during daytime. Drank lemonade in the gardens. The kids stood in the fountains (other people were too, so I figured they wouldn't get shot).

A man approached Husband with some English passports he had 'found'. He wanted Husband to go with him to a phone box to phone the owners. Husband said he would use his mobile at which point the man became very aggressive and snatched them back. I took photos of him, which I later showed to some police who were in the cathedral square but they were completely disinterested.

Dinner in a restaurant at the top of *La Rinascente* which is a shopping mall selling designer stuff (pretty boring unless you like that sort of thing) but has a very interesting food hall at the top, and a restaurant on the roof. It was lovely, we sat in the balmy evening air overlooking the gargoyles on the Duomo. Very atmospheric.

Had drinks (and hot chocolates) in the hotel bar and played cards.

Day 4

We had breakfast and packed, then got a taxi to the airport. There was a thunder storm, which pleased Bea and I as it meant we could use our umbrellas and mac (this holiday has been all about posing: it's what you're meant to do in Milan). We were going to the airport to collect a hire car, not to catch a flight, which thoroughly confused the taxi driver. Collected hire car and drove to Lake Como.

***

Lake Como 2009

Drove 1½ hours from Milan to Lake Como. Checked in to *Grand Hotel*, Menaggio. The hire car is a rather smart Mercedes, so Husband is happy.

The hotel was lovely, with pretty communal areas and a balcony in our room overlooking the lake and surrounding hills. Very pretty.

Found a bar that was open late, for lunch.

Strolled around the town while kids swam in hotel pool. We found a shop, and bought the boys a crocodile to replace *Croccy Dee*, the inflatable from Taormina. Am not sure why we did that.

Dinner in hotel, nice 4-course meal. The Italians have starter, first course, second course, and pudding. Friendly staff.

Walked into town and played crazy golf. It was a cold evening. I hate playing golf.

Day 2

Got up early and went to gym. Then felt ill all day (exercise obviously bad for me).

We were late into breakfast so the buffet was rather depleted. Lazy day.

Day 3

Didn't go to gym. (No need to over do it.)

Hotel were having a Gala night, so were putting up some (slightly naff) decorations.

Ate lunch in a square in town. Como has lots of hotels, along the road next to the lake. There is a main town, which has traditional Italian squares and a few shops. I didn't think it was especially pretty, and the main focus is the lake. Strolled around but it was too hot to walk for long.

Dinner was nice but we had a grumpy waitress who threw down food, spilt drinks and scowled a lot. Probably does too much exercise.

Sat on balcony and watched fireworks across the lake.

They played classical musical, and it was magical, watching the reflections play across the water.

Day 4

Drove along the side of lake and into Switzerland. Took about 2 hours.

Beautiful scenery, even the kids thought it was good: "Looks like one of those posters which you know isn't real. But it is!" There are green fields, and mountains, and the bluest lakes I have ever seen.

Went to St Moritz. Bit false, mainly hotels and designer shops. Had a lovely homemade soup and cheese sandwich lunch in a cafe.

The family all went on a train and cable car up to the peak to look at the Alps. They said the scenery was brilliant.

I got off the train at the first stop and tried to find the storybook Heidi's house. No helpful signposts and I wasn't really sure what I was looking for. The only possible contender I saw was pretty big. My image of Heidi's grandfather was not multi millionaire. Maybe he extended it when her books became popular.

It was fairly chilly. I met other walkers, who were all wearing full hiking gear complete with boots and walking poles. Wondered if my silk skirt and sandals was inappropriate clothing for mountain walking. Pretended I was local, and stared at them as if they were over-dressed annoying tourists.

Walked down through pine forests, listening to cow bells. It was a mix of very lovely (as it grew warmer on the lower slopes) and a bit scary – because I was on a mountain all by myself without a clue as to where I was, in a silk skirt and sandals. I figured I only needed to keep aiming downhill, and eventually I would reach a town.

When I got back to town my legs were shaking from walking downhill for so long! (Maybe I do need another gym visit.)

Went to Co-op and bought chocolate and cokes.

Drove home (after we managed to pay the car park ticket. The machine only took euro notes and we didn't want swiss francs as change).

On the way back we stopped at a lake. It was totally perfect. Husband and the boys stripped off and swam. Lots of squealing when they realised how cold the water was! Luckily no one had a heart attack and we made it back to hotel slightly damp, very hungry, but feeling we had had a good day.

The dinner was very nice again.

Day 5

Husband went to the gym, then restocked his protein with egg and cheese for breakfast. (No comment.)

Morning by pool, lunch in bar next door.

Spent the afternoon at *Villa Carlotta*. This is a villa (duh), built in the seventeenth century for a Milanese marquis. It is now a museum and botanical garden.

The gardens surrounding the villa are very lovely and we spent some time wandering around. It would have been more enjoyable in a slightly cooler season.

Day 6
We took the ferry across the lake to Varenna.

The ferries stop right next to the hotel and you constantly heard them announcing all their stops. It wasn't particularly intrusive, they were only at certain times and not late at night, but whenever I now think about that hotel I hear the chant from the ferry information in my head. Shame they weren't chanting something useful.

Varenna is a little town on a hill, full of picturesque lanes and old fishermen cottages.

We walked around and then bought slices of pizza which we ate on stone steps leading down to the water. We found a cafe next to the lake and had some very good pancakes before getting the ferry back to Menaggio. Husband and Bea both bought bags.

After dinner we walked into town.

There was extremely loud music in the car park next to the hotel until 2am. It was like trying to sleep in a night club. Gave up and danced on the balcony for a while.

Day 7
Woke tired and grumpy. Husband escaped to the gym (coward).

Morning by the pool, boys did not emerge from their room.

Drove to a viewpoint overlooking Lake Lugano. It was a long drive and a very confusing map. Ate a not very nice ice cream when we got there.

After dinner, a pianist played next to the pool.

Day 8
I felt ill. Packed and left.

Drove back to Milan for the flight home.

It was very difficult to find a petrol station to refill the hire car before we returned it. Finally bought extremely expensive petrol from a man selling 'especially refined diesel'.

Arrived at the airport in plenty of time. Spent 4 hours reading/chatting/trying to not mention the time.

Flew home.

A good holiday. I am rather in love with Italy, even though it has a lot of shops. I hope to visit again, especially the lakes. Perhaps I will try to learn a little Italian.

New York and Denver to Las Vegas 2010
(Children aged 14, 16 and 18)

Thursday
Flight from Heathrow. Husband used his Virgin Gold card to get us all into the executive lounge. Very nice, will forgive him for all those business trips. We made good use of the facilities. Bea had a haircut. We had cocktails and champagne, then a meal. Boys played snooker while we read papers and had coffee. Very nice.

Flew Economy to JFK. Not so nice. Flight lasted forever.

Arrived JFK. Got monorail to Avis. Rented totally massive car. After being awake for about 36 hours, I was not at my best when presented with a map and asked:

"Okay Annie, which way?"

Drove to Hilton, in Montvale, NJ – and no one was murdered (though it was close a couple of times).

Hotel seems nice, but I am way too tired.

Friday
Our hotel includes breakfast in 'the butler's pantry'. This turns out to be a smallish room, stocked with bagels, cereal and porridge (which the Americans call 'Oatmeal').

Got bus into Manhattan. Checked into W hotel in Times Square. Very trendy. Suite. Bathroom had a glass wall, very strange – who wants to watch someone using the toilet? The children were quite vocal about this.

Looked down into Times Square. There are lots of giant billboards, filled with lights and adverts which change every few seconds. An explosion of colour. It's noisy too – even in the hotel, you hear cars beeping – American drivers use the horn a lot when driving.

Walked around. You feel like you are in a movie set in New York. So many people, everyone rushing, shops you can get lost in, sirens and cars beeping, smells wafting from all the fast food places and delis, steam rising from big orange columns.

Ate at *Smith and Wollensky*. Husband and Jay shared a huge steak (half a cow). I didn't think I could eat that much meat, so ordered chicken. When it arrived, I was a little shocked to find it was exactly that – a chicken. As in, a WHOLE, family-sized chicken. Wow! Delicious food but ate too much, and still left loads.

Excellent red wine, probably drank too much of that as well. Fun evening, ate and laughed a lot. Didn't see anyone famous.

Saturday
Breakfast at Starbucks.

We all queued outside *Abercrombie and Fitch*, waiting for it to open (it was a new shop). I cannot possibly explain to you why this seemed a good thing to do on our holiday – or on any day, in fact – and I have no excuse at all. Perhaps Bea persuaded me while I was under the influence of too much red wine. The experience was every bit as awful as it sounds. I even had an argument with a woman who pushed in. Can't quite believe I did either of those things, embarrassing.

Went Downtown. Saw Statue of Liberty, China Town, Little Italy. It's nice to just walk around, looking at places.

Lunch in a diner. So American! Had booths and everything, just like being in a Jack Reacher novel. Emm had Philly cheese steak. Very NY.

Got bus to Woodcliff Lake, then taxi to Hilton.

Dinner at *Applebees*. A comfortable restaurant, reminds me of Beefeater in the UK, but with lots of sports paraphernalia on the walls. Bea got told to move further from the bar – I always forget how strict the US drinking laws are.

Shopped.
Really, really tired.

Sunday

Church at *Cornerstone Christian Church* in Wyckoff, NJ. Saw a few people we recognised from when we used to live here. Good music with a band, interesting talk, friendly people.

Went into city with some friends. Ate at a Mexican restaurant. They kept bringing us huge platters of food. Really nice, though I was still feeling tired, and everything was a little unreal. I'm hoping my conversation made sense.

Walked through Central Park and round the zoo. Very hot. Central Park always surprises me, such a big park in the middle of the city. Saw lots of places I recognise from films. The zoo is small and smelly, but nice if you like zoos (which I do).

Back to friend's house. Take-out pizza.

Monday

Pancakes at *IHOP* on Route 17. Perfect! Quantities still huge though. It is not possible to only order one pancake, they come in stacks. All the coffee everywhere is 'bottomless' (free refills) which is wonderful. Coffee in the US is different to coffee at home. It's less bitter I think.

Went to a friend's pool. Swam, chatted, relaxed. BBQ chicken and corn with friends. Then went to Paramus Park Mall in the evening. So big! Dairy Queen ice creams, then said goodbye – always sad.

Tuesday

Gym and swam at hotel. I didn't exactly work-off all those big meals, but I felt better.

It's a nice hotel, very inexpensive and convenient being so near the city but also – because it's in New Jersey – you can see a little of 'real' America too. Breakfast in hotel lounge. Bagels – I had forgotten how fantastic the bagels are in NY. They are huge (of course) and soft, and are perfect with cream cheese and coffee.

Drove round Upper Saddle River, saw the house where we used to live. Remembered all the traffic laws – like having to drive slowly past schools, not being allowed to park on the street at night, only parking in the direction of traffic, having to stop if you see a stationary school bus – whatever side of the road you are on. Also all the 'unwritten' rules, like watching the opposite traffic lights and moving the *very second* your light turns green, or you get honked. We got a lot of driving tickets when we first arrived here to live, in 1998.

Went to Summit, met some other friends. Sandwiches from a deli for lunch. Had forgotten how easy it is to get nice food in US. Summit is nice, lots of trees, lots of typically American houses, clean and peaceful.

Went to town pool. In US, most towns seem to have a town pool. You have to be a resident of the town to become a member but can then invite friends. It's where people meet their neighbours and spend summer afternoons. It doesn't really have an English equivalent.

Wednesday
Breakfast. Packed.

Jay informed me that if you hide shampoo they keep leaving more. (Horrid image of hotel shampoo stashed in mini fridge comes to mind.) Bea added that it doesn't work with hairdryers. (Not sure how she would know that.) The boy's swivel chair was in the bathroom. They told me they had used it in a game. I decided not to ask… (Tip for parents of boys: If it's not dangerous, illegal or mean, then you are probably happier not knowing.)

Newark airport. Awful.

Flew to Denver.

Collected another car the size of a caravan and drove to *Best Western* in Dillon. The motel is next to a lake. Very pretty.

Ate in an American Restaurant. Nice. Food here is so easy. It always tastes great, the portions are always huge, the service is usually friendly.

Thursday
Beds do not compare well with Hilton, bad night's sleep.

Husband went for early walk and came back with coffee for everyone. Sometimes I remember why I love him.

Breakfast bar in hotel. Jay used internet in lobby. I looked at views across lake.

Supermarket trip. Family stocked up on bottles of water and Gatorade. No one in the family likes Gatorade, we never have, so I really have no idea why everyone insisted that we buy some.

Drove. Went through a dodgy town. Listened to audio book. Drove.

Drove some more.

Denver to Vegas is shorter on the map.

Amazing scenery. Amazing weather. Few rain showers, fantastic clouds, snow at one point when we were really high. Mountains, lakes, trees, rivers, cattle ranches.

Stopped at *Bongo Billy's* deli (yes, real name) and bought sandwiches. Boys bought food from a *Subway* opposite.

Had ice creams in Ouray. Cute houses, looks like a cowboy film set. Spent some time wandering around. Interesting curiosity shops. There was also a woman who kept screaming. I have no idea why, perhaps she had mental problems, but it was a little perturbing.

Drove up a steep mountain pass – scary. Brilliant red rocks. Followed annoyingly slow lorry.

Pizza Hut in Durango.

Arrived at Holiday Inn in Cortez. Really nicely decorated with lots of ethnic American Indian stuff.

Friday
Slept well.

Breakfast not so good. Polystyrene plates and plastic spoons. Husband burnt finger on bagel. I put sugar on oatmeal, then discovered it was mushroom soup (don't know how I missed that one).

Got petrol.

Bea spotted meerkats. But they aren't really meerkats, must be cousins. I think they're prairie dogs, disguised as meerkats.

Found track to *Valley of Gods*. This was not easy, and we drove along someone's driveway at one point. I think the map was wrong. Luckily, we didn't get shot. Saw amazing rocks. Road very rough.

Back on main road. Totally straight, no bends for many miles.

Saw eagles eating a dead horse.

Ate snacks for lunch. Boys did Indian chants.

Looked at American Indian stuff on stalls next to road. Interesting, but too expensive. There are lots of these stalls beside the road, and they all seem to sell much the same thing. I found my interest in looking at them far exceeded the rest of the family's. Especially Emm's, who threatened to throw himself off a cliff at one point if we stopped to look at more Indian stuff.

Went to a visitor's centre. Looked across a valley to an ancient town, built into canyon wall. It looked like a toy town because the canyon is 4 miles across. It was hard to get any perspective on it, there was nothing to compare it to, so the wonder of it was lost.

Drove to Tuba City, checked into *Quality Inn Motel*. (I wonder how they came up with that name.)

Lots of American Indian stuff. Emm was so pleased.

Ate in restaurant next door. All the other customers were Native American Indian. Not sure if that's a good sign or not. Nice pink lemonade. Very pink.

The menu had a food poisoning warning at the bottom, which rather put me off my dinner. Have they had lots of cases of poisoning and feel the need to cover themselves?

Bad night due to motel having a blocked toilets problem (not ours). Maybe related to food poisoning warning on menu.

I notice that no one, at all, drank any Gatorade all day. Just saying.

Saturday
Went to Indian Trading Post. Interesting, some good stuff.

Drove to Grand Canyon. Found really good place to stop, amazing views. Saw eagles soaring. Beautiful.

You cannot help but be amazed at the size of the canyon. It deadens all sound and sucks you into its peacefulness. Best if you avoid the main car parks which are touristy. We have visited before, but it still fascinates.

Drove to Las Vegas. Queues at Hoover Dam, because the authorities were checking for terrorists.

Drove down *The Strip* (which is the main street, where all the hotels are). Slightly heated discussion about where to go, but we found the correct carpark eventually.

Checked into *Mandalay Bay* hotel. Nice room, telly in bathroom (should you be the sort of person to whom that would appeal).

Met my sister who has come down from Calgary. We ate dinner in *Blues* restaurant, and I tried to stop the boys watching a pole dancer in the casino opposite.

Mandalay Bay is nice if you like massive hotels. It was clean, and the rooms had everything we needed. There was a lot of colour and very patterned carpets. And a slightly enclosed, recycled air, feel. It's not a good place if you suffer from migraines.

Sunday
Starbucks breakfast.

Went to the pool, weather is incredibly hot, though all buildings are slightly too cool due to the air-conditioning, so you need to bring a cardigan. You remember you are in a desert as soon as you step outside of the hotel, which is a lot like entering a blast furnace.

Lazy river was nice, but too crowded. You felt slimy wet bodies all around as you floated along, which I found unpleasant. The children didn't seem to mind though. It was too hot to sit outside really. I did have books to read, and there were towels and sun-loungers, but within minutes of settling down, you wanted to go back inside. Or join the masses of slimy bodies in the pool. Not really my sort of thing.

No one drank any Gatorade.

Lunch in a diner. Huge portions again. We will all have huge stomachs soon, so will waste less when we eat out.

Walked to other casinos:

Luxor – impressive (though males rather distracted by bikini clad girl in lobby).

Excaliber – pretty castle outside.

MGM – boys remembered the Rainforest Cafe from when they were little. I think there also used to be lions there, though perhaps they have been moved because a tiny cage is cruel. Or maybe we just didn't see them this time.

Too hot to walk further.

We dressed up in pretty heels (okay, not the males) and went to a Chinese restaurant in the hotel. They gave us a private room (must have been because they were impressed by the pretty heels).

Las Vegas seems different to when we visited in 1999. It seemed smarter then, everything looked new, and most people were well dressed. Also, all the food was very cheap due to hotels making their profit primarily from the casinos. This time it felt slightly old. Lots of people were very casually dressed, and the food was pricey. It felt like it was trying too hard. The casinos didn't feel excitingly low lit – they just felt dark, as if they couldn't afford any more light bulbs. Or perhaps they hoped we wouldn't notice the worn out carpets. I might copy this idea when I don't feel like doing housework and we have guests.

After dinner, drove to *Bellagio*. Amazing lobby, like a giant garden. Watched fountain/music display.

Monday
Coffee and donuts in room.
    Swam, chatted, relaxed.

Drove to *Venetian* to pick up theatre tickets. Ate in their Italian restaurant. The waiters were arguing, so it wasn't the best atmosphere. Nobody was shot though.

Saw gondoliers, and giant toffee apples. It was very well done, and you felt as if you had stepped into a storybook.

Went to Phantom of the Opera show. We were nearly late, because traffic was so bad, and we crawled there, watching the time tick past, wondering if our tickets would be wasted. The show was short, but good scenery and singing. (I was a little confused, and thought we were watching *The Phantom of the Opera*. But we weren't, we were watching a *show* of *The Phantom of the Opera*, which was just a few extracts and the more popular songs. If I had understood beforehand, and had the correct expectations, I would have enjoyed it more.)

Drove home past erupting volcano and fountain display.

To date, we have seen: 4 brides, 2 Elvis', 2 showgirls in a carpark. The Gatorade is still unopened.

Tuesday
Donuts and coffee.

Packed.

Swam and sunbathed, and nearly died of heat stroke.

Drove to airport, which is right at the end of The Strip, so very easy.

Nine and a half hour flight home. Ugh...

I decided to leave the Gatorade in Vegas.

Rome August 2011
(Children aged 15, 17 and 19 years)

Saturday

4:15 am, taxi arrived. Emm in a panic because had planned to get up at 3:30 but hadn't. Then the insecure taxi driver refused to drive via the lanes, and there was a blockage on M25, so I was somewhat stressed by the time we arrived at Gatwick.

In security check we got sent to a faster line. Boys remarked that security in this lane obviously weren't checking properly. Luckily no one heard.

Nice breakfast at *EAT*. Emm gave economics lecture over strength of Euro.

Good flight, taxi to *Hotel Genio*. Quite small but a good position.

Pizza/pasta lunch. Walked around.

Hotel is right next to *Piazza de Nevona*, which is a totally brilliant square with fountains, artists, etc. Saw an old man pretending to sing opera while miming to a hidden CD. Very funny. Gave him some money just because he made me laugh.

Had a quick look at some Roman stuff. Quite warm.

Dinner at brilliant restaurant, very rustic. *(Old Bear: Via dei Gigli d'Oro 3)* Had a litre of sangria. Played cards while waiting for meal to arrive. Extremely sleepy. Nice dinner, with tasty food and friendly service. Husband ate loads of bread so he was happy.

Sunday

Up early. Lovely breakfast on roof terrace, looking across Rome. I had pineapple juice (which I hate) and warm milk (which I hate). Need to learn some more Italian.

Walked across a bridge and along river. Beautiful. Read guide book and tried to plan rest of week *(Tues: Vatican, Wed: Colossium, breakfast each day at 7...we'll see.)*

Walked to St Peter's Square. Watched the Pope on a big screen. He gave benediction in lots of languages (quite impressive). It was hot but sort of nice. Saw that square was built over the original Roman race track, which is where they crucified St Peter. That felt strangely significant.

Found a restaurant. We waited there with drinks while Husband ran back to hotel to collect Emm (who had declined Pope trip). Nice lunch.

Back to hotel. I had a nap. Boys in our room while their air con is fixed, so not a very good nap.

Tea on roof terrace – this terrace is a nice place to escape to, and feels sort of 'Italian'. Boys collected Subway and we bought drinks and fruit from a Spar.

Walked to Spanish Steps. Very pretty but very crowded, so there was no atmosphere. There were tourists from the whole world there, jostling to take photographs. Jay took photos of his feet. (Why?)

Went back to square. Nice music, lights, stalls.

Back to hotel. Tired.

Monday

Up at 7:00. Met Jay and Emm for breakfast. Walked to Garibaldi statue but didn't find it. Ended up in a botanical garden. Was deserted and very run down. Highlight was giant bamboo and some ducks crossing the road.

Wrote postcards. Subway lunch.

Went to *'Time Machine'*, a historical cinema. But they'd had a power cut, so it wasn't working.

Walked to Trevi fountain. Very crowded. Amazing little church behind it, full of angels, paintings, gilt, candles. The church was much nicer than the fountain.

Ice cream in Navona Square, which was lovely but expensive. I guess really you are paying for the view and the atmosphere, as it's rather lovely to drink coffee and eat ice-cream in a pretty Italian square. Wandered around.

Dinner: Tried to go back to same restaurant but it was shut.

Walked up a street of cafes, each one had people outside trying to entice you in. There are lots of these streets in Italian cities – narrow lanes with tables and chairs outside, a few plants, a menu for you to compare (though you sometimes get a more realistic impression by looking at the plates of people already eating there).

One woman said they had a special deal – starter, pasta or pizza plus a drink for 11 euros. Went inside. When we came to order, she said that the 'special deal' was only for lunch times, so we had to order from the evening menu, which was not so special. When I ordered a glass of red wine, she said the wine in the menu wasn't very nice, she would open a special bottle for me. Suspected price was going to spiral upwards. We left.

Ate in a friendly but hot cafe in same street. Portions were quite small for the boys, but nice food, and the menu inside was the same as the menu displayed outside, so we didn't feel conned. Husband drank shots while paying.

Walked around. Rome is very romantic at night. Bought Husband a hat, and the boys some silk ties.

Tues
All awake for 8am breakfast so could get an early start for Vatican. Long queues. People were arriving after us, and pushing in, so boys made a long line and blocked them (embarrassing but effective).

Firstly, we walked through St Peter's church. This felt more like a museum than a church. Too many tourists taking photos. No music. No candles.

Couldn't get into Sistine Chapel because need to pre-book for mornings. Boys didn't climb tower due to very long queues.

Pizza for lunch.

Went to back to Sistine Chapel. Extremely long line of hot people, shuffling through narrow corridors. Some amazing art en route but rather tempered by need for fresh air and water. When there was something amazing, some sculpture by Rodin, or a particularly beautiful painting, there was no opportunity to stop and appreciate it, you had to keep shuffling forwards, pushed by people behind.

Chapel itself was smaller than expected. Brilliant art but did feel very like cattle herded into a pen. Escaped after about an hour.

Kids drank from a fountain in a random square – so they'll probably die.

Ate at *Hard Rock Cafe*. Fun. Also cheaper than most places in Rome, though possibly not particularly Italian.

When boys realised drink refills were free, they drank loads. Eventually waitress dumped two jugs on the table and disappeared (to weep).

Wed
Breakfast 8am, then taxi to Colosseum.

We managed to avoid massive queues, by Husband going to information desk and then paying for an audio tour. This allows you to walk straight in without buying a separate entrance ticket. As we walked past the hundreds of people standing in line, I did feel a bit guilty, but the offer is open to everyone, though not especially well advertised. We had to wait at a separate, 'Guided Tours' entrance, which had almost no queue at all.

Outside, there were men dressed as gladiators. They persuaded people to have their photo taken with them, then charged them 5 euros EACH! Some people were cross and argued, but most people just paid. Lucrative scam.

The Colosseum was interesting. It's less preserved/restored than the one in Verona but you could see underneath the chambers. You could imagine all the terrible, and wonderful, things that had happened there.

McDonalds lunch. Ice creams and cards on the roof.
Restaurant dinner.

Thus

10am, walked to *Piazza del Popolo* with Bea and Jay. Saw two matching churches. I am not sure why anyone would build two churches, both huge, right next to each other.

Had coffee and milkshakes in a bakery.

Saw Augustus' tomb, all fenced off.

Passed a cool fountain that was a wall of water.

Subway lunch on roof. The boys were given a free one, because they have been such good customers!

Went back to *'Time Machine'*. It's a 5D cinema – a really good idea, nice to look at, but it doesn't quite work. It tells the story of Rome, from when it was a barren wasteland, through to modern day. The seats move, and you feel as if you are in a time machine, watching the city change. The whole cinema had to stop because someone felt travel sick.

Walked to Hard Rock Cafe.

Pleasant walk back to hotel. I bought a Vespa fridge magnet.

The family played cards on the roof, and I tried to read, but it was too dark.

Fri

Husband and I walked to Garibaldi statue – we found it this time. Good views.

Pizza lunch next to Pantheon. Looked round.

My head was bad, so I went to bed.

Ice cream in 'our' square.

Dinner at *Old Bear* again. Another good meal.

Sat

Taxi to airport. Picked up a hire car, which was big and ugly. Drove to villa.

***

Villa near Rome

Saturday 13th August 2011

We arrived at the villa too early, so went to a cafe for lunch while we waited. The cafe was pretty, and friendly, and there were plants everywhere. They gave us free Champagne.

The villa is lovely, very large and comfortable. We had to leave a 44€ security deposit, which seemed excessive, but as the villa is so lovely Husband decided it was fair. The garden is beautiful, with flower beds and a big pool and outside seating, and fresh herbs growing. There's a big oak table in the kitchen, and the cupboards are stocked with food and drink, which they said we can eat (though that seems unusual, so I don't expect we will).

It's owned by Florinda Bolkan, who was well-known for her acting in the 60s and 70s. There were large photos of her everywhere. She was wearing clothes in some of them.

Sunday
Swam and ate and watched DVDs.

Monday
Swam, read, slept, sunbathed.

Went to Bracchiano for dinner. It was nasty and unfriendly. Left, and went to a pizza place, which had plastic tables but was friendly. The pizzas were good.

Watched DVD.

Tuesday
Slept late.

There was a big frog in the swimming pool. It was dead.

Went to a supermarket. Bought food, and swim suit, hat and goggles. We have not bought holiday gifts for anyone, which seemed fine when we were in Rome, as we had another week of holiday, but there are no shops here, so it will be a problem. Am hoping Mum will like some Italian biscuits.

Everyone chose their own box of ice-creams for the freezer. Bea's were horrid. Emm's were nice, so we all started to eat them. He hid the rest in the bottom of Bea's box.

Cheese and stuff for lunch.

Swam and read.

Steak and salad made with fresh herbs for dinner (it seemed like too much effort to go out and try to find somewhere to eat). I have found that booking a beautiful villa in rural Italy or Spain is not entirely good. Although the house is often beautiful, and you can look at 'real' little towns and villages, and drive through lovely countryside, there are not necessarily good places to eat. I think a villa works well if you want to cook, but if (like me) you hate cooking and would rather have a break on holiday, then villas in remote places are not ideal.

Wednesday
Husband and I went for a drive around in big ugly car. The area seems to be made up of unfriendly hamlets. Felt unwelcome, even in shops.

Went back to supermarket (most exciting part of the day). Husband bought a leather briefcase, and we looked at leather jackets for the kids – possible Christmas gifts.

Thursday
Went back to buy leather jackets. Only Bea fitted in one.

We ate in a restaurant near the villa. The owner was very concerned that we didn't speak much Italian, and asked another customer to translate. The meals were nice, but the atmosphere was very tense. At one point, a bat flew in (but I think that was unrelated).

Friday
Packed and lazed around.

Husband and I went to a town and had coffee in a square. This is what one is meant to do in Italy – I am not keen on isolated villas.

Lunch at the pizza place again.

Flew home.

Sorrento August 2012
(Children aged 16, 18 and 20 years)

Monday
Boys' alarm failed. They woke at 4:45 in a panic (I'm not sure they had packed.)

Left home 5am, one hour delay at Gatwick, then flew to Naples. Boys checked out *High Life* magazine for drugs.

Husband sorted hire car while we collected cases.

Drove to Sorrento. Managed to miss a 'No Entry' sign and went the wrong way down a one-way street. Within seconds, two policemen (who had been hiding) hurried over, and fined us 39€.

Staying at *Hotel Bristol*. All rooms have sea view and balcony.

Had sandwiches at pool side bar.

Evening meal was lovely, though slightly rushed as the next course arrived the second we finished eating each one. Perhaps the waiters had somewhere to go. Friendly service. Delicious ice cream.

Walked into town. Lots of little shops selling leather goods and lemon products.

Tuesday
Breakfast really nice. Lots of fresh fruit, breads plus cooked stuff. Husband tried to plan activities. Not sure we were helpful.

Views are so beautiful, want to absorb them.

Went to pool on roof. Nice but it's very over-looked. We were issued with a single towel per day by pool attendant. Not allowed to leave pool via side, rather than steps. Not allowed to take inflatables into pool. Not allowed to reserve loungers (which is mainly good, deters people from leaving a towel at dawn to reserve best chairs. But does mean you have to guard your towel when swimming, or predatory pool man reclaims them!) Not allowed to do shoulder stands. Not allowed to jump in.

Not sure my boys and the pool attendant are going to be friends…

Walked into town and bought calzones and stuff for lunch. Saved about 75€ on hotel price. Ate on balcony.

Read, snoozed, swam. Husband started campaign to have inflatables allowed in pool. Am hoping it doesn't last all week.

Boys seem to swim mainly under water – unsettling when they loom below me as I'm struggling to reach the side.

Another nice dinner.

Played *Catan* in the lounge. It's a really nice lounge, lots of sofas and a piano for Jay to play. Emm won. Of course. Actually, we all nearly won at some point. It was an extremely long game.

Wednesday

I got up early and went for a walk. Left Husband to wake the family.

Sorrento is at the top of a cliff. The main town area is full of narrow lanes, and tiny squares, and interesting shops where locals sell their crafts. Some things are very expensive, all are wonderful to look at. Our hotel was further along the coast, and walking anywhere involved a steep hill.

Returned to find Husband engrossed in a book. I woke family.

Swam, read, swam. Lunch. Swam, read, swam.

Dinner, then played cards in the bar. Musicians playing jazz.

Thursday

7am breakfast then Husband and I drove to Pompeii. We went years ago, when the children were small and unhappy in the heat, and I promised myself that one day, I would come back without them. This was that visit.

Everyone else had a late breakfast and lazed.

Pompeii still interesting, still dusty, still incredibly hot. But there is something about it, seeing the grooves in paving stones where chariots drove, seeing streets that are pretty much intact, seeing gardens, which takes you back in time. Most houses are complete to the first floor, and you can easily feel how crowded the ancient city was. The ancient Roman people become real, it is so easy to imagine how life was. But it is very hot.

Went to huge supermarket on way back to Sorrento. My feet hurt, next time will wear proper shoes, not sandals. Finished reading *The Book Thief* – a brilliant book.

Friday
Up early and went to exercise room. It's very hot in there, was nice to swim afterwards.

Went to breakfast. Everyone asked me why my face was so red.

Checked evening meal menu. Planned day (we're doing nothing, so it didn't take much planning).

Swam.

Played *Catan* on the roof lounge. There are comfy chairs and big umbrellas, so it's a pretty space to be in, but it was still too hot to be completely fun. Swam.

Nice dinner, then walked into town. Bought gifts, which was easy as there are so many shops selling soaps and trinkets. Sorrento has lots of inlaid wooden crafts. There are also leather goods – and every Italian town I have ever been in has shops selling handbags.

Bit cooler tonight, might rain.

Saturday
Gym at 7:30 with Husband. Painful. Breakfast.

Bea ate slowly while Emm sang "We're not getting any younger". She ignored him.

Lazed, read, swam. Males played cards (extremely noisily) in smoking room.

Walked into town and collected pizzas. Ate on our balcony. Bea was put in charge of rubbish disposal. Was banned from throwing it onto neighbour's balcony or flinging it off roof. Have horrid feeling I am going to find abandoned pizza boxes in unsuitable place.

Pizza boxes currently in corridor. Not a good sign.

Lazed, read, swam.

Family joined with an Irish family to play games in pool. They used Jay's rolled up tee shirt as a ball (well, it's not an inflatable). Jay said ants had found some food he was saving. Ah.

Pizza boxes still in corridor.

Another nice dinner. Watched Olympics – Bolt won relay.

Sunday
Gym and swam.

Breakfast. I love the breakfasts here. Today there were pancakes.

Swam, read, lazed.

I began to feel that I needed to *do* something, so walked into town with Husband. Had a coffee. Was nasty. Drank it in a little square surrounded by typical Italian houses listening to Olympics on a television in a bar.

Bought lunch. Had an espresso. Was perfect.

Lunch on balcony. Emm had done a workout in gym. Seemed to have trouble lifting his arms.

Monday
Left hotel, drove to Puglia.

Puglia, Italy 2012

Monday:
Drove from Sorrento to Puglia.

Mammoth journey, took forever. Loads of traffic – most of it on the wrong side of the road whilst over-taking at least one car and two scooters on a blind bend. Also had a detour due to a forest fire.

Nice lunch at a service area – freshly cooked burgers and nice sandwiches.

Arrived in Torre Canne about 4:30.

Spent a long time looking for *Hotel del Levante*.

We unpacked and looked around. It all felt very foreign after the pretty Sorrento *Hotel Bristol* and it was much less luxurious. The carpets and furniture felt a bit cheap and worn out. However, it was clean, and the pool and beach were excellent. I hope the dinner is good.

***

Dinner was okay.

We played cards for a while (I hate playing cards) then I went to bed. Slept well even though it was quite noisy. The rest of the family stayed up.

Tuesday:
Got up and walked along the beach to the lighthouse. There were lots of men setting up stalls on the beach selling beachwear and toys. Hotels were setting up their chairs on the beach, ready for guests. It was a nice time of day to walk.

Met the family for breakfast at 9am. Coffee at breakfast was nasty, but the hot chocolate was good. There was a buffet breakfast with a good range of fruit, cakes, cheese, eggs, etc.

Some people took food from breakfast to eat later – which I am not sure was ethical, but seemed very commonplace. So we passed Grandmas smuggling bread in their bags on the stairs, and teenagers with pockets full of cheese. The hotel staff didn't seem at all bothered, so perhaps they include the cost of a 'smuggled lunch' in the bed and breakfast price.

We then had a big discussion about that evening. The hotel was holding a *Gala Night* which involved paying an extra €15 per person to 'cover drinks' (we had already paid for dinner in our 'half board' rate). This was quite a lot for all of us, and we had to pay even for those who wouldn't drink. It was rather a long discussion, and we didn't really know what to do. The hotel were pushing the evening as a big event, but we'd seen the one in Lake Como on a previous holiday, and it had looked a bit naff. In the end, we decided to risk the money and attend. I do hope we don't regret it.

We went to the pool and swam. The hotel has a big pool, and a smaller one for children. Both are right next to the beach, so you can switch between sea and pool as the mood takes you.

We were invited to play volleyball. We lost, but not too embarrassingly.

Went in sea – until Husband told me that there might be jellyfish. (We did not see any jellyfish the entire holiday, so he may have been lying because he was bored with me swimming.)

Pizza lunch from pizzeria next door.

Went to Gala night. It was brilliant so I am very pleased that we did. I will try to describe it all for you:

In the pool, they had set up a floating giant waterlily, which had a fountain coming from the centre. There were lights in the trees, tables with ice sculptures, flowers and candles everywhere. All very beautiful.

As the evening grew darker, we sat at tables around the pool, listening to the sea.

There was a huge buffet – which we thought was the main meal – but then they served dinner! The whole garden had been set up with little tables, each one serving a different food, so you could wander around, filling your plate. Lots of food, lots of wine.

There was a band with a singer, then there were fireworks.

They brought out a massive Chinese lantern – the size of a parachute – which they lit using a blow torch, and set off to float above the sea (we were a little nervous at this point in case it set fire to the guests, but luckily no one got burned. I feel this would have rather spoiled event).

Finally, there was music, and everyone danced. Lots of other people came onto the beach to watch the dancing – I am assuming they walked up from the town. Was great fun.

Wednesday:
Very sleepy.

Another late breakfast at 9. Then I went back to bed, my family went on beach.

We went into town, just as everywhere was shutting, so perhaps not the best time. Husband bought a ball. Bea didn't buy a jumper (yes, a jumper. Why? It's boiling hot!) Everyone felt hot and grumpy.

Drove back to hotel. Husband only went wrong once, family very restrained in their feedback.

Hotel man looked very depressed when we gave him another car to fit into his over crowded car park (maybe he drank too much last night too).

Spent the afternoon in the sea and pool.

Boys took inflatable boat into sea. They didn't float to Corfu (lucky, would have been inconvenient).

I swam with Husband for a while, and did not get stung or eaten. The sea has big waves, though is not too rough to swim.

Read and had an ice cream and an espresso next to the pool. Felt very contented. This is what holidays are for.

Dinner was slightly dysfunctional (the staff must have been tired from the previous night).

The house next to the hotel had a party. Extremely loud music for much of the night. Not much sleep again – so not what I was hoping for.

Thursday:
After breakfast went to *Alberobello*, which is a historical town nearby.

Saw lots of *trullo*. These are little round white houses, which were first built in the fourteenth century. The Count, who owned the land, told all his workers to build them because they could be quickly dismantled when the land was inspected, and he could avoid paying taxes. They were pretty, but it was too hot for them to be interesting for long.

I bought a cushion cover for my collection. It was more expensive than ones bought in Asia or the rest of Europe or US! That is Italy.

Bea didn't buy a bikini (but at least she was now looking at weather-appropriate clothing).

Friday:
Breakfast at 9. Did nothing all day, very pleasant.

Saturday:
I walked along the beach before breakfast. I really like that beach. It was packed with whole families, mostly Italian, from grannies to babies. Sellers walked up and down with swimwear and beach toys. Everyone was relaxed and enjoying themselves, no one cared about what they looked like.

After breakfast we drove to a zoo but it looked a bit naff and over-priced. Drove on to some caves. Caves are not my favourite thing. They tend, in my opinion, to be all the same. They are dank holes in the rock, sometimes big, sometimes small, but always just holes in the rock. I wandered around gift shops and had a coffee in the shade and read, which was much more pleasant.

The family went into the caves and said they were excellent.

Had lunch at the cave place. It was not overly efficient service.

Drove back to hotel.

Got petrol – always an adventure in small town Italy if you don't speak the language. This time, we had to pay in advance. Worked it out eventually.

Sunday:
I decided to stop worrying about people 'stealing' from breakfast. Everyone seemed to do it, and were very open about it. One old lady even took foil with her to cover her plateful.

Day by sea and pool. Boys played volleyball against various teams. The hotel staff wander around, inviting people to join in various games. It's ideal for a family.

Enjoyed the sea. It had big waves again.

Nice dinner today (they were sometimes a bit random).

Monday:
We packed.

We asked to keep one room until we left in the afternoon, so we had a place to store things, and could shower before we left. Everyone moved their stuff in.

We swam and played on the beach. Made sand animals on the beach, and lots of people passing by stopped to look at them. Clearly the Italian word for "Dragon" is "*Crocodee*"

Showered, pizza, played *Catan*.

Flew home. Good holiday.

At home, the freezer had turned off, and had been blowing warm air for two weeks. The smell was amazing. Not the best welcome home I've ever had, if I'm honest.

Dubai November 2012

Husband and I went to Dubai for a work trip (his work, not mine). We were staying in the Sheraton Hotel in Dubai Creek.

The Sheraton Hotel was lovely, with a beautiful foyer, and our room had great views across the creek to the city. When it was clear, we could see all the main skyscrapers. When it was hazy we could watch the boats lined up in the creek.

Day One:
Husband was working, so I decided to try and find the *gold souk*. I don't speak any Arabic, so was nervous about using public transport on my own. I wanted to visit somewhere I could walk to, and according to my map, this would be possible.

This was also my first visit to a devout Muslim country, so I was unsure of what was appropriate to wear. I asked the concierge, who assured me that I didn't need to cover my head unless I planned to visit a mosque, and my dress (long sleeves, high neck line, long skirt) was sufficiently modest. She said I was safe to walk around on my own but it was very hot, so most women didn't walk.

I set off, armed with a map, and an iPhone which I didn't know how to use. The hotel was right next to the creek, so for a while I was distracted by all the boats unloading. It was hugely interesting to watched relatively small boats, which were stacked high with everything from plastic chairs to washing machines. It was amazing that some of them had made it across the sea, they seemed much too heavily laden. The whole place was busy, and some of the boats – which looked almost homemade – were tiny.

There were also lots of men. While I was staring at the cargoes, they were staring at me. It felt uncomfortable so I moved on.

I found a shopping area on a main road. Stopped to look at small supermarkets, and shops selling plastic shoes and cheap handbags. All the other women were wearing black *abayas* (long cloaks that cover other clothes) and despite the heat, I decided to do the same, as I found all the men stared at me and I didn't like it.

Found a cheap clothes shop, and bought a long black tunic and *hijab* (black headscarf). The tunic was fine, but I didn't know how to tie the hijab and my attempts looked silly. (I looked more like a washer woman from a child's story book!) I would have asked a random woman in the shop, but no one seemed to speak English. Decided to wear it anyway. If I had found a full *burqa*, I would have bought one. I love the thought of being able to hide. (Would have been great for the school run when the children were young, or for nipping to the shops in pyjamas.)

Lots of the shops had interesting textiles, and fancy shaped coffee pots. There were also lots of mosques. Whatever your religion, you cannot deny that mosques are pretty. I once read that the castle in Disneyland is based on a mosque, and I can see why.

I found the area where my map showed the g*old souk* should be, but I couldn't see it anywhere. Tried to find someone who spoke English. Failed. Also, most of the people serving in the shops seemed to be men, and I felt uncomfortable approaching them. The men in Dubai stare.

Then I spotted a small shop where they took in sewing, run by Chinese people. I went in and asked if they spoke Mandarin, which they did. Excellent. They said I was actually right next to the *gold souk*, but at the back. They pointed out how to find the entrance.

I looked around the *souk:* window displays full of gold. Also, a lot of dodgy-looking men, suggesting I might like to follow them to buy a fake watch or designer handbag. I didn't. The whole *souk* seemed to have only men in it. Some wore European style clothing, some wore traditional white *thobes* (Arabic dress.) I saw very few women and they seemed to all be wearing full *burqas* and be escorted by men. I wondered if I was breaking some rule, though the hotel had said it was okay to wander around on my own. I felt very uncomfortable, even in my black dress and badly tied scarf (I wasn't exactly a fashion icon).

Left the souk and tried to find my way back to the hotel. Got thoroughly lost. Found a tiny spice *souk*. A very friendly man (who spoke excellent English) saw me peering in, and showed me round. It smelt wonderful and was very interesting. There were tables piled high with brightly coloured powders. I thought about buying some frankincense (just because I had never seen it before). Didn't. Then spent the rest of the trip wishing I had, and also knowing I would never be able to find my way back again.

Continued to be lost for some time. There were lots of people, so I wasn't worried, it felt safe. Found a main road. It was busy, full of cars and also a man pushing a hand cart. Found the waterfront. It was beginning to get dark. Was a single female allowed to wander around after dark? I had no idea.

There was a call to prayer. It drifted across the water, a lovely sound I thought. All the men stopped their activities and knelt on little prayer mats to pray. I didn't see any women praying and wondered why.

I realised I was at the wrong waterfront, this was not the creek where my hotel was. Managed to find someone in a shop who spoke English and got directions. I walked next to the river, watching the daylight fade, past the ferry terminal where people were waiting, along to where the cargo boats were being unloaded. Returned to the hotel unscathed.

Husband finished work. We had dinner in the hotel, then got a taxi to the main part of the city. Saw the skyscrapers (but I think you had a better view from our hotel). Went to a shopping street and I bought a cushion cover for my collection. Also bought some gifts and a weirdly shaped tea pot. I bought a white *throbe* and a *ghutra* (checkered headscarf) and *egal* (black rope you tie scarf with) for the dressing-up box at home. Because someone is sure to want to dress like an Arab at some point in the future.

Day Two:
Husband didn't have to work, so we got a taxi to Royal Mirage Hotel for breakfast. It was beautiful.

We walked around a bit. It was very pretty, very clean (and very 'fake'). There was even a *souk*, but a rather sanitised version of the ones I had visited (and a lot more expensive).

We had an extremely nice breakfast sitting on an air-conditioned balcony. They brought a big tray, laid with silver pots, pastries, fruit, juice and eggs. We sat in the shade, listening to the sea, enjoying the beautiful decorations, the luxury of it all. A moment to remember.

We left via the main reception area, which had the darkest black men I have ever seen, dressed in costume, opening car doors as they arrived. I asked if I could have my photograph taken and they were very friendly. I wonder if they mind that their job is just opening doors for rich people and being looked at as a novelty. Maybe they are just happy for the money, or are students doing it temporarily. I hope so.

Went back to our hotel. Drove via a beach which we went to look at. Not allowed to take photographs because of modesty laws.

Day Three

We had arranged a trip through the hotel with Arabian Adventures (arabian-adventures.com) and were going to see the desert. We were advised to wear sturdy boots for walking on the sand and trousers for when riding on camels. Very exciting!

We were collected from the hotel by a silver 4×4. We then drove to two other hotels, and collected other tourists, before driving off to the Dubai Conservation Desert. We then met up with several other Land Rovers, all identical. They stopped and changed the tyre pressure, then we set off.

First we were driven to a small camp where we watched a falconry display. This was the same as every other falconry display I have seen, but there was something about watching it in a desert which made it more exciting.

Then we were taken for a short camel ride. Great fun, if somewhat smelly. The key advice would be, lean back hard when they stand up. Camels really stink. After the ride, you stink a bit too. The camels also had mouth guards, so I am guessing that they bite. My children will be pleased to learn that I do not wish to ever own a camel.

Then we went *'wadi bashing'*, which basically involved driving very fast across the dunes. It was not unlike being on a roller coaster. I was grateful for the seat belts and roll bars, not that we needed the latter. One man felt car-sick, which added a little tension to the trip.

We stopped to take photographs of the sunset. I think it is the most beautiful thing I have ever seen. The whole desert seemed to change colour as the sun dipped.

We then drove to a camp. It was lovely, all set up in the style of a Beduin camp. We sat on cushions around long low tables and watched belly dancers in the candle light. We were then given a *shisha* supper, which was delicious. Although we didn't know anyone else, there was a lovely atmosphere, and people chatted and were very relaxed. (Perhaps it was sharing the common bond of not being sicked on by the poor travel-sick man!)

Finally, we were all returned to our hotels. An excellent day from start to finish.

Bitez, Turkey, August 2013
(Children aged 17, 19 and 21 years.)

Monday:
Taxi arrived 7:15. Boys ready – that's a first!

Taxi driver drove two sides of the triangle at end of our lane. Family remained silent. Lots of eye-contact.

Made it to airport with no other detours. Flights okay (slight dispute at check-in over weight allowance, followed by some frantic repacking, but we won't mention that).

Collected hire car – pretty white Mercedes with silly foot brake. Many, many, miles on clock.

Drove to villa. Nice. It has white floors, everything seemed clean, and it has air-con (essential). Dispute over room allocation so they drew lots and Emm won the double room. Our room (also double – we didn't join in the lottery – we're paying) has a balcony over the garden. The garden has a pool and seating, the rest is full of fruit and vegetables. I'm not sure what some of the plants are.

Turkey has bad drains, so lots of signs explaining you *cannot flush toilet paper* and have to deposit it in a bin. Horrible. This caused some family discussion.

Nice meal at a beach-side restaurant, The Lemon Tree.

Tuesday:
Walked along beach path. Lots of cafes with tables stretching almost onto the beach, big cushions on beach where you can sit and order tea, little shops selling beachy stuff.

From our villa, we can hear the 'call to prayer' from mosque next to beach. It's a nice sound I think.

Swam in pool. Played *Catan*.

Met Friends (who are staying nearby) and had dinner at The Lemon Tree again. Three-course set meal 38TL. They gave us free cocktails at the end.

I had lovely apple pie for pudding, with surgical spirit flavoured ice cream, which was somewhat odd. (If I'm honest, it wasn't listed as that flavour on the menu.)

Wednesday:

Lazed around. Kids introduced me to *'Flow'* on my iPhone.

Tried to read by pool but boys much too loud and splashy so retreated to balcony. Pleasant.

Went to Bodrum with Husband. We went on the local bus – such fun! It stopped wherever people wanted to get off, the price was displayed and people just threw money into a little basket next to the driver. Everyone chattered to each other, and there was a wonderful atmosphere of neighbours meeting for a chat. They all smiled at us.

Bodrum was nice. Pretty harbour, men outside mosque washing feet, call to prayer, lots of ethnic shops, street sellers, cafes.

We had a Turkish coffee. Not completely disgusting – an experience. Not sure what one is meant to do with the inch of sludge at the bottom. I don't think I ever need to try one again. It was served with a glass of water, which we didn't drink as it was probably tap water, but we weren't sure what it was for – to rinse away the taste after drinking the coffee? I think it's an acquired taste, as I have a friend who loves Turkish coffee.

Went back to villa. Don't think boys had moved since we left.

Husband decided to allocate jobs (so I can have a break from housework). Emm refills the water bottles from the giant one we buy at the supermarket. Bea sorts the dishwasher. Not sure what Jay does. Husband empties the bins (containing used toilet paper). Boys now call him *"Shit Man"*. Husband rather disgruntled, and can be found muttering *"international business executive"* under his breath.

Nice dinner in restaurant over looking the sea. Perfect warm breeze, palm trees, comfy seats. Food was okay. Most of it arrived actually on fire, which seems to be a Turkish custom. Also discovered that *"tirimasu"* means '*chocolate synthetic sludge*' in Turkish. Worth avoiding.

Thursday:
Went to supermarket again. Buying milk is a challenge. A picture of a cow on the bottle does *not* necessarily mean cow's milk. Have tasted some very sour liquids this week.

Drove to Yalikavak to meet friends. Wandered around a brilliant market. So much colour. There were fruits, and fabrics, and flowers, and heaps of spices. You just wanted to stand and absorb the colour and scents.

Jay bought some Turkish Delight.

I bought a cushion cover: "You Turkey, I Turkey, I give you a very good price. I not make up English price. You know what I say?"

Had dinner next to the sea. Very pretty, lots of candles, and waves splashing right next to us. After-dinner entertainment was...unusual. A strong man picked up people; then another man gave volunteers electric shocks. The boys joined in with Turkish line dancing. It was all good fun but not necessarily what you ever need to see a second time. (It wouldn't have taken very long for them to learn the dances I feel.)

Walked along the quay and looked at all the huge yachts.

Back to villa about 1am.

Still not sure what Jay's job is.

Friday:
Extremely lazy day, did nothing.

Jay washed up a pizza tin – maybe THAT is his job. Emm moans every time someone has a drink from the water he has refilled. Not sure he fully understands his role. Bea has instigated a lot of rules around the dishwasher loading, might try some of them when we get home.

Dinner at Lemon Tree. We were tired, so didn't accept their after dinner drinks this time. Worried this might be considered insulting.

Watched *Jack Reacher* film.

Saturday:
Went out for breakfast. We tried sitting on big colourful cushions under palm trees on beach – they look so pretty, so 'Turkish'. Way too many ants. We moved to a table in the restaurant garden, which was less comfortable but also less itchy.

Husband and I shared a Turkish Breakfast: cheeses, fruit, dried fruit, breads, honey, yogurt, olives. Very nice.

Jay had 'Full English' which was not very English, though did contain pork (but not bacon) and eggs.

Bea had pancake and hot chocolate. Good choice.

Wandered around the shops. Jay bought a wooden trinket box. I bought another cushion cover. Everyone very friendly. This is beginning to typify Turkey for me – people are incredibly friendly and welcoming.

Went back to Bodrum on bus and met Friends.

Wandered around the shops (too many, I hate shopping) then had dinner. Some restaurants have very aggressive salesmen outside who try to 'entice'/force you inside to eat. It is a shame, because on the whole, this is the most friendly country I have ever visited.

Walked to an ice cream parlour. Great ice cream.

Bus back to Bitez.

Sunday:
Went to a bigger supermarket (a Carrefour). Bea and I chose a slice of cake at the deli counter – it looked fabulous, tasted synthetic.

Husband bought snorkels for the boys. Children's ones. Think they were cheap. Pink and orange. Boys were not delighted.

Did nothing. I read on balcony, family swam in pool. I was annoyed, because someone's bonfire was blowing smoke at me and it spoiled the air. Then looked up, and realised there was a HUGE forest fire on the other side of the hill, you could see the glow along the horizon. A helicopter and water plane were flying over and dropping water. The sky was black with smoke and the pool was full of ash. Rather exciting. Hoped it wouldn't burn its way to town.

Went to dinner. Mine was horrid. Returned to villa. It hadn't burned down.

Monday:
Up early (8:30) and met Friends in Yalikavak.

Hired a boat. Not very expensive for nine of us and absolutely brilliant. We could sit on deck, in the sun, or go into the little cabin if we wanted shade. There was a washroom (fairly basic) and a tiny kitchen and eating area. The cost of the boat included a skipper and a person who cooked for us (I think she was the skipper's mother).

Spent the day swimming in coves, diving off the boat, sunbathing. Water really deep, so jumping and diving very safe. Sea quite choppy in places so the spray came right over the front. Lots of squealing and holding on tight.

The boat people catered for us. We had salad and steaks for lunch, a fresh fruit snack, then Turkish tea and biscuits.

Husband swam with his phone (his work one) to take photos. I sooo hoped he would drop it. Nearly drowned due to laughing so much.

A really happy day. There was even a little 'ice-cream boat' that came round the coves. Jay swam across to check prices, then we all had one. Husband ate his while floating in the sea.

Went back to town very salty, with wild hair - Husband called it: *"happy hair"*.

Tuesday:

Went for a drive. Recognised one of the bays that we visited yesterday in the boat.

Found an old church. It's the first church I have seen in Turkey. When you think about how much this country was part of the early church, it's sad that there are so few Christian churches here today. It was locked up and disused. I'm not sure whether the law here allows Christians to meet in churches.

Went to the ice-cream parlour in Bitez. They had sold out of nearly everything, and then got the bill wrong.

Swam.

They played *Catan*.

Had dinner at The Lemon Tree.

Wednesday:
Met Friends by beach and had breakfast. Very relaxed.

I ordered a banana crepe. When it eventually arrived, it had no banana inside, just a long slice of melon. It was a bit odd – melon and pancakes don't really go together, so I called over the waiter to ask why it wasn't banana. The waiter (who clearly didn't believe me and was claiming it was a banana) took it back to the kitchen. He returned to inform me that the chef said they had no bananas, but he could cut any fruit I wanted into a banana shape. I had a very nice *plain* crepe with ice cream and chocolate sauce.

Swam in pool then had a drive around area.

Stopped at a kebab restaurant. They didn't speak any English and we spoke no Turkish (all the restaurants near the beach speak excellent English). We looked at the menu, and a man came to help us order, but we couldn't really understand each other. Then the waiters arrived with many plates of salads and meat kebabs and pots of yogurty stuff. We had no idea what was going on. Husband worried about the bill, and went to try and have a discussion with the man who 'almost' spoke English. He decided it was probably okay, so we ate. All delicious. The final bill was tiny, such lovely food for such a low price.

Boys went to watch an Arsenal game in a bar on beach. I hoped they wouldn't get attacked.

Thursday:
Bought Turkish Delight to take home as gifts. Opened one box – there is much less Turkish Delight than I was expecting. Pretty boxes though...

Walked past The Lemon Tree, and the owner invited us for coffee. Nice coffee. Had a nice chat too. In 'real life' he is an engineer. He's owned the restaurant for six years.

I went back to villa and changed into a long skirt and headscarf, then went with Bea to look at the mosque. It felt kind of scary, I was worried we would do something wrong by mistake and be shouted at, though there was an English sign on the door explaining that visits were allowed as long as it wasn't a prayer time.

Inside, it was just a room. I had been expecting something else, something more ornate or 'foreign'. It was just a room, with a carpet on the floor, an indentation in one wall which marks the direction of Mecca, and a section which is divided by a large white cotton curtain. It looked like a sheet. I assume that the women pray behind it so they are separate from the men. Outside there was a place for people to wash their feet. (We have seen men washing their feet when the call for prayer is sounded.)

It was interesting – very plain, certainly did not feel either 'holy' or 'evil', it was just a room.

Swam in sea. Cold. Ate at Lemon Tree.

Friday:
Drove two and a half hours to Ephesus. Interesting scenery.

Ephesus (*Effes*) was brilliant. I was very excited to go, having read the book in the Bible – Ephesians – so many times. There is a sense of wonder about visiting towns named in the Bible, to see that they really existed.

It was hugely interesting to actually see places you can read about, to walk the same distances, to see the walls of the same arena, to imagine how it must have looked. It makes *Acts* and *Ephesians* come alive in a whole new way. Smaller and less hot than Pompei – it didn't have the same 'wow' factor, but was worth visiting.

Dinner at Lemon Tree.

Saturday:
Got up late, then walked to the beach for coffee. Got directions to a bakers. Everyone here is so friendly and helpful.

There is a toothbrush living on the dining table. Why would that be a good place?

Sunday:
Home.

I loved the part of Turkey we visited, and hope to go again one day. My main impression was of friendly people – it is the most friendly country I have ever been in. I'm not sure what will happen with the politics in the future, but I hope nothing bad happens to the people who we met, as they were all very kind and welcoming to us.

China September 2013

Before leaving the UK we had to get visas to visit China. This takes much longer if your trip includes going to Tibet. You can apply for the visa online. In the space where it asks who has invited you, it is acceptable to put the name and address of hotels where you will be staying. We went to the embassy in London to collect the visas.

Friday:
Taxi arrived at 11 (Husband still packing – now I know where the boys get that from) and drove us to Heathrow.

Virgin flight to Shanghai. Sat opposite a boy who I swear is an actor but who claimed he worked for Ebay.

Shangai airport was very efficient. We had to give 'customer feedback' at immigration by ticking smiley faces.

Taxi to Le Meridian Hotel (艾美酒店) on *Nanjing Dong Lu*.

Note: *Taxi drivers do not speak English nor can they read the English version of hotel names. If you do not speak Mandarin, there is a man at the taxi rank who will translate for you, but you will need to queue. It is much faster if you go online before leaving home and print off the Mandarin name from the website.*

Driver was friendly and found my bad Mandarin very amusing. Chatted a bit.

Le Meridian Hotel was lovely (we have stayed there on previous trips). The lobby is dark, with pools of water and orchids. I thought the pools of water were black glass discs – nearly got a wet foot! It also smells lovely, a jasmine perfume. Our room had great views down towards the Bund.

Had tea at the hotel, then walked down *Nanjing Dong Lu*. This is a main shopping street and whilst the shops are fairly ubiquitous, the signs are all in Chinese script, and there are street sellers selling unusual fruits and trying to entice you to buy fake designer goods (which is illegal, so best not to buy). Walked through the 'Peace' (Fairmont) Hotel. They were having a tea dance. One day I want to stay there, it looks like a lovely old colonial hotel.

Walked along the Bund. This is the water front to the Huangpu River. Across the water you can see the amazing skyline of *Pudong* (the financial district). Along the Bund are all the old colonial buildings from Victorian times, it's like stepping back in time. It's lovely to walk along, beside the river, in the evening, seeing the lights and watching the city prepare for the night.

We walked back to the hotel via the lanes (I would not want to do this alone at night, though it might be safe). There were lots of interesting shops, street hawkers and food stalls. One food seller was very insistent that I taste some fruit she was selling, she kept just *telling* me to taste it. So I did. How stupid – I can't believe I did that. Worried I would be ill for rest of the trip.

We ate dinner in the hotel buffet. This was a mistake. The food was lukewarm, not especially nice and cost a fortune. Next time we will eat in the lounge, which is included on Husband's loyalty card.

The hotel lounge has drinks and hot snacks whenever we want them, and also has a full breakfast and evening cocktails. It has big comfy sofas, with great views towards the river.

Went to bed exhausted. A really, really long day (actually, two days rolled into one). However, I didn't sleep until about 4am. Not good.

Sunday:
Breakfast in the lounge. I had a pastry. Husband had everything, including pork dumplings. Great coffee.

Went up to the hotel bar and took photos of Shanghai. It's a good view, and lots of non-guests go there just to take photos.

Walked along the Bund, then the old part of the city. Weather is great, very comfortable for walking. Found some more alleyways: tiny shops, stalls selling swatches of lace, fruits, stalls full of eggs, fish swimming in large plastic containers, meat, hens and ducks (alive) with their feet tied or in wooden crates (no water to drink, poor things). If you bought one, they took it to the back of the shop and killed and plucked it. One even had a 'plucking machine' which looked like a big metal barrel. The meat was not refrigerated, but was incredibly fresh. (I know my Chinese friends in England don't like that the meat they buy in UK is several days old. They like to buy meat the day, if not the hour, that it is killed.)

It was all hugely interesting as long as you didn't 'think' or 'feel' too much. I think it is essential to remember that China is a different country, with a whole different culture and history. It would be wrong to make value judgements I think, when visiting as a tourist.

We bought cans of lemonade. Before coming, I had bought a box of wrapped straws online. I always carried a few in my bag, so it was possible to drink from a can without actually putting any potential germs into our mouths. (Still can't believe I ate that fruit...)

Saw several street sellers selling plain notebooks. Bought one for 10RMB (£1) Why didn't I buy more? Great for scribbling notes in.

Went to hotel gym and pool. China now has a law that you must wear hats in public pools. Bought a couple (£3 each).

Decided to be brave and go out for dinner, to a restaurant we had seen down a side street. It was very Chinese. There was a choice of starters: chickens feet, turtle heads or gristle. We picked a few 'safe' dishes and had a lovely meal, loads of food and all for only £15.

I'm not sure how well you would manage if you didn't speak any Mandarin. It would be completely fine in larger hotels, where everyone seems to speak excellent English. People here are very good at understanding very bad Chinese, but in shops and restaurants they speak absolutely no English at all and in smaller restaurants they may not even have a menu in English script. I guess that's why most people opt to visit China with an organised tour.

Monday:
Very little sleep again, finding the time difference difficult to adapt to. I tried a traditional breakfast of fried dough sticks. They involved more oil than I was hoping for, and weren't great. (I had hoped they would be a variation on a fresh donut. They weren't.)

We walked around the People's Park (人民公园). Interesting to see old men playing *mah jong*, people practicing *t'ai chi* and children catching huge coy carp from the pond. (I am pretty sure they were not meant to catch the fish!)

Found a book shop. Stocked up on Chinese books – they were so cheap. Will blast the weight limit on flight home.

In the evening, walked to see the fountains outside the museum. They are floodlit but look much better from above, through the hotel window. The park was rather foreboding at night, I'm not entirely sure how safe it was to walk there.

We saw a man in the street lying on a trolley. He was very disabled and was begging. I find the beggars here upsetting. I have no idea what charity is available for them, if they need to beg to survive, or if it is a huge scam and they are 'organised' by criminals (which is what I understood was the case in Mumbai with children begging).

Bed. No sleep. Really, no sleep. And not for a good reason. I could never be an international business traveller.

Tuesday:
Posh hotel car drove us to Rainbow Bridge (虹桥)

Railway Station to catch train to Beijing. Scrum (literally) to go through security at entrance to station.

Used station washroom. You have to take your own toilet paper, but it was fairly clean. Found out which platform we needed, and waited for gate to open.

Assumed there was going to be another scrum to enter platform, so didn't bother to queue. A mistake, as everyone stayed in line when the gates opened. Joined back of queue. Was a bit concerned, as we had red tickets, and most people had blue ones. Checked we were in the right place. We were.

Train was nice. The seat was big, with plenty of leg room. We put our cases in the luggage rack at the end of the carriage. If travelling by train, try to avoid sitting at the front of a carriage as you only get half a window.

Do not sit next to the toilet.

There was a tap that dispensed hot water, and lots of people came to refill their drinking flasks. (Chinese people drink a lot of hot water. When my friends come for 'coffee' in England they usually just want boiled water.)

There were hostesses who brought round drinks and snacks. Food could be bought from the dining car.

I think the train is a great way to travel. You could sit and watch the Chinese countryside whiz past at 300km/hour. Seemed to be mostly small fields of sweetcorn, rivers with fishing boats and white ducks, factories of grey cement, ugly blocks of flats and many, many new developments. We saw whole new towns complete with roads, and factories, and houses, being built; but no people.

There were lots of very guttural sounds on the train. Lots of throat clearing and gobbing – this is something you have to get used to in China, they have a *"better out than in"* ethos.

Arrived in Beijing. Got a taxi. Here, no one spoke or read any English, there wasn't a desk for foreigners to ask for help, so it was essential to have the hotel's Mandarin name.

A half hour ride was only £5.

Staying at St Regis Hotel. Beautiful.

Went for a stroll. Husband looked at Arsenal shirts, as everything is much cheaper here.

Had a drink in the hotel's press bar. Very nice, lots of dark wood, textures, leather seats, candles and books.

Ate (English food) in hotel restaurant.

Watched a film then went to bed. Slept for 2 hours. Oh dear.

Wednesday:
Had a coffee but no breakfast.

Got underground train to *Tian an Men Square*. Underground was very easy, clean and safe. Only cost 20p for a ticket. All bags go through an X ray machine when you enter the station. The trains have an underground map next to the door, and a light shows which station you are at, so it's really easy to track your route.

Tian an Men Square is big. Really big. With no shade. There are pretty buildings (the old city gates) where the old walls used to be, before they bulldozed them. They have bulldozed a *lot* of the ancient city.

We looked at Mao's mausoleum, but didn't go in. (I am completely confused by Chinese history in relation to Mao. I would recommend you read 'Mao's Great Famine' by Frank Dikotter and then try to understand why modern day Chinese people still revere him. It would be like if people said that Hitler did a few things that were very wrong, but basically what he did for Germany was good. I really do not understand the logic.)

In the evening, went to *Wangfujin* Road. Found a really cool market. Really crowded. Fresh (still moving) scorpions on sticks waiting to be deep fried. All kinds of snacks, ranging from bird foetuses to insects and sea creatures.

We weren't tempted to taste any, but it was really interesting. So much noise and colour and people packed together. Lots of people (Chinese people) were taking photos of the snacks, so we felt very comfortable taking pictures.

There was such a sense of excitement, definitely worth a visit.

Saw a choir singing outside the cathedral.

Wandered round some of the larger shops, which was mostly boring unless you enjoy shopping, which I don't. Did visit a cool jeweller's shop and looked at the jade, which was beautiful.

Thursday:
Went to *DimSum* restaurant in hotel (very nice and very good price.)

My stomach was bad, so I just had some *congee* (米粥) which was perfect, very plain – like a porridge made from rice.

Went to The Forbidden City (故宫).

Bought the wrong tickets in the wrong place and ended up in the garden next door. Found a back entrance into city but still had to queue up for the correct tickets.

Finally made it. It's big and initially interesting, but goes on for longer than you want it to. It is all in individual courtyard sections, so it is hard to get a sense of the size of the whole thing. The front few courtyards were well preserved, repainted and clean. The back courtyards were faded, dusty, with grass growing in the roof gutters. (I think I preferred the later courtyards.) It was all very elaborate and impressive, and wasn't too crowded or too hot (lots of seats in shade if you needed to rest).

It was very interesting – though in my opinion, not as interesting as the alleyways. Not much beats seeing people eating scorpions!

Went to *Häagen-Dazs* shop for ice cream. Perfect.

After dinner, drank hot chocolate and watched a big storm.

Tried to find a launderette on internet, as we need to do some washing (hotel laundry prices really high – would be cheaper to buy new clothes). We failed. Everyone has heard of *Chinese Laundries* but they don't seem to exist in Beijing.

Friday:
Am finally sleeping for most of the night.

Pollution very bad today, you can hardly see beyond 200 yards. The air feels heavy when you breathe, I expect it causes problems if you have asthma.

We tried and failed again, to find a launderette. Asked a few people. It seems you either take your clothes to an expensive Chinese laundry/dry-cleaners or travel a long way to a launderette (there is one at the university) but they do not have dryers. Decided to hand-wash stuff.

Walked around *Qian Men Da Jie* (前门大街) It was slightly 'plastic, touristy, rebuilt' but was colourful.

Found some interesting alleys which were more real. We saw women walking back from a bath house. There are lots of toilet blocks. I assume the houses do not have individual plumbing, and people wash in communal wash-houses, a bit like when you camp in England.

We went in the old pickle shop (smelly) and a Chinese medicine shop (which smelt unexpectedly of chemicals. I had expected it to smell of herbs but it was much more clinical.)

Saturday:
Up early, then went to meet a guide and driver who we had booked through the hotel. The hotel had warned them that I speak Mandarin and they 'tested' me before we set off. This has happened a few times. As soon as you speak Mandarin anywhere, they tell all the other staff. I am guessing that they are so used to European visitors not understanding them, that they sometimes say things they shouldn't in front of them.

We had wanted a driver to take us to the Great Wall. However, it was only possible to buy one of their 'packages', which included trips to other places. I think they make some of their money by tourists buying things at the places they are taken to, which the guides then receive a share of.

We drove to the Olympic Stadium and took photos.

We were taken to a jade factory. Not as boring as it sounds. Bought a jade ring.

They made a lot of fuss about jade being as hard as diamond. They neglected to mention that there is a lot more of it, so the price should reflect that...

Drove (finally) to the Great Wall. The driver (plump woman) looked like she was falling asleep and made many deeply guttural noises. Think she had a cold. It was rather off-putting.

We got a cable-car up the mountain. The wall was renovated in many places, though still had whole steps missing. It was not so much a 'wall' as a series of staircases. You walked up a lot of steps, then down a lot of steps, then up again. The steps are quite narrow for great big European feet. It's definitely a place to wear flat, comfortable shoes.

It was a beautiful clear day (I think not worth going if the pollution is bad). We could see Beijing on the horizon. The mountains were beautiful, green folds that went on forever.

Returned to car and our germ-ridden driver.

Drove to a 'farm' and had lunch in an empty restaurant. Tasty. Was European style Chinese food (real Chinese food is nothing like the food served in our restaurants in England).

We looked around a craft shop. Bought a Christmas bauble.

Walked straight past our guide – I didn't recognise her, which was embarrassing. (But my Chinese friends in England assure me that all English people look exactly the same, so maybe it is okay.)

Found our sleepy driver, and we drove back to the city. Took ages. The traffic (and driving) was terrible.

We were taken to a tea room. A pretty young girl taught us about the Chinese Tea Ceremony. Very interesting, definitely worth going to a tea room if you can. She showed us how the pots and cups are all warmed with boiling water, and how to hold the cup correctly. We tasted oolong with ginseng, jasmine, black tea and 'flower' tea which has a dried flower that unfolds in the hot water (looks really pretty, tastes pretty horrid). We looked around the shop afterwards. All very expensive. Didn't buy anything. Awkward.

Eventually, they took us back to the hotel. I expect they were rather annoyed that we hadn't been enticed into spending loads of extra money. But we enjoyed the day. Though not the germy bits. Or the driving.

Sunday:
Had coffee.

Went on underground to *ChongWenMen* church(崇文门堂). They were very friendly and welcoming. They had headsets with English translations (someone sat in the basement and translated the service while it was actually happening). This was one of the government sanctioned churches. It was allowed to conduct services how it wanted, and the congregation were allowed to advertise and invite friends. They were not allowed to meet anywhere else (for example, no 'street preaching') and their main leaders were appointed by the government (so difficult to know what their actual beliefs were).

However, I found it a friendly place and the message preached was definitely Christian, if not perhaps especially evangelical. Attached to the church was a bookshop, which was fabulous. It had many authors who I recognised (such as John Stott, R.T. Kendall) all in Mandarin translations. There seemed to be no restrictions on buying them, and the shop was crowded. I bought a couple and also a CD, am hoping it's not too awful.

Went back to hotel for a *dim-sum* lunch. Husband happy, he likes the *'All you can eat for £15'* lunch-time deal! I had a chop sticks issue with an exploding dumpling.

Went back on the underground to *JingShan* park (景山).

It's directly behind the Forbidden City, and has a hill that overlooks the city. In many ways I preferred this to the city itself because you get a real sense of the size of it. We stood there, looking down at all the tiled roofs, and you could imagine how it would've been when the emperor lived there.

Some people were singing folk music, so we had an ice-cream and listened. Not a pleasant noise. I think Chinese music is an acquired taste (and I haven't acquired it).

Another main attraction of the park was a tree where an emperor had hung himself. Pleasant setting I guess.

Walked back to *Tian an Men* via *hutongs*. These are the traditional style of house in old Beijing, and consist of a small courtyard surrounded by buildings (which all seem to be grey). Many have been demolished, and rebuilt by rich people, and many are government owned. This is a cause for contention amongst Beijing residents. Some people resent that so much history is being eradicated by the government and they would prefer the old *hutongs* to be restored and lived in by normal people.

We visited an extremely expensive supermarket. Saw caterpillars and sea-cucumbers being sold (things cost hundreds of pounds). There were many, many sales assistants, we felt rather swamped. Bought some bubble bath – which did not cost hundreds of pounds. They may have been disappointed.

Dinner in hotel. Husband had spicy noodles, which he splattered everywhere so had to ask for a fork. Glad I am not the only messy eater.

Monday:
Got a taxi to the Summer Palace (颐和园).

It was quite a long taxi ride but still only cost £7. Saw some interesting parts of the city from the taxi window.

The Summer Palace was brilliant, my favourite place in Beijing. There were lakes, and hills, and pathways through trees, and lots of traditional Chinese roof-tops and bridges.

We hired a pedal boat and went on the lake. Then we walked around the edge (which takes a long time, it is massive). We went up and down lots of steps looking at temples and pavilions, all beautiful and all very oriental. There were lots of traditional Chinese bridges, and willow trees draped across the water. We felt as if we were in a painting.

We then took an uncomfortably hot and crowded underground back to the hotel. Definitely worth avoiding subway during rush-hour.

Tuesday:
It rained and we did very little.

Went for a walk to try and find a station which is on the front of one of my books.

Saw some bits of the original city wall and some rather naff parks.

Went to 'The Friendship Shop' which was in the guide book and which was awful. Worth avoiding. Very tacky and over priced.

Wednesday:
Decided to visit an animal market that was in the guidebook. Got a taxi to *Shi Li Dong Tian Bridge* (十里洞天桥).

No one seemed to know where the market was, and the bridge was at the intersection of some fairly major roads. Abandoned taxi and looked around a stone market. This was really interesting, lots of jade, which we now knew something about since our factory visit. Bought a jade bracelet. (However, a year later, after it had been left on a windowsill, the 'jade' had faded from dark green to yellow, so although the man selling it claimed it was real jade, and although to my untrained eye, it looked like real jade – it wasn't.) Had to haggle. Learnt that if you offer too low a price it is insulting and the traders will not barter with you. Seems to be best to let them give a starting price and then tell them it is too expensive. If you learn no other Chinese, learn to say: "It is too expensive" in a shocked voice. It sounds like *"Tie Gway Ler"*.

Decided to try and find the animal market and asked a policeman. At first he said there was no market, then when I said I wanted to see little birds and insects he laughed, and pointed to where we needed to walk (it was right next to the bridge but slightly hidden).

It was brilliant, amazingly Chinese. As you walked in there were shops selling huge coy carp and other fish. In the actual market, there were little wicker baskets containing crickets, which you could hear chirruping as you walked around.

There were traditional bird cages with birds, kittens, terrapins, squirrels, mice – just about everything. There were also lots of walnut stalls, some in the green fruit, some polished and some strung onto bracelets. There were tables of carved wood, polished stones, pipes, shoes, cages, plants. A whole mix of interesting stuff. The stall holders were friendly, and when I asked if I could take photos they laughed at my accent and then posed for the picture.

Found a new tube station, which was not even on our underground map. Got an extremely crowded train back to *Jiang guo men* station and the hotel.

Went to visit some friends who had a house on the other side of Beijing. Was very interesting to visit a 'real' Chinese home.

As it was nearly time for the moon festival, we took some moon cakes. These look like small pork pies but inside they have lotus paste and a hard boiled egg yolk (to symbolise the moon). Everyone goes back to their home for the moon festival and takes gifts of mooncakes. You can buy them in China Town in London too.

Went out for dinner. Delicious. They ordered for us: pickled cabbage with slices of garlic, aubergine, chicken and cashews...Lovely meal, lovely evening.

Thursday:
Up at 7:30 and got a taxi to the north railway station. Catching the train was much less worrying than last time.

Caught a train to Xi'an. Journey uneventful.

I didn't much like the look of Xi'an as we went in a taxi to the Hilton. It looked much poorer than either Shanghai or Beijing. There was nothing pretty, and it looked very run-down and neglected. It reminded me of an inner London council estate.

The Hilton Hotel was in the old part of the city, within the old city wall (which is still standing). It isn't near the terracotta warrior museum but I think it is a good place to stay if you want to see a glimpse of real Xi'an.

We arrived at the hotel at the same time as a coach full of American tourists. The receptionist was somewhat stressed and complaining (in Mandarin). She was moaning to her colleague about all the foreign people, and not exactly being very complimentary. When she showed us to our rooms, I thanked her, in Mandarin, and she was suitably embarrassed and asked if

I had understood her comments (which I had). We got very good service after that.

Our room overlooked an apartment block. It was shabby but very interesting.

Walked around. Xi'an felt dirty. It made Turkey's drains seem good, and the general aroma was unpleasant. We saw fishmongers preparing and cleaning a fresh delivery (some of which tried to escape). Had to walk through a lot of fish guts on the pathway.

Decided sandals are not suitable for Xi'an, will buy boots.

Friday:
Breakfast buffet in hotel. They have an open kitchen, so you can watch the chefs at work while you eat, which was rather fun. Husband had noodles (I think just because he saw them being prepared!)

Went shopping. Shops much the same as anywhere else in the world. Except in large department stores, you have to take what you want to buy to an assistant, who gives you an invoice, which you take to another till to pay, and then return to the first place to collect what you are buying. It was a bit confusing but they were very helpful and friendly.

Bought some warm clothes (Xi'an was much colder than Beijing) and some sturdy boots for wading through debris.

I found everyone to be very friendly and they wanted to chat. Most people I chatted to had never left Xi'an, not even for a holiday. They all laughed at my bad Mandarin and called other people over to come and listen. Then they would talk. Sometimes they asked me to repeat things, just because it made them laugh! They had never heard a non-Chinese person speak their language before, and they found it immensely funny. They were also friendly and welcoming, and happily explained things to me and answered my questions. I began to change my mind about Xi'an, I like it. It has a 'realness' to it.

We went on the city wall. It cost £5 to go up, and at the top you could hire tandems or bikes. It was very wide, as wide as a major road, and fully walled, so it felt completely safe. We hired a tandem. It took us an hour and a half to cycle around the whole wall. It was brilliant. Some excellent views of the city, and lovely to be able to exercise outside.

After dinner we walked to a night market but it was just like Hitchin market, where I grew up. Just stalls of cheap clothes and plastic shoes and fruit and veg.

Xi'an is a very 'real' city. People seem to live a lot of their lives outside, on the street. We would walk past arm chairs pushed onto the pavement, with old men playing cards; see women chatting and sewing; watch welders making food carts. People were poor, but open and if I smiled and said hello, they would often start a conversation (usually laughing at my pronunciation).

Saturday:
We got a taxi and went to see the Terracotta Warriors.

Walked through a plaza to buy tickets, trying to dodge the very persistent tour guides. They kept telling us that we needed a guide to show us the way and explain things or we would miss interesting things. In the end we gave up, and accepted one. Then she would NOT stop talking. It was like walking with a bossy radio and no 'off' button. I did not need to be told where to stand to take a photograph, or where to look. I had read the guide book before coming and she was just irritating. Her English was excellent, but she spoke with an American accent, which was also irritating.

I was also unimpressed with the warriors. Perhaps because I had heard they were brilliant, and so I was expecting something as impressive as the Grand Canyon. It was like going round a museum where all the exhibits are identical. Maybe I was missing something. We were on walkways above the army, so it was hard to get a feel for their size and there was no 'wow' factor. It felt sterile. (I never much liked museums as a child either.)

The next two exhibits were just lumpy mud, because they haven't even dug them up yet. It was hard to be interested in earth, even though this earth had a sign telling you that underneath were more warriors. Though several people were still taking photos. (These are the sort of people who you dread visiting after their holidays, when you have to sit and look through 4 million photos of boring things – like the ground which has warriors underneath.)

Then there were opportunities to pay to be photographed next to fake statues. Opportunities to pay for the signature of the farmer who found them – poor chap. He lost his farm and job and now sits and writes his name all day. We could buy the book (a scintillating read I'm sure) buy a rather ugly ornament, or even buy a tee-shirt with a warrior on. We managed to resist the temptation. The guide then dumped us, as we were obviously not a good source of revenue. I was not sorry.

I ate a moon cake and we walked to the exit, which was through another market. It was rather crappy but did have lots of fox fur and bear skins, which at least was different.

Our taxi had waited. We drove back to the hotel.

The museum is in a very different part of Xi'an. There were mountains in the distance, trees, fountains, lots of orchards and fruit sellers. It was pretty, but I think I preferred our rather scruffy, real life area.

Sunday:
Breakfast. I tend to eat boring English stuff (bacon and eggs). Husband tends to eat everything (bacon, eggs, noodles, fish, bread, dumplings, pastries, etc).

We got a taxi to a church we found on the internet. The first taxi refused to take us there (said the road was too narrow and drove off).

There was an old lady at the gate. She welcomed us and bowed. The church building was quite big but it wasn't very full. The service was all in Mandarin. The hymns were on a big screen, which made it easier to join in (Husband sang the 'Amen' at the end of each one). The sermon (exactly one hour) was quite difficult for me to understand, I could only really understand the main gist of what she was saying. It was very formal.

The congregation was mainly women, most were taking notes. There were several people coming and going during the service. At the end, a girl came and hugged me, clearly excited at having visitors. It was rather touching. We looked at their bookshop but they only had about six. I bought a jade cross for my mum.

After lunch we got a taxi to the drum tower. Didn't go up it.

Walked around the Muslim quarter. Amazing mosque, really worth a visit. Very old, very Chinese. Lots of round doorways, and pretty roofs. There was a street market with some interesting textiles (bought a cushion cover for my collection). There was street food, and a lot of walnuts. This was an interesting part of the city, full of bustling life, with lots to look at.

We saw builders balanced on bamboo scaffolding, throwing tools to each other. Not sure there is much 'health and safety' in China. We saw old men with their tummies showing (it seems to be normal to roll up your tee shirt if you are hot). We saw toddlers wearing trousers with slits in the front for easy toilet access. We saw people gambling on the street, kites, old men chatting, traffic and bikes in every direction and sometimes on the path. People stared and laughed openly. Raw humanity, no pretence. I loved it.

Monday:
Breakfast. Husband didn't hold back again. Chatted to a couple from Hong Kong who are stranded due to a big typhoon.

We got a taxi to Big Goose Pagoda. There was a fountain show, but we had missed it.

We walked around the garden, which had excellent statues. We saw people carving writing on a wooden sign. It was so neat, it looked like it had been printed. They just used a razor blade and a nail to chip out the characters. So talented.

We paid to go into the temple.

We paid again to go into the pagoda. Buddhists are clearly not shy about taking money. The pagoda was basically just a lot of stairs. I was unclear why it was necessary to go up them. It's a boy thing (like church towers in Norfolk. I have never understood the need to go up those either).

We spotted another Starwood hotel (Westin) so went inside for lunch. It was clean and peaceful and safe. I love seeing China, but it is lovely to have breaks from all the new culture every so often.

Paid to go into a park. It was not very nice. It felt fake and slightly broken and smelled of sewage. It had been advertised as *the Xi'an equivalent of the Summer Palace.* It wasn't.

Tuesday:
Caught a flight back to Shanghai. Stayed at Royal Meridian again.

Wednesday:
Caught flight back to England. An amazing holiday.

Lake Garda, Italy August 2014
(Children aged 18, 20 and 22 years)

Wednesday:
We arrived at Hotel du Lac du Parc, booked through Citalia.

I had recently had brain surgery, and couldn't fly, so Husband and I drove there via France, Luxembourg, Germany and Austria. It was a lovely drive, really interesting and the traffic was okay.

Met the family there (they flew). I was relieved they made it, as we'd had lots of texts about the boys persuading Bea that they should all go out the night before the flight. When we arrived, they were sleeping on the sofas in the lobby, waiting for their rooms to be ready. I expect the hotel staff were delighted to have them there.

I walked around the hotel grounds, and got a bit lost. Very pretty gardens with lots of little ponds with bridges and ducks. There are chalets in the grounds where you could stay (seemed to suit people with young children who prefer to self cater).

I was feeling ill, so had dinner in my room. The family ate in the hotel restaurant then played cards in the bar. Hotel is nice, I think we'll have a nice time. It has some very pretty areas, but also seems relaxed and friendly.

Bathroom light seems to be permanently on, which is a little odd. There doesn't appear to be a switch.

Thursday:
All had breakfast on the terrace. Very nice food, with a lots of choice. There are different food-stations, and you wander round and help yourself. Nasty coffee and juice from a machine. Then we realised that other people were ordering drinks from the waiters. We copied and then had very nice coffee and fresh juice.

There are dogs here which is nice. Someone has allowed their dog to wee in the lift, which is not nice.

Went to pizza place opposite hotel for lunch. Villa Aranci. Very nice, rustic setting, not too expensive. Boys had tankards of beer, I had some nice wine.

I slept (still feeling very 'fuzzy' after my op). Everyone else swam. The hotel provides blue swimming towels, which is good (some hotels do not allow you to remove towels from the rooms).

Nice dinner in restaurant, and I managed to stay for the whole meal today.

Family went to watch a jazz concert in town, I went to bed.

Friday:

Pouring with rain, which was disappointing. Lake Garda seems to have its own climate, and it is often grey here, when the sun is shining in nearby towns.

Breakfast, followed by a relaxed day doing very little. While I was resting, the maid knocked on the door. I opened the door, forgetting to cover the big ugly scar across my head with a scarf. The maid didn't flinch or faint or anything, which was nice, and made me feel a little more confident. Usually I wear a scarf, looking like someone from the 1950s. I'm wondering if the fashion will catch on, and by the end of the holiday other guests will be wearing headscarves.

Husband went for a run in the rain. We then went for a stroll around the town, but it started to pour with rain, so we went back to the hotel.

Lunch at pizzeria again.

The family swam, and I went for a walk. I didn't get lost, which was excellent.

Nice dinner, then had hot chocolate in the bar and played games. Everyone discussed the bathroom lights, which are always on, in all our rooms. None of us has managed to find a light switch. Perhaps it's a safety feature.

Saturday:

Raining again. Family went to hotel gym or read/slept.

Went to Co-op near hotel and bought food for lunch. Ate on balcony (each room has a balcony overlooking the garden). Emm chose beer, Nutella and crisps. Great diet.

Family played *Catan*, then swam. I walked into town. Saw a band.

Sunday:
Not raining. Excellent.

Breakfast, then family swam.

Walked into town and looked around. The town is set next to Lake Garda, and there were some lovely lake-side cafes. The town has a big square, and shops in the surrounding streets. It was quite busy, and away from the lake had more of a 'real town' feel, where real people would live and work. There were also some nice shops selling touristy things.

Found a switch under the mirror in the bathroom. This operates the bathroom light. Informed family.

Nice dinner. The restaurant staff are really friendly. They have noticed that Jay eats the most, so always give him a huge portion.

Monday:
Another cloudy day. Gave up on pool when it started to rain. The weather is very disappointing, we hoped that Italy would be warm and sunny all summer, this is not so different to English weather.

Walked into town (5 minutes) and got a ferry to Limone. It was very windy on the ferry, wished I had worn something warmer.

Limone was a pretty town. It had some nice little shops for buying trinkets, lots of tubs of flowers and pretty buildings. There was a pretty square, and views across the lake. Had coffee and ice creams, then got the ferry back.

Jay told us that going to reception to say that you have lost your key card for the fourth time is embarrassing.

Tuesday:
Bea did the 'ice bucket challenge'. The concierge (male) seemed delighted to throw a bucket of iced water over her.

Drove to Verona. Stayed at Romeo and Giulietta hotel (booked through Citalia). We had been told that parking was provided. They showed us on a map where we would probably find a parking space (which is not what we were expecting) and gave us a permit.

Watched Madam Butterfly in the arena. Is such a magical setting. This time we took cushions to sit on, and bottles of drink. They confiscated the bottles, though we were allowed to pour the drink into plastic cups. They said it was due to the health risk from glass bottles. However, there were people wandering throughout the arena selling glass bottles of drinks, so was somewhat inconsistent, and probably more to do with them not wanting to reduce their own sales than a safety issue. Husband listened to the opera while lying horizontally across the spare seats. I am sure he appreciated the music and didn't fall asleep.

Wednesday:
Returned to Garda.

Husband and Jay took big inflatables to the lake, and floated around on the waves.

In the evening, I was too ill to go into dinner. The staff were very accommodating and let Husband order from the restaurant menu and then bring it to me on a tray. So much nicer than having to pay for room service. They also started to ask if Husband had murdered me, as they had not seen me for some time. Husband suggested the head waiter might like to join them at the table, so he sat down in my place for a while.

While I was eating, alone in my room, the walls started to shake and the furniture rocked from side to side. I texted the family, who were all downstairs in the dining room, to ask if we were having an earthquake. The family all rushed upstairs, thinking I was having a funny turn. They assured me I was imagining things and should stay in bed. They then went back to finish their meal.

After dinner, they went to Riva, and danced in a square to a live electro-pop 70s Euro band. It is the beginning of a Robin Hood festival, and several people are dressed in green.

Thursday:
Another sunny day so family relaxed at pool.

News reports were all discussing the earthquake tremors from the previous day. I was very pleased that I'm not going mad after all.

Also delighted to notice another guest wearing a headscarf.

Saturday:
I finally felt well enough to go into dinner. It was fun but clearly the family had become rather out of control in my absence:

Emm received a menu with additional comments, such as: "Okay but sauce no good," scribbled next to each dish – the head waiter was adding his own recommendations.

Jay confided that he has now lost his room key six times, so has 'borrowed' the cleaner's one.

Sunday:
Emm has been to keen to try the little "make your own tart" things at the buffet breakfast. Unfortunately, the pastry case (which in fairness, does look remarkably like a small ice cream cone) turned out to be cardboard. It is for collecting jam in, not eating. He realised on his first bite. We were all very kind and didn't laugh at him or mention it again.

Breakfasts were really nice (as long as you don't eat the cardboard containers). There was an extensive buffet, and in one corner was the 'egg lady' where you could line up and ask her to cook eggs, omelettes or pancakes.

The hotel garden has a place where you can hire canoes, so I took photos while the others hired a couple of boats. The lake, surrounded by villages and mountains, is such beautiful scenery.

Monday:

During breakfast, Jay's room key fell out of his pocket. (I have lost count now.) A nice lady pointed it out.

The family drove up into the mountains around Garda. They said it was cold. They took some great photos of the views.

We left for our long drive home. This was such a lovely hotel, with friendly staff. Even being ill here was nice because they had such a relaxed manner. It was clean and pretty, with lovely meals and lots of activities, most of which we didn't manage to try.

I definitely hope to stay here again. Next time I will hire bikes, and get the ferry to all the little towns around the lake and maybe walk up a mountain or two. I will, however, pack some warmer clothes.

New York March 2015

Husband had a work trip in New York, so I decided to tag along. I knew it had been snowing (even more than usual) so chose my clothes carefully: no thick sweaters because all rooms, restaurants and taxis would have heating on full, very thick coat because outside would be freezing, walking boots because paths would be wet and salty. This all worked well except that I hadn't thought about the journey. As we walked through the exec lounge and sat in first class on the plane, everyone else was wearing suits and smart shoes. I pretended I was part of Bear Gryll's production team and dirty walking boots were completely normal footwear. Think everyone was fooled. Except for Husband, who banned the woolly hat until we had left the airport.

Stayed in the Chatwal Hotel on 44th Street between 6th & 7th Ave. Very nice place to stay, comfortable and clean with excellent facilities and art deco furnishings.

We strolled around, which is my favourite thing to do in New York. There were piles of snow heaped in the gutters and all the paths were very wet. I liked looking up, seeing all the different levels of rooflines. Lots of huge billboards flashing brightly lit adverts. The streets smell of roasted chestnuts and hotdogs as you pass the vendors. It was so cold, any exposed face actually hurt.

Went to Duane Reade – useful if you travel with someone who snores and need earplugs; or are feeling unwell and need medicines; or have lost your luggage and need make-up and toiletries. They also have food for when at 4am you're wide awake because the time zone is different.

Passed the New York Public Library, which I have seen many times but never actually been into, so decided to go inside. It has a beautiful entrance, you walk up marble steps into a marble lobby with many staircases.

I walked upstairs and came to a hallway with a beautifully painted ceiling and lovely carved door frames. Went into a room, where people were working at long tables and portraits lined the walls. There were no books. I had seen the library in a film where they had burned books to keep warm, so I was pretty sure there should be books. Unless they had burned them in real life?

Explored a bit further. Still did not see any books. There were lots of doors, which were locked. Found more paintings and a book in a glass case. Began to find this amusing. Were there books in this library? I wondered if the architect had got carried away with making it all look lovely and had then decided he did not want it spoiled with lots of books. Maybe the initial brief had been unclear. Guessed this may have caused some arguments, especially as the word *'library'* had been carved above the entrance.

Asked a guard if there were any books. He directed me into a room of map books. Not really what I had hoped for. Saw lots of people studying microfiche, but no books.

Decided to go back to the entrance and ask at the 'information' desk. Felt a little surreal to ask: "Are there any books in the library?"

However, found a very helpful little man who looked like he should have been selling magic wands. He explained that actually this was a research library. He told me that most books – novels etc – are kept in the library opposite. He then clearly decided that as I was foreign, I may not understand what a library was, so went on to explain that residents could obtain a library card and could both read books or even borrow them and take them home for a week or two.

Managed to keep my expression interested and surprised. Thanked him and left. I still have a feeling that I somehow managed to miss a huge room full of books, but I never found it. Beautiful building though.

Went to bed about 5pm. Woke about 3:30 am. At 4am, gave up on sleep and got up. Decided to try and find a deli or diner for some breakfast. It was snowing quite heavily, so very happy to have my sturdy walking boots and big coat. Did not expect to meet anyone, so pulled on jeans and coat over pyjamas. Felt rather adventurous to stand in Times Square wearing pyjamas!

New York at 4am is very nice. It is still brightly lit and feels very safe. (I wouldn't go down any small alleyways but main streets were fine.) Lots of people were around – mainly shift workers and homeless people I guess.

Found a deli and had bagels and coffee. Nowhere in the world does bagels and coffee like New York. Perfect.

Walked past the *ABC* studios. They have a window into the studio, so you can watch them filming the breakfast show. We were joined by a lady who became very excited to see *Mary Mary* about to perform. Apparently they are famous gospel singers. We joined her in waving excitedly, and they looked pleased and waved back. Luckily they didn't know we had absolutely no idea at all who they were.

At 8:30 NY time, we went into the hotel restaurant and had pancakes and more coffee. (I was showered and dressed by now, in case you were wondering.) Had a stack of pancakes and maple syrup. Another New York essential. I figured this counted as lunch, if I stay on BST.

In the afternoon we met some friends. Got a taxi (they allowed us to fit 4 people) to Central Park. It was so pretty with all the snow.

We ate in *Tavern on the Green*. This is a lovely restaurant right in the park. Inside there are lots of art deco furnishings, outside are twinkling lights, reflecting on the snow. It had comfy seats (makes a big difference to a meal) and an open kitchen, so you could watch the chefs. We last ate there in 1999, and it had a smart dress code, but now it is casual, so jeans were okay. Food was nice but my body thought it was 2am and could not cope with eating much. They packed up the remains of my dinner 'to go', which all restaurants in US seem happy to do and it takes the guilt out of having a small appetite. A lovely evening in a beautiful venue.

Didn't go shopping, but there is every opportunity if that's what you enjoy. It would at least be warm.

Another, colder, option is to visit the Intrepid Aircraft Carrier museum on the Hudson.

You could then eat in a typical American diner. I ate in the Diner on 11th Ave and W34 street. Had pie and coffee and pretended I was Jack Reacher.

A slightly more luxurious alternative with a much better view is dessert for $12 at The Mandarin Oriental on Columbus Circle. Afternoon tea is $48 (or $80 with a glass of champagne). If you want a window table (which you will) then be sure to book it when you make your reservation.

Another fun thing to do is to walk along The High Line. This is a disused elevated freight railway, which has now been turned into a park/walkway. In March, with all the plants under snow and in freezing wind, is probably not the best time to see it. However, even in arctic conditions it is interesting. You can see lots of old industrial buildings, there is random artwork along the route and best of all you can walk for nearly two miles without constantly stopping for road junctions. (Walking in New York is mostly slow and disjointed unless you are in Central Park.)

Being in New York is always fun, always easy and there is always something to do. Even a short trip is worth the jet lag.

Note: When I was in NY with my sister Ruth in 2018, we visited the library, and there were loads of books. I have no idea how we managed to miss them the first time – I think perhaps there was a whole floor we never visited.

Brazil June 24th 2015

Arrived in Rio after long flight. Really, really long flight.

We were met at airport by hotel driver. Bit of a squash fitting cases into boot due to two large gas canisters. I thought he had brought along his scuba diving gear (silly man) then learned that they were full of natural gas, it was a gas powered car (silly me).

The driver's ticket didn't open the exit barrier, so he reversed, drove around the carpark for a few minutes, and parked in deserted corner. We sat in the back, not moving, not speaking, not sure what was going to happen next.

He did NOT then draw a gun and ask for all our valuables, he just apologised and went to pay for parking. Clearly has watched different films about Rio to me.

Checked in at Sheraton Hotel. Discovered I had forgotten to turn off 'data roaming' on my phone and had already been charged £26:04 for excess internet. Good old 3 Mobile. (Not nice.)

Hotel however, is nice. Our room overlooks beach and has a little balcony. Husband complained sea was too noisy (such a romantic).

Showered, ate a burger, slept really well. Until 4am – oh dear.

Wednesday 17th June
Opened curtains and watched dawn break over the sea. Beautiful.

Rio de Janeiro was named by the Portuguese who discovered it. They thought they had found a river (*"rio"*) and they arrived in January (*"Janeiro"*). Good idea, except it wasn't a river, it just looked like one.

Ate breakfast in the hotel. Friendly staff, good buffet, ate overlooking sea. Tried some pretty tasteless papaya and some very nice melon. Coffee was disappointingly average.

Walked to Ipanema beach. Saw Corcovado Hill, with big Jesus statue on it. *"Corcovado"* means "hunchback" (I hope you're enjoying all these Portuguese insights as much as Husband did.) Saw a 'muscle beach' with people working out, doing pull-ups, etc. Lots of muscle. I can understand that having a gym on the beach is fun to use, though I would be too embarrassed by being watched to enjoy it. The muscle we saw seemed to be enjoying being watched though. I paddled in the sea (cold) feeling very white and unfit.

Saw people playing volleyball. Beach not too crowded. Sun gradually burnt off cloud and it warmed up, though didn't get too hot. Saw coconuts for sale and some growing in trees. You can buy fresh coconut milk at beach stalls.

Husband discussed birds on beach (feathered variety). Interesting shape, big and black and white. Tried to look them up in guide book but it concentrates mainly on nightclubs. Surprising really.

Lunch by pool. I used my best Portuguese (first time I have used it) and ordered a mineral water, still, no ice. I received a water, sparkling, with ice. Considered it a success (they understood the water bit).

The hotel staff spoke some English but in the rest of Rio, only Portuguese seems to be spoken. Occasionally we found someone who speaks Spanish but really you need some Portuguese or a lot of sign language. They pronounce things differently to both European Portuguese and to Northern Brazil, where the "d" is soft, sounds like a "j".

Sun disappeared behind hill disappointingly fast. By 3pm we were sitting in the shade.

Had cocktails in the bar. The traditional Brazilian cocktail is *Caipirinha*. It's made with cachaça (an alcohol made from sugar cane) sugar and limes. Very nice.

***

Thursday 18th June

Got to Rio airport very early. This was lucky, as check-in on airport computer took a while. It printed out boarding cards which resembled the crunchy variety of toilet paper – lots of perforations. One machine had run out of paper, so we had to fetch someone to refill it. It then spat out all the last few boarding cards and half of our one.

Flight okay. Landed in Recife and collected our luggage. My bag appeared to have been run over, it even had tyre marks going across it. The zipper no longer works, but I don't think anything had been lost. I will wrap duct tape around it when we next fly, and hope for the best.

It was raining hard. Lots of aggressive people in airport offering taxis, which you just knew would turn out to be an expensive 'limo' service. Found official taxi rank. By the time the taxi arrived at hotel it had stopped raining but was so humid my glasses steamed up.

Area is very mixed. We saw some expensive cars and very nice housing. Also saw a family sharing a bike, small roadside stalls selling fruit, lots of concrete. When we stopped at red lights, people walked amongst the cars selling stuff (like steering wheel covers) and there was a man juggling in the road.

We're meeting a team from Tearfund, and staying at Cult Hotel. Has some interesting art – mainly phallic in style. It's clean but basic. No mirror in room but a massive telly. They seem to favour beige a lot. And it smells of mould (humidity a problem here). The hotel was booked on our behalf by Tearfund. I'm guessing they didn't choose it especially for the art.

Met the other people on our trip and had dinner in nice restaurant next to sea. Seem to eat a lot of carbs here – every meal comes with potato *plus* either rice or couscous. Tomorrow we're going to *Instituto Solidare*, who are one of the partners that Tearfund work with here. Main info we've been given about the area is the high murder rate. Super.

Fri 19th June

Just got back from visiting the slums. I just want to give you a splurge of words so you understand something of the day's experience.

We started off going to *Instituto Solidare*. This was on the edge of the city and was a concrete building with big gates that locked. We could see teenagers playing football in a large covered area. We were taken upstairs, shown into a classroom and joined by about six of the workers. We all introduced ourselves – I got to use my Portuguese, very exciting.

We then learned a little of their work.

There is a huge problem here with prostitution, drugs, and the violent crime that goes with it. Some of this rises from boredom, and the ease with which young children can be enticed into gangs. *Institute Solidare* aims to remove the kids from the streets, to occupy their time with lessons, sports, a proper meal, then they go to school in the afternoon and spend the evening with their parents. They are then hopefully, too tired to get into trouble.

We looked around the institute, then walked around the community.

The houses were small, unmade roads, lots of dogs. The river was where all the toilets empty. In the rainy season (June and July) the river floods, taking the sewage into the houses. Many of the houses had moved all their furniture upstairs. It was hot, lots of flies, lots of dogs wandering around.

We saw young men strutting, with hard faces, appraising eyes. There were children, cute, smiling, wanting to be in photographs. Then the other teenagers, the ones with thin faces, dead eyes, wasted bodies. As a mother, it broke my heart to see them. They have mothers, somewhere. They are feeding their lives into hungry addictions, dead before they have known what it is to live. I wanted to take them home, hated leaving them there.

We went to another *favela*. This one seemed much poorer, it felt unsafe walking around (we were told to leave all our bags and cameras in the car. We just took our phones for pictures.) The homes were made of cardboard, hardboard, odd bits of wood and scaffold. It smelt, litter was everywhere.

I photographed beautiful children sharing bags of crisps, giggling. They lived in the equivalent of a shack. Their father thanked us profusely for coming, was keen for us to take photos, smiled his gappy-toothed smile, seemed pleased we were there. Then he returned to moving all his furniture onto the flat roof, waiting for the river and sewage to seep into their home.

There were women playing a game with scraps of paper and stones in an empty water bottle – it looked like Bingo. It looked as if they were having fun, seemed a nice community activity. I later learned they were the main drug pushers in the community, waiting until later to make their sales. If they listen to what the church is telling them, become Christians, want their lives to change, then they will lose their livelihood. This is why the church is also offering the chance to learn new skills, new occupations so they can still earn money.

It felt hopeless. Yet there was hope. Tearfund are working with their partners to educate the people, to teach them about flood control, clearing up litter. They are teaching them skills so they can find work, things like making jewellery from discarded stuff, metal work. They are lobbying the government, trying to get better housing, more respect for the people.

It wasn't a horrid day, though I feel exhausted by all we have seen. We laughed with children who were playing a game with Husband. Some teenaged girls had done a play about clearing up litter, which they had performed to their neighbours in the favela. They were so proud of it, wanted to take us to where they had done it, sang us some of the songs. We chatted a bit and they laughed when I told them I have chickens and ducks. I wanted to scoop them up, bring them out of the *favela* to somewhere safe, somewhere that they won't probably end up as sex workers. I cant.

All I can do is pray, support the work that Tearfund is doing. And tell you about it.

20th June

Showered, breakfast then left Cult Hotel in Recife. Was glad to survive shower, which has electrical wires coming out the top, was hard to relax when using it.

Also left the room with some added duct tape, which Husband had used to seal the massive gap around the air-conditioning unit. It worked – we got no mosquitoes (which was important as they carry dengue fever here) but I'm not sure the bright red tape blended very well with the dingy brown decor.

Apparently all the electricity is slightly weird in Brazil. Was certainly a challenge to bring the correct power adaptors, as the plugs seem to change from region to region. (If you plan to visit, bring a range.)

We also left the rather sexual art displays at the hotel. On the first evening, the team leader led us in a time of prayer. It is the first time I have ever prayed next to a large statue of an erect phallus, while sitting below a painting of a naked woman (who definitely had not had 'a Brazilian'). Tearfund trips are always unexpected.

Drove for a couple of hours to Coqueral. Interesting drive, passed lots of small communities, people driving horse and carts, big lorries. Rained hard a few times.

Coqueral is a small farming town (1,500 people). The area did not really support that many farmers, the town was off a track beyond a track, most people were unemployed and on benefits. The pastor told us they were "less poor in money" than the people we saw yesterday but "more poor in the mind". I don't think he meant they all had 'special educational needs', more that a sense of hopelessness pervaded the town.

They had a lot of knife crime and alcohol addiction.

It is St John's festival time which seemed like our harvest festival, but is cultural, not religious. The children at the mission hall had decorated the hall with plaited banana leaves and dressed in costumes and make up. They danced for us, a bit like a barn dance. I certainly didn't feel the display was too short.

We then joined in, which they thought was hilarious, especially as most of us were wearing the 'aid worker' sensible outfit of long sleeved shirts, long trousers and massive walking boots (which look really ugly and are no good for dancing in, but when you're wading through raw sewage in the slums, fashion doesn't seem so important).

Drove for about 5 more hours.

Arrived in Afogados. Staying at Hotel Brotas, which is quite like a motel. Room full of mosquitoes and ants, so I'll use lots of DEET while here. Husband is busy rigging up a mosquito net to sleep under. Am hoping it doesn't involve anything too structural.

Monday 22nd June
Yesterday was a day-off, which was good. Had hotel breakfast: melon, cake and something like a set egg custard. Not unpleasant.

Saw a capuchin monkey in a tree in hotel garden. Very cute. Then had lazy day.

Drove around town, did very little. Didn't go to a church as they were all a distance away and started at 7pm and Tearfund has a policy that you shouldn't drive at night in developing countries for safety reasons.

It gets dark really fast here. Dawn is 5am, dusk is about 5pm and it's pitch black by 5:30. Same all year round. No seasons, except that June and July have more rain.

Today we drove to see three rural projects. The charity tends to work with women and teenagers. This is partly because there is a lot of domestic abuse and it helps to empower the women and girls if they have a trade, are not at home all day completely dependent. It helps them have a sense of self worth, have rights (at the very least the right to not be abused).

They have also found that when a woman earns money, she tends to use it to improve the whole family. If men earn money, they tend to get distracted and spend it on alcohol, gambling, etc.

The first project was a small farm. Originally it had provided food for just the family – sustenance farming. This left no safety net if crops failed, or they need more money needed for improvements, etc. The charity provided knowledge and tools. The women now produce enough to provide for their families and also to sell some.

We saw a warehouse where they were preparing the food – fruits, bread, honey – for sale. Some goes to market, some is sold to the government for schools and hospitals, and the proceeds are then ploughed back into more charity work in the community.

We went to see Rosa We sat on brightly coloured furniture in her little sitting room. The walls were bright red, strewn with pictures of Jesus and photos of her grandchildren. There was a large telly with a statue of Father Christmas on top. I wondered if her grandsons have the same sense of humour as my boys and they were 'gifts' or if she had chosen it.

The internal doorways had no doors, just curtains. There was no ceiling and you could see up to the roof tiles, which had big gaps in them. It wasn't a bad house – as long as it didn't rain. Not quite sure what happened to the telly when it did.

We went off round her garden. Saw lots of the normal crops (onions, marrows) and also bananas, cashew nuts, medicinal herbs. Her kitchen had a huge freezer, where the produce could be crushed, bagged and frozen. The charity had given her the crushing and bagging machines and helped sort out the irrigation system.

Drove to the next project. Saw big expanses of arid land with a few shrubs and tall spindly palm trees. Also saw lots of donkeys pulling carts of stuff and even two oxen pulling a cart of logs. Would be SUCH a cool photo. I have lots of blurry ones. Mainly of trees. We saw lots of animals as we drove: goats, hens, cats and dogs, everywhere we go.

Went to *San Jose do Egypt*, which translates as "Saint Joseph from Egypt".

Went to cafe for lunch. Everywhere much cleaner than I was expecting it to be. We were advised to not eat the salads, which was a shame as they looked fabulous.

Went to a bakery. The charity had again provided equipment and education. It was MILES. From anywhere. Was so glad they had a toilet (very bumpy track to get there).

We got out of the van, and the heat from the sun was boiling, so hurried into the bakery. Then we nearly melted. Was like entering a furnace. The heat hit you like a wave.

Drove to a bee farm. Looked around the farm. Tearfund had provided funding for wells to be dug so production could increase (it's a semi arid area, lots of cacti) Saw the bees. Saw turkeys (which really do 'gobble').

Tearfund had again provided some tools and some knowledge. They had also helped to provide wells – again, it was a very arid area. The work of Tearfund here seems to be based around *helping the people to help themselves*, to help them improve their skills and to understand that they need to produce more than they eat, so they have some to sell and can earn money.

Then we had one of those horribly awkward moments, when the granny on the farm called us all into her house, and sat us down for drinks and snacks. She had prepared vats of juice for us, all prepared with local water which would have made us ill. Luiz had disappeared, she had gone to a lot of effort, we didn't want to offend her, nor be ill all night. I used my best Portuguese and apologised that we couldn't drink it because…had to mime last bit, my *Duolingo* app never taught me how to say that! Thankfully Luiz came back and explained a bit better. Felt bad. Difficult situation. Escaped to car.

We drove for miles on unmade tracks. Passed lots of small farms. They have no address, no street names. Also the area is about to be flooded as they are building a huge dam. All the farmers will have to be rehoused. (Our bee farmer and fruit juice granny will be okay, are out of range.)

Drove back to Ant Hotel.

Tuesday 23rd
Spent day in car, driving from Afogados to Recife. Six hours. Tried hard to not need washroom at the service stops, when finally relented it was the cleanest public washroom ever.

Went to restaurant for lunch. Was a buffet. Unlike yesterday, this time I knew that I had to weigh the food BEFORE I started eating it, as it's paid for by weight. (Don't ask about yesterday.)

Checked in at Cult hotel. Same room, duct tape still safely in place.

Walked along beach front. Despite the warnings everywhere, even behind every room door in the hotel, we did not see any sharks. There was even a man swimming and I waited for a few minutes, camera poised, but nothing, not even a fin.

Went to a market. Was either setting up or closing down. Bit naff. Didn't buy a cushion cover. Walked back along front. It was getting dark and we wondered if it was safe to be walking around.

Started to rain, then poured. Very warm, so rather nice. Until we remembered were travelling the next day and had no way to dry clothing.

Wednesday 24th
Early flight to Rio. Before we left, when we came to check-in the bag the airline had destroyed on the flight out, the same airline made us sign a disclaimer, saying that said bag (now secured with duct tape) would not be their responsibility if duct tape should fail. So wished my Portuguese was good enough to have explained that THEY caused the damage in the first place! Shall compose a letter when I am home. Cannot really recommend TAM airlines, not for customer service anyhow.

Bag arrived in one piece, I did not have to pick single items of clothing from conveyor belt.

Taxi to Caesar Park Hotel. A few days holiday now. Am really tired.

The hotel is lovely. It's right on Ipanema beach, brilliant view. Room is perfect, comfy beds, great shower, complimentary bottles of water as well as all the normal chocolates on pillow, bathroom stuff etc. Staff spoke good English.

Checked out the pool – more of a foot spa really. Restaurant and pool on roof, so great views.

I asked about crime/safety in Rio. Was told that after dark (5:30 pm) I should not walk anywhere on my own but in a group, if we kept to well lit busy streets, we would be fine. I did see single women walking on their own, but maybe they looked less like tourists than me.

Thursday 25th June

Walked around corner and ate breakfast at Armazen cafe. This is a chain of cafes, we saw a few of them. They serve good coffee and a range of sandwiches and cakes. The warm apple and walnut cake makes a good breakfast.

We walked up to *Rodrigo de Freitas* lake. Hired bikes (£15 per hour, plus took our hotel address as security) and cycled around the lake on the cycle paths. It only took half an hour. Fun.

We chose a place for lunch from the Lonely Planet guide book. It had been demolished. We chose alternative place; but they only did full meals and we weren't that hungry. Returned to Armazen cafe.

Got a taxi to old part of city. Drove past Copacabana beach, saw sand sculptures and street entertainers. Nice colonial houses in old part. Also lots of major road work - maybe for 2016 Olympics.

Ate dinner in Satyricon restaurant (rumoured to be Madonna's favourite). Husband had eaten there 5 years ago and still talks about the lobster bisque, served inside a hollowed loaf of bread. Not sure it lived up to his memory.

Friday 26th June

Had booked a tour through the hotel to *Ilha Grande* (big island) with Trips in Rio.

We were told we would drive from the hotel to a village, get a boat to the island, then hike for three hours through lush forest to beautiful beaches. This was all true.

However, they omitted to tell us a few things:

Friday is the WORST day for traffic in Rio. It took us two hours to leave the city and about three hours to get back in the evening. Alecs, the tour guide, did a coffee and washroom stop (nice clean facilities) so it was okay, but it wasted a lot of the day.

As we drove we saw police had stopped vehicles in various places. They carried machine guns. There's a VERY strong police presence in Rio. On the boat another passenger had a hand gun. Turned out he too was a policeman. (Owning a gun is illegal in Brazil except for police.) Also saw more amazing wall art/ graffiti.

When we met Alecs, he advised us to go back to room and change into sturdy shoes, long sleeves etc, as we needed proper hiking stuff. This should perhaps have been a warning that our gentle day strolling might not be so gentle.

The hike was long and steep. We basically walked/ scrabbled/ climbed for over an hour UP a mountain track. When we remembered to look up, it was beautiful but it was hard going, narrow paths, slippery clay covering rocks, very steep. Needed to concentrate on not falling.

We then walked/ slid for an hour down the other side. Finally reached the beach to find the track ended on a *ten foot high rock, with a rope*. No other way down. Had to abseil down to the beach.

Beach beautiful and had cafe with loo. Only permitted a quick rest, then trekked for another *hour and a half* to next beach. No abseiling this time – it's surprising what you come to appreciate. The next section was not such a steep walk, though it did begin with climbing a 45 degree slope of granite. Not so easy with tired legs and sand slippery shoes.

Made it with no major injuries, though I did slip at one point and jar my wrist. Luckily didn't slip into one of the trees coated with four inch long spikes (which they used to use in blow guns as weapons).

Arrived at second beach. Saw black vultures (probably waiting for exhausted hikers). The third, most beautiful beach, was a further hike, then a return to second beach for boat out. We opted to stay at second beach.

On way back to Rio, car ran over an abandoned cone (heavy traffic, safer than swerving to avoid it). Was removed from under car by man with shovel at petrol station.

Satnav kept recommending we leave the traffic jam and take a side road. Alecs said the route would take us through two *favelas* and might not be safe. I'm glad he didn't, felt I had had enough adventure for one day.

Saturday 26th June
Compared aching muscles over breakfast at Armazen cafe.

Morning on beach. The hotel provided a lounger, towel and sunshade (for free). Along the beach there are various first aid stations. These are numbered and called '*Postos*'. People tend to gather around a specific *posto*, though there is no 'rule', you can go anywhere. They are mainly just good places to meet people.

The beach is interesting, lots to watch. Many vendors walk up and down and you can buy almost anything without leaving your beach chair. There were lots of bottoms in string bikinis, some beautiful, and some suffering from the effects of gravity. A band came and played Samba (nice) then stood next to every chair in turn and refused to move unless given money. They were very persistent (not so nice).

I watched the surfers and wished I was young and athletic.

We got a taxi to Sugarloaf Mountain. Cable car to first mountain, where there are two routes: The green path takes you quickly to the queue for the next cable car. However, if after 4:30, it's better to walk the other route and take your photographs first (because it will be dark on the way down).

At the top was a viewing gallery, cafe, toilets and gift shop. Plus amazing views of Rio. The *Christ the Redeemer* statue was behind a cloud; it looked like ascension day!

Went to *Porcao*, a *churrascarias* restaurant. If you are in Brazil, you must go to one of these, they're very traditional. There was a buffet full of salads – some hot, mostly cold. You paid a fixed price (plus drinks) then helped yourself to the salad. Then the waiters walk around with massive skewers of freshly cooked meat, whole legs of lamb, great steaks, etc. You were given little round cards with *'sim'* (yes) on one side and *'nao'* (no) on the other. If the green *'sim'* side was showing, they came to the table and sliced off pieces of meat onto your plate. You had little tongs to hold the slice while they cut it. It was great fun. It suited me because I don't like too much meat, and usually restaurants give me too much and I have to leave it. It suited the males because they ate a small farm's worth of meat. Drank Bohemian beers, chatted, laughed, great evening.

Sunday 28th June

Armazen cafe shut. Walked to a *confeitaria*. You go to a small kiosk, say what you want to eat/drink and pay for it. They give you a receipt. You take the receipt to the counter, they read it and give you what you have ordered. You then either eat standing at one of the small round tables in the centre, or take the food away. It was quite exciting waiting for the food to arrive to see if we had said what we thought we had. Language practice with added tension, because your breakfast depended on it. I had a very sweet banana bread and a small bitter coffee. Perfect.

Saw a teenaged boy going through the bins looking for food. Too sad. Rio is full of contradictions: the very rich living alongside the very poor.

Took some money and offered to buy him breakfast. When I spoke to him he flinched, like a wounded animal. It is not right, to be so broken when so young. He was fairly spaced out, probably high on something, but he managed to order something at the kiosk and went to collect it.

On Sundays, they shut one side of the road along the beach. The whole city (almost) turns out to walk. It feels a little like one of those disaster movies, where everyone is walking in the same direction, escaping the tidal wave or giant snake or something. Anyway, we joined the walkers and went to Copacabana beach. There were kids, grannies, bikes, dogs, wheelchairs, whole families. Wonderful.

Stopped to take photos: fishermen, sand castles, vendors, palm trees, surfers.

Felt something on my leg. Looked down to find yellow sludge across back of my legs. Instantly a man appeared, with cloths, offering to clean off the "dog shit" (his terminology, not mine). Husband shoed him away. We got out copious quantities of wet wipes. It smelt like mustard. Cleaned up and walked on. On return walk, we saw lots of empty sachets of mustard thrown on the floor. Obviously a scam – if we had accepted help from the 'cloths man' we probably would have then been expected to pay him.

Monday 29th June
Coffee and cake at Armazen cafe.

Taxi to Cosme Velho to catch the '*trem do Corcovado*' up to the *Christ the Redeemer* statue. Another ride through Rio full of cafes, artistic graffiti, bars and gates around all the first floor offices, homes, and car parks (which are locked up at night). Lots of people with dogs (which they are really good about cleaning up after, the dogs here are well cared for). Patterned tiled pavements (pretty, but takes some skill to walk in heels). Tree lined streets.

There was a queue for the train but not a huge one – June/July is winter, which might be quieter. We waited 45 minutes and it cost 51 Reales each. The train has open windows and goes through a hilly forest. We used lots of DEET but to be honest I didn't see any insects at all. It is best to sit on the left of the train (with the mountain behind you) when going up for some cool glimpses of Rio.

At the top station there was either a lift or steps up to the statue. There aren't many steps and the view is amazing. There are little gift shops too, perfect for that plastic flip-flop keyring you have always wanted.

The platform at the top was crowded but not terrible – again, I've heard it's worse in the summer. There were lots of people lying down to take photos, so you had to look where you were going, as trampling on them would be unfortunate. The best place was down a few steps at the front of the statue.

To be frank, I am not sure that I like a big statue of Jesus (not keen on crucifix jewellery either). It feels vaguely superstitious. There is also something faintly incongruous about having a huge statue of Jesus, who spoke so radically about equality, love, social justice, above a city so full of inequality and crime. However, the views are fantastic and when you come to Rio you kinda have to visit it.

Went to supermarket on way home. Tried to buy brazil nut biscuits for mum. Failed. Do brazil nuts even come from Brazil? Bought her some dark chocolate (cacao is grown here) and some pistachio biscuits, which are Italian. But I tried.

Went to beach. I mainly watched people, it's a busy beach. You could do a whole week's worth of shopping on this beach. The vendors come round, calling out their wares, carrying heavy bags (they pad the handles with towels but even so, in the heat, walking across the sand, it's a tough way to earn money). You can buy coconuts full of milk, beer (draft beer no less, from a huge barrel with a tap) cigars, sarongs, kaftans, swimwear, hats, cheese (which they carry on skewers with a vat of boiling oil and then cook them for you at your beach chair), shrimps (also freshly cooked), tattoos – not sure how they do those – might have just been the transfer sort. Lots of people here have beautiful tattoos, a whole limb covered in intricate pictures. There were also books, ice-creams, nuts (not brazil nuts), and sweetcorn (cooked in a tub of boiling water, served in the green leaves, with butter).

The sand is full of pigeon footprints, groups of young men kicking footballs, sun-loungers, girls with rounded bottoms in minuscule bikinis, tall waves carrying surfers towards the beach. By 4pm there are long shadows and a cool breeze. By 5:30 it's beginning to get dark and it's black by six.

No one stays on the beach after dark, if you walk you stay on the well lit path next to the road.

We ate at Pomodorino, an Italian restaurant. The main courses were nice but the puddings were excellent. I had the chocolate, orange and grapefruit tart. Perfect.

Tuesday
Flew home to a very sunny UK.

Malta and Gozo August 2015
(Children aged 19, 21 and 23 years.)

Saturday:

Taxi at 5am. Always stressful as everyone has set alarm for 4:30, knowing it will take half an hour to get ready. Lots of tension over bathroom space.

Taxi and flights okay.

Landed in Malta. Hired car through Avis, a Mazda 6. A very battered Mazda 6. As we left the airport, understood why it was battered. No one stops at junctions, you just have to try hard to avoid them.

Jay map-read. Not easy, as map had no road names and there were lots of unexpected one-way roads. Also roundabouts were marked on map, but did not appear to actually exist. Bea and Emm gave regular input, Husband ignored most directions. No idea how Jay remained calm (this is why I REFUSE to be the map reader).

Malta has lots of flat roofed buildings made of pale limestone. Reminded me of being in Palestine (not that I've actually ever been to Palestine).

Arrived at *Meridien Hotel*. Nice lobby. Had drinks while they prepared our rooms and looked at views, which are brilliant, across a bay to a church. Rooms nice.

Walked around town and bought water. Tap water in Malta tastes horrid, though is safe to use for ice, washing salads, and cleaning teeth – unless you are particularly sensitive.

Even at 6:30 pm, it was really hot; sweaty within minutes.

Ate in *Villa Restaurant*, which is part of the hotel. Meals around €30 per head for starter and mains. Very nice. We sat on a veranda overlooking water, tiny lights in trees, beautiful. Bea told me that next to the sea you don't get mosquitos so won't be bitten. This is not true.

Sunday:

Breakfast. Amazing buffet, had pretty much everything. Family sat and chatted to each other on Facebook.

Planned day. Hotel is at St Julian (which explains why I couldn't find it on map in Valletta. Another reason why I no longer map read).

Valletta has a Crusaders fort. Caught bus. Very easy as Valletta is end of the line. Tickets cost €2 each and are valid for two hours (so you can get on and off buses with the same ticket within that time).

Valletta was interesting, busy and hot. More limestone flat-roofed buildings, flags, cafes, gift shops. Malta has lots of *Festa* - each town has a Saint, and one weekend each year they decorate the town, have a parade, let off fireworks and are generally festive.

We looked round the free bits of the fort because the bits you pay for are basically museums, and we don't much like museums. Plus we could see lots just from the free bits. Great views. Loud canons at midday.

Fort was built in 1556, by the knights from the Order of St John. Later, in 1798, Napoleon invaded and kicked out the knights. The Order still exist today - in the UK they are St.John's Ambulance Brigade, though the order itself is based in Rome and answers only to the Pope.

All hot, so decided to go for lunch. Got enticed into a cafe by man on the door. Had nice lunch in warm air-conditioned dining room (was less hot, but not really cool). Prices in menu differed from prices advertised outside but not by much (always worth checking though). Food nice and cheap. Toilets nasty. Service friendly.

Went round the Grand Masters Palace. Cool painted ceilings and suits of armour. Lots of 'Do Not Touch' signs. If you're tempted to try on a helmet when no one is looking, don't bother – they're glued onto the modals. *Weapons Room* had lots of weapons (not unexpectedly, you might think) and was very hot.

Got bus back to St Julian. Friendly lady on bus told me that you can buy a weekly ticket for €21. Actually, everyone on Malta is friendly.

Walked to next bay and checked out restaurants. Everyone seemed very young and trendy (am informed that the use of word "trendy" proves that I am old). Ate ice creams next to sea.

Swam in hotel pool.

Walked around bay to *Eat* restaurant (not part of the UK fast food chain). Very nice starter. Bea and I had cocktails which looked nice, but mine was fairly low alcohol. Main courses okay, but not great. When bill came, waitress said their credit card machine didn't work. Emm-the-economist informed me this was a scam. Either that or she was a bit daft to not tell us at the beginning, as we may not have been carrying enough cash.

Monday:

Nice breakfast. Family communicated by mobiles again. Might take a book tomorrow.

Drove to Mdina and Rabat. Mdina is the walled city within Rabat. Jay in charge of map again. Lorry ahead of us hit a tree branch, which then fell and blocked the road. Jay made up detour. Arrived in Mdina, which was surprising as Jay admitted that at no point was he sure which road we were on. Did not stop him making decisive decisions at every junction, we were fooled. Apart from Emm, who labelled him the *'Helen Keller of map readers'*.

Emm requested that we not walk around in the midday sun. We arrived in Mdina at 11:50. It was hot. He hardly mentioned it at all.

Walked to St Paul's grotto in Rabat. It started to rain. Was only about five drops but all males complained. Fear we may be holidaying in Sahara next year. Emm complained that the name 'Rabat' is stolen from Morocco, and St Paul's Cathedral is stolen from London. He then walked around muttering about looking for the *Maltese Eiffel Tower* and *Statue of Liberty*. We ignored him.

St Paul's grotto was interesting, cool and dark, especially the catacombs. Not good if you don't like confined spaces but excellent otherwise. Some of the best stuff is down narrow unmarked tunnels, so worth taking a boy with a clever phone, or a torch. Tall males complain a lot.

Used toilets in museum. Nasty. Toilets in Malta also rarely have paper, so worth carrying your own supply.

Bought cushion-cover for my collection. Has Maltese cross on it. Happy.

Ate lunch in *Bottegin*, Palazzo Xara in Rabat. Was okay and cheap.

Drove home. Got thoroughly lost. Bea took over map reading and took us in a big circle past some bamboo. Fired her and reinstated Jay/Helen Keller, who took us all around the coast. Was scenic if not exactly direct.

Played *Game of Thrones* board game in the bar. I never actually understood the rules but everyone else seemed to enjoy it. Drank beers (which helped).

Tuesday:
Breakfast at 9.

Husband collected a plateful of Maltese food: pickled herrings, pea pastries, cheese. Ate a few mouthfuls, then collected a plateful of English breakfast food to 'dilute' it with. Told him he's getting portly. He did not appreciate feedback.

We didn't go to the Hypogeum in Paola as you have to book and there are no vacant slots for the next 20 years.

Drove to Hagar Qim to look at *Mnajdra* temples. Arrived 11:55. Emm again hardly mentioned "midday sun" at all. There was an interesting 4D film before the monument (my kind of history, short, informative and no long boring information boards to read). Temples were unusual. And hot.

Drove back to St Julian with no detours. Jay told us: "It helps if you know where you are when you start." Explains a lot.

Checked out, and then ate lunch in hotel lobby. Nice food.

Drove to ferry at Cirkewwa. I cannot begin to tell you how my family pronounce the names here...

Arrived at ferry terminal in good time. They leave every 45 minutes, so only had to wait about 10 minutes but in the hot sun it felt like forever. Was surprised by how big and near Gozo looked – like a peninsula across the bay.

Jay gave directions, but the other two quite vocal. Conversations like:

Jay: Take the next right.

Bea: This one, this one, turn right now.

Husband: I'm not going up that one, it's too narrow. Right, which way now?

Emm: I think that's wrong anyway.

Jay: It's not wrong, I know where we are exactly. Probably. Okay, if there's a roundabout take 3rd exit. But there wont be; roundabouts are only on the map, they never exist in real life here.

It is also hard to see 'no entry' signs as the sun has faded them all.

Gozo has more flat-roofed houses and domed churches. Very pretty. Met villa man in square and went to villa in Xaghra, pronounced 'Shara'. My family never managed that. It was very luxurious.

Drove down winding road to nearest big supermarket.

Walked from villa into centre of Xaghra, about 10 minutes unless you got lost. Several people sitting outside chatting. Square has a few restaurants to choose from.

We ate at *Oleander*. Very friendly and welcoming. Food nice, especially the baked brie starter served on figs and walnuts. Delicious. Husband and Emm raved over the tomato, capers, olives and peppers bruschetta. Jay agreed it was delicious – and he doesn't even like capers, or olives, or peppers. He isn't very keen on bruschetta either. All too full to eat our main courses. Had Limoncello shots then walked home. Didn't get lost.

Wednesday:
Lazy day. Unpacked, did washing. Cooked pancakes and bacon – all takes ages in unfamiliar kitchen. Kitchen is beautiful but rather lacking in equipment. Used salad bowl to make batter. The only coffee maker seems to be a Nespresso machine (but no capsules) or a cracked cafetiere – which I don't fancy using. Think maybe a dog mauled it at some point.

Pool boy came. He was about 70.

Got cinema room working. This is a long room built under the pool, so is dark and cool. It has black leather sofas that recline, and a big screen and sound system. Note to self: never allow Husband to install a fancy sound system. He has it loud enough for the whole town to hear. Claims bass is set too high.

Played *Game of Thrones* board game. I still don't understand the rules. Much testosterone-fuelled arguing and making of alliances. Was a very long game...Lucky we weren't in a beautiful villa with views across a valley full of sunshine...

Of course, the best thing of all, is that long after the game FINALLY ended, it could be discussed at length, each move analysed, much advice given. Shoot me someone.

Strolled into town. Picturesque square/church rather spoiled by extensive building work. Found a small supermarket 5 minutes walk from villa. It opens at 6am, so ideal for buying stuff before breakfast.

Ate at *Oleander* again. No one really enjoyed their meal. Maybe it's just too hot to enjoy eating.

Thursday:
Lazed, swam, ate ice-creams. The ice-creams were like rocks so turned down the freezer.

Pizza for lunch. Tasted mainly of plastic.

Drove to Xlendi. Parked in car park behind the shops. Everywhere we went was much less crowded than resorts in the UK. There are not many spaces in the car parks but there are always some. The shops and cafes run along the waterfront. It was very crowded with a shingle beach. There were buoys marking where was safe to swim (easy to get run over by a boat when swimming in Gozo).

We walked along a rock wall to some steps down into the sea. Swam/snorkelled. Mainly saw small shoals of fish. Water really salty (stung eyes) and very deep.

Drive home was difficult, winding roads and lack of signs. Apparently, roads were designed to be confusing because the island was raided so many times, and they hoped invading foreigners would get lost. They succeeded.

Ate in *DVenue*, another restaurant in the square. Actually, the best restaurant we found in Gozo. They had a good fresh fish platter. Nice meals.

Walked back to villa and watched *Harry Potter* (not my choice) in cinema room.

Friday:
Walked to local shop and bought local honey, eggs and milk. Made pancakes. There is also a bread van that comes from the local bakery and drives around the town honking its horn at about 10 every morning. Stops in various places. Nice crusty bread.

After lunch, went for a drive.

Drove to Dwejra Bay. Beautiful. There were rocks down to deep blue water, *Azure Window* (a big hole in the rock which was very crowded with people taking photos), several ice-cream vans, stalls selling tourist tat from Africa, St Anne's chapel (more modern than expected).

You could look down onto the Inland Sea. This used to be a huge cave, but the roof fell in, so now it's a giant rock-pool surrounded by cafes and full of boats for hire and divers. Took photos.

Drove through St Lawrences. Took photo of church, which was very ornate, lots of red and gold. All the churches here have a basket of material next to the door, so you can cover your shoulders.

Drove back to Xaghra via Ghasri, Zebbug, Xwejni Bay, Marsalforn. You can imagine how my family pronounce these names.

As we drove, I saw interesting rock formations, and salt pans, but was told I had exceeded my photograph limit and the car was not stopping.

Getting into Xaghra was a challenge, due to closed roads, and no helpful *Diversion* signs. Also, Gozo DOES have cul de sac/ no-through-road signs, because I have seen some. However they obviously did not buy enough, because mostly they are unmarked, and you just have to turn round when you get to the end. Got home eventually.

Ate several ice-creams.

Played *Game of Thrones* with the males. Husband's turns are like advert breaks in the US – you can write diary, read a book, cook a three course meal and still not miss any play. Boys had coded talks to discuss the rules in secret (like I would've cared). Bea sunbathed and talked to Boyfriend.

Ate at *DVenue* again. Finished with complimentary limoncello shots. Weekends get busier, so we booked a table for Sunday.

Saturday:
Quick breakfast, then drove back to Dwejra Bay. Worried about hair being dry in the salty water, so I put suncream in it. Bea asked me why my hair was blue.

Walked down some steep steps from the first car-park, to a cove where Fungus Rock is (big rock where they used to collect a plant – which apparently was not a fungus). Water wonderfully deep, you could just float around wearing a snorkel, lost in an underwater world. The route into the water was via sharp rocks, so we wore swimming shoes (bought for about £5 from Amazon before we came and they worked really well). Saw rocks and seaweed and shoals of fish.

Jay asked me if I knew my hair was blue.

Bacon and egg lunch at villa.

Played *Game of Thrones*. Each move took 27 hours.

Watched *Pitch Perfect* in cinema room. Still not my choice but not as bad as you might think.

Cooked steaks (horrible) and had them with red wine (nice) and salad (okay) in fancy dining room/wine cellar which has been carved out of the rock below the villa. Very atmospheric.

Hair no longer blue. But suncream made it very wiry, was not a good idea.

Sunday :
Made pancake batter, then couldn't light hob. No gas. Annoying. Husband checked barbecue outside and managed to light it. Took ages to heat up but then worked fine. Was rather lovely to eat breakfast outside, overlooking the valley. Sent text to villa man who changed gas bottle later that morning.

Walked to church. Service was in progress but other people were going in, so I slipped into the back. Was incredibly hot in there. Very full church, lots of families. No order of service sheet, or hymn books, or Bibles. Service all in Maltese, it was like listening to Arabic: couldn't understand a word. After 10 minutes, with sweat trickling down my back, I gave up and slipped out again. I'm glad I went – I don't know how else to make Sundays different – but there seemed little point in staying long. Pretty church though, with lovely painted ceilings.

Husband went to cake shop, *Cafe Reale*. There is an Italian man who owns it. He gets up early every morning and bakes wonderful cakes. We tried a selection. My favourite was the Bounty cake.

From about 11:30 to after 12 each day, there is lots of canon fire/fireworks across the valley. Bea suggested they are the midday canons and the Maltese are not very good time-keepers. Husband suggested that maybe a bird had got lost and strayed across Gozo and we were hearing the hunters. (Hunting is a problem here, there are not many birds left now.)

Played *Game of Thrones*. Each move took 29 hours. Clearly one major difference between the genders is that females can decide future moves DURING someone else's turn, hence taking much less time when it's time for their move. Plus they don't actually care that much. Wine helps.

Dinner at *DVenue*. Good again.

Saw a blue light on a roof. I told Bea they have blue stars in Gozo.

Monday :
Husband went to buy water and milk. Hard to find full-fat milk here. Today bought 2.5% fat. I think the darker the blue of the carton, the higher the fat content. But not necessarily.

Discussed family chores, as Husband has decided everyone should help (that idea went so well last holiday). Bea and Emm are responsible for all dishwasher duties. They immediately formed a trade union, and appointed Bea as spokesperson. Spent some time discussing terms and conditions with Husband, who tried to instigate penalty clauses but Bea told him it contravened European law. So glad he started this. Jay (in charge of rubbish disposal) kept offering to strike in support of Bea and Emm. It would be so much easier to simply do the jobs myself.

After lunch walked to square. Full of dusty roadworks, so continued round the corner to a little cafe. Had ice creams and coffee. I had a *Malteser* ice cream – clearly from Malta. Hot walk back to villa.

Went to Victoria as Bea wanted to buy gifts (Yaay shopping, my favourite). Very windy. We were told a storm was coming: "With 110 lightening strikes in Tunisia already."

Shops all rushing to get their displays inside. We went to *Maldonado Bistro*. They didn't open until 7pm, but kindly let us go in early and have drinks while we waited.

The menu had 12 different bruschetta. This kept family occupied for 50 minutes – just the choosing bit. You may have not noticed, but my family enjoys negotiating/discussing/persuading. Strong opinions. Not my genes. Bea tried a *Kinnie*, which is advertised everywhere here. It's a bitter orange drink. Very bitter.

Bruschettas were huge when they arrived – half a loaf. Very nice. Great atmosphere (down in a wine cellar) and friendly service.

Drove home. The streets are pretty at night. Saw several blue lights on poles. Boys told Bea it was an alien invasion.

Tuesday:

Drove to Xewkija - pronounced "shewkeeya". But not by my family.

Saw the third biggest dome in Europe, except one in Malta also claims this. One is higher and one is wider, so there is some dispute. Sounds like my family. The Rotunda is nice, quite simple inside (apart from the massive dome). It was built over a smaller, more ornate church, which they moved to the side by numbering all the stones and moving them individually. It is now a side chapel.

The main church has some good modern art, including two statues made of papier-mâché by Alfred Camilleri Cauchi. I like papier-mâché, and made a rather fine mask when I was at Junior School. Not that it really compares.

Went to small supermarket next to rotunda (husband has developed a peach addiction). It started to absolutely pour with rain, ran to car, soaked. Drove home through Victoria, which is like the moving staircases in Hogwarts in *Harry Potter* books – whichever way you go in you can never find the correct route out.

Lunch. Thunder storm.

Males decided they wanted to build sandcastles on Ramla beach. As it was cloudy and cool, Bea and I decided to walk there. Started to follow road signs, then realised that they directed traffic along major roads, so followed map instead. Reached a ridge where we could see beach but it was unclear how to get down to it. By this time the sun had reappeared and it was very hot.

Two stray dogs joined us, happy to have some company and walked with us, waiting at every bend for us to catch up. We ignored them but they came anyway, it was rather nice. Took an hour to reach beach (nice walk if *not* sunny).

Found males in far corner of beach building 'Venice'. Bea and I had a drink in the cafe for 17 hours while the males finished their sandcastle. Drove home.

Swam. Pool very cold when full of rainwater. Ate ice creams, which are still too hard. Realised the "fast freeze" button had been left on by previous guests. Slight moment of panic from Husband when he realised the *Cisk* beer he'd put into the freezer to cool down was still in there. I moved them to fridge.

Wednesday:
After breakfast, drove to Victoria. Walked to citadel. Great views, could see all around island.

Went into the battery, which led to the silos (huge grain storage areas, like great caves.) Very interesting. The silos are connected by a dark narrow tunnel (from when they were turned into a reservoir) so now you can walk right into them. Jay and Bea sang a chant, harmonising with their echoes. Was magical.

Then saw the rooms used as WW2 shelters. They were under the reservoirs, so if they'd been hit, everyone would've drowned. Not such a good idea.

Didn't pay for the museum. Didn't pay for the prison, but did put Jay into the stocks outside. Didn't see a Christmas tree ornament to buy. But did see some traditional lace. Shop owner said it was the last of her stock as all her suppliers were now in their eighties and younger women won't sell their work because it earns about 50p an hour. Seemed too mean to buy any.

Had lunch back in Xaghra at *Cafe Reale*. They have the BEST iced coffee. Still not losing weight.

Males decided to return to beach, we stayed here to swim, but then the pool man arrived so we couldn't. Annoying.

Males returned late, very happy, had built a brilliant castle and had been joined by another family, who were somewhat younger, so they could pretend they were building it for the children. Husband did suggest a post-dinner drive to show me and Bea, but unfortunately he drank too much *Cisk* and was over the alcohol limit. Such a shame.

Nice dinner again at *DVenue*.

Back at the villa, I looked across the valley. All the towns are now full of blue lights on poles. Apparently they represent Mary (not aliens) and I assume are ready for the 15th, which is Assumption Day. There is a strong Catholic presence in Malta.

Thursday :

Husband booked a boat for Friday afternoon, at Xlendi Watersports, €80, 4 adults, 2 hours. The boys are keen to go out on a speedboat. I am not, so might stay and write.

Drove to Calypso's cave. This is where Ulysses was put under a spell by the witch Calypso when returning from the Trojan war (if you enjoy Homer).

It was confusing to find on maps, as there's also a viewpoint and you can't tell which is on the road. Followed signs. Brilliant view of Ramla beach and out to sea. No cave. Searched around a bit (while husband checked sandcastle with zoom on camera). Found some disused steps and some scaffolding holding up a rock. I think Calypso's cave has collapsed. This is a pity as it's in all the guide books and sounded interesting, perhaps they will repair it.

Went back to square for more iced coffee with cream at *Cafe Reale*. While we drank, we watched the building work and cars narrowly missing each other in the square. I must say, Gozo has a LOT of building work, they seem to be rebuilding the whole island.

Back to villa in time for 12 noonish canons. Gozo also has a lot of canons.

Went to the salt pans at Xwejni Bay. Very interesting. Shallow pools, which were cut by hand, to collect seawater. When it dries they harvest the salt crystals and sell it. (Gozo sea-salt.) The salt pans were first cut during Roman times.

Walked around Qolla-L-Bajda. Weird rock erosion and a cave. White clay cliffs eroding fast, beach littered with great chunks of fallen cliff. Cove was interesting, but a bit smelly.

Evening meal in Marsalforn. Ate in *Menqa L'Antika*, which had good reviews, but either we were unlucky and went on a day when they had staffing problems, or they wrote them themselves. (I think probably the latter.) Good menu but food didn't really match descriptions.

Friday:
Pancakes for breakfast.

Did shopping for weekend as everywhere will be shut for the public holiday.

Walked to *Cafe Reale* for coffee and cakes. Bought take-out pizzas for lunch.

Family then left to go boating. I don't much like boats, so elected to stay home and read/write/swim.

When they returned, they said the afternoon had gone well. Husband had pre-booked the boat by phone, and they found the office easily. The man spent a long time explaining where the hidden rocks were, marking them onto a map. He took a credit card number as security, and then they left.

Husband passed the important map showing all the rocks to Jay, who put it safely onto the wet seat next to him, and then watched in horror as the wind carried it away, into the sea.

Bea said there were a few calm discussions, where everyone was very understanding, and then they continued. All they could remember was: the worst rocks are marked by a yellow buoy. They gave all yellow buoys a wide birth.

They returned unscathed, no one drowned and they made up some best-seller songs about being in a speed boat driven by an accountant.

Ate in *DVenue*. Very nice. Again.

Saturday:

Today was the day of the *festa* in Victoria. It was surprisingly hard to find out details/timings but found them eventually (gozonews.com is a good source of information).

Decided to go to the 2:30 horse racing. It began at 2:10, which was a surprise. So was the number of people wandering the crowded streets, seconds before the first horses came galloping down. Most races were horse and carts, like Roman chariot races, three in each race, hurtling down the main street in Victoria.

There was a ten minute pause between each race, which feels a long time to wait in the hot sun.

In the evening there were fireworks, which we watched from the villa across the valley.

Sunday:
Today Bea had to go home (only 2 weeks off work). We took her back to the airport in Malta, felt strange going back, the roads are much busier. All the timings with ferries worked well and it was a three hour round trip. You only pay for car ferry when returning to Malta, not on the way out, €15 for a car plus €5 for each passenger.

Omelette lunch, then watched Arsenal/Palace match on telly. Such a thrill.

Went to windmill in Xaghra. Used to be a 'community windmill'. This means that when the wind was blowing in the right direction, the windmill owners blew through a shell to let the town know, and everyone brought their grain to be ground.

Went to San Blas Bay. Very steep walk down, though an enterprising local did run a taxi service to the beach for anyone who didn't want to walk. Walked past some interesting small agriculture growing in derelict buildings, was like a Hobbit village. Amazing views. Saw figs, prickly pear, grapes, lemons. Beach was small and sandy. And not, in my opinion, worth the long hike down to it.

Ate in *DVenue* - never disappoints. Strange not to have Bea with us.

Didn't go to church this week. The day was nice but it didn't feel special, different. Didn't feel like Sunday.

Monday:
Big breakfast - lots of food in fridge to be eaten.

Went back to Dwejra. Had a boat trip. You get the boats from the little Inland Sea, €4 per person, takes 15 minutes. We went through a narrow passage in the rocks towards open sea. One woman got scared by the waves and deep water, so the boatman returned her to shore. She was apologetic and embarrassed but we were pleased - meant we got to enter the cool dark narrow bit twice for free. Mr Boatman pointed out deep blue water (it looked dyed) cool orange coral, caves, interesting rock formations. Excellent trip, not expensive and short enough for me to not get bored.

Found Blue Hole, which looks a lot bigger in guidebook photos. Saw Qawra Tower which the Knights built to guard Fungus Rock; but the car refused to stop at best photo stop on the hill. Went into the glass shop which had some surprisingly beautiful glass. I like Dwejra, it's busy, interesting and there are some really cool natural features. Scratchy rocks really mess up leather shoes though.

Came home via the craft village in Gharb. Males all pleased and excited when I suggested this, and I didn't feel hurried at all. Several small cabins housed various leather goods, various arts, lace, and local food products that you could taste. Bought some fig jam for the mothers.

We ate as much of the left-over food in the fridge as we could. There are also two bottles of wine. Without fail, when we arrived at a holiday villa, Husband buys two bottles of wine. We then spend the whole holiday eating and drinking in restaurants and bars, so the wine sits there until the last evening, when we debate what to do with it. This is a family tradition.

We swam, and went back to Ramla beach for a last sandcastle build, while I read.

Both our normal restaurants were closed, so we ate at *Breeze* - another restaurant in the square. The food took forever to come, and was then tepid, and we had to sit right next to the road. Not a great last meal.

I like Gozo. It's surprisingly empty but has a good range of restaurants and cafes. It has some pretty towns (I think St Lawrence is the prettiest) and some spectacular scenery. Plus, the signs and menus are all in English and the weather is hot. I hope to visit again one day.

Tuesday

We left the villa in good time. All the various ferries and roads were running as expected, so we arrived at the airport in plenty of time for our flight. In the waiting room, there was a piano, so Jay played. The other passengers filmed him on their mobile phones, which was great fun.

Flight was delayed by an hour.

When we eventually got on the plane, the boys were next to the emergency exit. The steward showed them how to operate the door, in case of an emergency. They assured her they were able to operate it.

When she left, they suggested to each other that perhaps they should have a practice. I could hear the woman sitting next to them, in a very anxious voice, saying that she thought that was unnecessary and they shouldn't touch the exit unless told to. I decided to not rescue her. Sometimes I don't protect the world from my family's humour.

Bangkok October 2015

I went to Bangkok for a couple of days. Husband was working there, so I decided to tag along.

We arrived Thursday night, COMPLETELY exhausted. It was a bad moment, 10 hours into the flight to Singapore, when I thought, "Ah, two more hours and we'll be there and I can get to the hotel and sleep…" then realised that we weren't doing that and we were catching another flight after we landed. Felt awful. I was flying premium economy (on airmiles – which is why I went via Singapore, direct flights get booked up) so the seat wasn't tiny but it was *so* noisy. Didn't sleep at all.

There was a sign at passport control, telling people that Thailand is a Buddhist country and the things that are disrespectful/illegal (like wearing a tee shirt with a picture of Buddha on it, buying a Buddha head, having a tattoo of Buddha). I thought it was a good idea – it's easy to cause offence by mistake.

Hotel (St. Regis) is lovely. Quite plain, but very clean and luxurious. We had a nap for a couple of hours, then went for a walk. It reminds me a lot of Xian, lots of people being busy, quite a dirty place but with an 'honest' feel to it – nothing pretentious. By the time we went to dinner, I had got over the long journey and had decided it WAS worth coming.

Dinner was nice, just ate normal food in hotel restaurant – too tired to be adventurous.

Went to bed about 8pm, slept really well for two hours, rest of the night bit of a struggle. (I think we are 7 hours ahead of UK time.)

Friday morning, husband went to work early (was in the office at 7:30 am.) I went back to sleep until 8:30. Then I decided to be brave and go to breakfast on my own. I hate doing stuff like that! I was standing in the lobby looking lost when a man asked if he could help. I said I just wanted a pastry and a coffee, not a full breakfast. He told me I could go and get a pastry from the buffet and he would bring me a take-out coffee. I sat in the drawing room – big comfy sofas, lots of dark wood – and ate my pastry. Much nicer than being in scary dining room on my own.

I went for a walk to see some Buddhist stuff. Not quite brave enough to use train or taxi on my own, so just walked. Everyone here speaks Thai, which sounds like Mandarin but is completely different and the writing looks like squiggles. Weather is cloudy/rainy/hot and humid. Walked for hours, brilliantly interesting. Lots of small industry – people carving doors, welding, etc. Everyone very friendly, feels safe here. Found some Chinese people to talk to. Not many foreigners apart from in the tourist attractions.

It rained hard, more rain than I've ever seen before, I was paddling as I walked, the water went right over my shoes, was glad I was wearing short trousers. I had an umbrella but it did very little to stop the rain, which gushed down the edges and splattered me as I walked. It was warm though, too hot for a coat. I rather liked it. Husband's map disintegrated so I'll have to try and find him another one before he finds it. There was a covered walkway, so some of the way was relatively dry.

There are lots of elephant statues everywhere. I went to Golden Mount, which is a man-made hill with a Buddhist temple on top. Had very good views of Bangkok. Also had a coffee shop near the top, it seemed slightly incongruous to see Buddhist monks in their orange robes, drinking in a coffee shop.

Saturday we got a taxi to a floating market (two hours out of Bangkok). It was really interesting, so glad it didn't rain. There were lots of stalls around the edge of the river. If you showed any interest in anything, they put out a hook and towed your boat in. There were also floating stalls and boats selling snacks. Not sure how they managed to deep-fry dumplings on a boat, but they did.

It was really crowded, sometimes the boats got jammed and had to be pushed apart. Lots of colour and smells and noise.

Everyone is meant to turn off their motor when they enter the market and use paddles but our boatman didn't, which spoilt it a bit.

Afterwards we were offered the chance to go and ride on an elephant. It was very tempting, I would love to do that. I just had this feeling though that the elephants wouldn't be kept very well and that possibly it was cruel. I felt I didn't want to ride on an abused elephant. It would have been upsetting to see, I like elephants, so we declined.

Had lunch at hotel then decided to go to Royal Palace. Arrived just after it shut, tried to blag way inside, failed. Walked around a bit. Lots of big photos of royal family on various buildings. The Thai people are very patriotic, we saw several cars with "Long live the king" as bumper stickers. I also read that it's a huge insult if foreigners don't stand up for the national anthem when it's played in cinemas.

Went to Wat Pho, the oldest and biggest temple in Bangkok. I expect if you had not recently been around several other temples, it would be rather spectacular. I'm afraid it just felt like 'another museum' for me. The art was amazing but I am a bit beyond being amazed by temple art now.

Tried to get water boat back to hotel but it was all a bit confusing and we were tired. Got a taxi. They all refused to do it by meter and wanted 300 baht to take us (always good to negotiate fares in Bangkok before a trip, especially the tuk-tuks, which are well known as rip-off men). Decided that as 300 baht is only £6, we would take one anyway.

Sunday, early trip to airport. Seems like I arrived a week ago. I like Bangkok. The people were all friendly and smiled a lot and I felt very safe walking around on my own. I probably wouldn't feel so comfortable with young children – you did have to be aware all the time. (I was nearly run over by a motorbike at one point. I was on the path and he came up behind me to avoid the traffic. He smiled and called "sorry, sorry" so I didn't really mind, but I was glad I wasn't walking with a child.)

Maybe I will try to come for longer next time.

Singapore October 2015

Flight to Singapore uneventful. I was in economy, next to a man who twitched continually and behind a woman who pushed her seat right back as soon as we'd taken off and then kept stretching her arms up and putting her hand over the screen in front of me. Resisted urge to slap both of them.

Also resisted the meal: plastic scrambled eggs. I just ate the bread roll and dessert, which was garnished with a strange plastic looking fruit. I bit it. Think it really was plastic.

St. Regis hotel in Singapore – pretty much exactly the same as the one in Bangkok.

I slept most of the afternoon. Then we got a taxi to the old part of town to an old colonial hotel, Raffles, famous for the cocktail *Singapore Sling*. Had one in the long bar – very traditional in a sort of Disney, pretend way. It was very pleasant, all clean and very atmospheric with lots of dark wood, ceiling fans, sacks of nuts on the table, with nut husks all over the floor. The cocktail is tall and sticky with froth on top and served with a pineapple chunk and a cherry. Mine was sadly lacking in discernible alcohol.

There is currently a lot of air pollution in Singapore – a 'haze' as they call it (it looks misty all the time). This is pretty bad and causes itchy eyes and breathing problems when it's at its worst. It's caused by people burning great swathes of land in Indonesia.

The people in Singapore and Malaysia are furious about this, especially as it happens every year. They have to close schools, cancel flights and avoid going outside when the pollution is at its worst. The Indonesian government are making plans to stop the problem but from reading the papers (which are in Singapore, so possibly a bit biased) they make plans but don't actually change anything. This is a problem that seems to have occurred every year for about forty years.

On Monday I walked around the historical part of the city. I got a taxi to Raffles hotel, then walked past St Andrew's cathedral – I could have been in England. The buildings are very European in style, with steps and pillars, and lots of white stone and red brick.

I arrived at the National Gallery but couldn't work out the doors. They appeared to be bolted shut from top to bottom. The sign said the gallery was open but I tried pushing, pulling and sliding the glass doors – they did not move. I suspect this was my fault. However, peering through the glass, the gallery did look very empty, so perhaps other people had problems getting inside too. Seems to be bit of a design fault for a door to not open (is rather the defining point of a door, separates it from a wall).

Abandoned non-opening doors and walked to river, crossed a bridge to Fullerton Hotel. This has the absolutely best sculpture outside. Walked along quay. There are lots of tiny restaurants, the whole world in one lane. I passed English pubs, Spanish taverns, Chinese restaurants (these had the biggest shellfish outside in great glass tanks). It was a little like being in the Epcot Centre at Disney. There were good views of the Marina Bay Hotel (which looks like it has a giant boat perched on its roof) but it was too hazy for a decent photo. Several people were wearing face masks to keep the pollution out.

I followed South Bridge Road up to China Town, passing Park Royal Hotel. This is opposite Hong Lim Park, but actually there was more stuff growing on the hotel than in the park – green blankets of plants spilling over every balcony.

I passed tailors claiming they could make a suit in six hours, Chinese sign-painters with canaries singing in cages, a Hindu temple with shoes littering the street outside, stalls selling silk, beads, masks, key-rings, lots of street food.

There was a mosque with a big sign outside, declaring that Islam is a peaceful religion and should not be judged by the actions of a few terrorists. I thought that was rather sad.

It was hot and humid, so I walked back to the park and drank a Sprite before getting a taxi back to hotel. In Singapore you cannot hail taxis in the street. (I spent a long time trying to do that on a previous visit. They ignore you.) You have to wait at a designated taxi stand, which is a lot like a bus stop. It's easiest to just go to a hotel foyer and wait for one to arrive. Singapore has a lot of hotels.

Singapore is clean and safe and has lots to see that is interesting. I did not though feel that I had seen the 'real' Singapore, I have left with no impression of the people who live there. Perhaps it is harder in a more developed city to see how people live and work, to glimpse the real culture beneath what is presented to visitors. I wonder if the same could be said of London, I wonder what visitors see when they tour our tourist attractions.

Sri Lanka May 2016

As we flew into Sri Lanka, we could see the extent of the recent floods. In some places they have had nearly 35cm of rain in a day. We saw destroyed roads, flooded houses, rivers that had burst their banks. Several people have been killed.

Immigration was efficient, then we collected our luggage and walked out through the Duty Free shop. In England (and every other country I have visited) this shop is full of chocolate and alcohol and cigarettes. In Sri Lanka, it's full of washing machines. And fridges. Obviously holidays abroad stimulate the local population into a frenzy of kitchen appliances desire.

As we drove to the hotel, we saw streets of shops selling spare parts for tuk-tuks, cars with whole shrines on their dashboards, lots of flooding. We passed Hindu temples, golden Buddhas on roundabouts, giant statues of Mary. There were people hanging clothes to dry on wire fences, trees, anywhere they could really. Many of the houses were very simple, made of corrugated iron and bits of wood. Some had cows in their tiny garden area.

Hotel is lovely: Galle Face Hotel, Colombo. It's an old colonial building, full of dark wood, carved elephants and ceiling fans. Our room has a balcony, right next to the Indian Ocean.

I feel a little like I have walked into a film set. At 5pm every day they play the bagpipes and lower the flag (a tradition from the 1800s when the British were ruling here).

This evening we walked along the sea front – a bombardment of the senses. Crashing waves and a babble of languages mingle with fried seafood and spun sugar. Children playing, kites flying, an ancient snake charmer, joined by his friend with a monkey, as the sun dipped behind the brick built pier, silhouetting groups of men and families.

I've never seen a snake charmer before. He took the lid off his basket and played his pipe and a snake – think it was a cobra – rose up. Then the snake got bored and started to slide towards us, so we left – he was bit of a naughty snake!

We ate dinner in the hotel buffet. Very nice, though the Sri Lankan idea of 'very mild' for a curry is somewhat different to mine. We watched a man frying hoppers – they're bowl-shaped pancakes, made with flour, egg, coconut milk and yeast. Delicious. You fill them with something savoury and roll them up to eat with your *right* hand (using your left hand – the toilet hand – is a bad mistake to make).

Thursday and Friday
Husband went into office, I worked in hotel room, putting through the changes my editor had suggested for my book, *Hidden Faces*. When I needed a break, I stood on the balcony and absorbed the sea and palm trees. Not bad at all.

Went for a fast walk along sea front. Lots of families, groups of boys in white tunics walking home from their Madras, street vendors, stray dogs sleeping in the sunshine. There's a big Buddhist festival over the next three days and they're decorating the streets with giant lotus flowers and lights and flags.

The weather goes from bright sunshine to complete deluge in a flash, you can watch the storms coming in across the sea. There are signs up warning people not to swim because of dangerous currents and poisonous fish.

Saturday
We were both ill. Food poisoning. Ghastly. Cancelled trip to see elephants. But at least we both had it at the same time, so only lost one day of holiday. Annoying because I have been very careful, drinking only bottled water and eating only hot cooked foods. Makes you thankful for toilets.

Sunday

Walked past the green and the harbour to fort region. This area was more official, lots of armed gates, groups of military. Saw the old customs house, onion shaped roofs, faded Victorian mansions. It is similar to Mumbai, but less intense – fewer smells and colour, less noise, less people.

If we stood still, even for a second, a man would emerge from nowhere, always wearing an open necked shirt, and asked where we were from and would we like a tuk-tuk, a tour, or a cup of tea.

We passed several booths decorated with lanterns and sculptures – I think for the festival, it looked like it might be a competition. Saw a tiny old lady sweeping. Husband raised his thumb at her, told her the booth was "very good." She smiled at him, no teeth, scant hair, ragged clothes, but a beautiful smile. Her whole face lit up. Precious moment.

Looked round the old Dutch hospital – now a complex of gift shops and cafes. Got a tuk-tuk back to the hotel. Agreed price beforehand (very important) but when we arrived, he said he had no change and gleefully showed us his empty wallet. Husband said it wasn't a problem and the driver could wait while husband went into the hotel and got some change.

Had a drink in the bar, under ceiling fans. Watched crows stealing food from the buffet. Listened to them screech while the sea bashed against the beach and the wind stirred the palm trees. Worth coming.

Got a tuk-tuk to Pettah region. Here they have a station and streets of market stalls. A rabbit warren. It was one of those experiences that feels scary but actually, as long as you kept your wits about you, it was just interesting. The people wanted to sell us stuff (at inflated prices) not murder us.

Hunted for a cushion cover. Not easy with no local language. Tried miming and got shown lots of bedding and pyjamas. In the end I bought some fabric, very ethnic, will make cushion cover when I get home. One seller offered to sell husband "a better tee-shirt," which I thought was hilarious but husband found less amusing.

Walked back to hotel along sea front. Loads of people again, all very happy. We are the only white people. I like it here.

***

A Day at the Pinnawela Elephant Orphanage

We hired a driver from the hotel and spent the day driving to the orphanage. It was really worth the time and money, as saw so much. We paid about £25 entry and local people paid about 50p each. They are quite open about this, they charge lots more for tourists.

We saw the elephants in the main area, then crossed the road and went to the river. There are lots of shops for tourists. Then we heard the elephants start to approach.

"Move out the way!" shouted the man as the elephants approached the river.

I thought this was bit of an over reaction, there was plenty of room for him to pass, but I did move slightly more to the side.

Then I realised more elephants were coming behind him. And more...

Great lumbering beasts, so big, so intent on getting to the river. A bit like a crowd of nine year old boys rushing to play, very likely to knock someone with their shoulder by mistake. But these shoulders were huge, I would be toppled and crushed within seconds. I moved further back, up some steps leading to a cafe. The elephants lumbered by.

I cannot explain how exciting it was. The thrill of a brass band that vibrates deep inside your being, the thrall of something wonderful and scary all at the same time. Best sight ever. They trooped down to the river and then behaved a lot like my family would. One stood away from the others and just enjoyed being in the river. One submerged completely and just lifted a foot from time to time. One squirted himself and anyone near. One was very task focussed and had a good wash. One tried to organise all the others. I won't name them...

We saw them at the Pinnawela Elephant Orphanage. I was slightly worried about how ethical it was – there were some chains and men with sharp sticks and quite a lot of shouting. But bull elephants are randy in the spring and need to be controlled, and I don't know anything about rearing elephants (clipping a duck's wings probably looks cruel to someone who doesn't understand) so I will reserve judgement. Certainly they looked happy as they went to the river. And there were lots of warning signs – they hadn't been tamed, they were still wild animals (which I like).

We saw babies being bottle fed and adults stripping leaves from trees. But nothing compared to the bath in the river.

The whole day was good – a chance to see more of Sri Lanka. We saw birds as vibrant blue as a slush puppy, paddy fields being planted with rice, pineapples growing on a bush, a woman leading three porcupines on a lead. And we stood in raindrops that felt like whole cups of warm water being thrown at us. But really, I just wanted to tell you about the elephants.

I like Sri Lanka. It has an *unspoiltness* about it. If you are planning to visit, come soon, before it changes.

Argentina 2016

As we flew into Buenos Aires, the horizon was red with dawn. A beautiful end to a 14 hour flight.

On the way to the hotel, we passed a demonstration. They had blocked two lanes of the road (the roads here are really wide) and they had banners (which were in Spanish, so I couldn't read them). People had just abandoned their cars in the road and gone to join them. Our driver said this happens a lot.

The hotel, Park Tower, is right next to The English Tower. Our taxi driver said this was because it was a gift from the English. The guidebook said it was because it looks like Big Ben. It doesn't. Opposite is the war memorial for the Falklands War (interesting choice of position). The politics are complicated, but the fact that so many young men died is heartbreaking, whatever your nationality.

We looked around Galerias Pacifico, which used to be an art gallery but is now a shopping mall. The walls were beautifully decorated. The shops were just shops, so didn't spend long in there.

We ate *empanachas* for supper. They are like mini fried pasties. Go well with beer.

The night wasn't terrible and I want to keep to UK time as it's such a short trip. We ordered room service coffee at 4am. The coffee here is very dark, the milk tastes like evaporated milk, so you don't want much. The room service menu has a separate price list. I'm guessing this is because inflation is currently 25%, so it saves them reprinting the whole menu every time prices go up. It was quite a challenge to get Argentinian currency before we came, and no one will buy it back from us when we go home. Most places accept credit cards or US dollars.

We walked to *Casa Rosada*, where Evita made her impassioned speeches from the balcony. I can't tell you how much it was enhanced by Husband singing all the Lloyd Webber songs in my ear, very loudly and slightly off-key. The palace is pink – according to the guide book this is because it's painted in cow's blood. I wish I hadn't known that, think I will stop reading guide book and make up my own reasons for things.

Crossed several major roads – multi-lane roads are a feature of Argentina. They do have lights to help you cross though. Saw a bridge which is meant to resemble Tango dancers. Husband suggested we could strike a Tango pose and take selfies. We didn't.

We got a taxi to *La Boca* region. We were told in the hotel that it wasn't safe for us to wander around, but there was one street, *Caminito*, which was full of tourists. We saw lots of painted houses, cafes with Tango dancers and singers, lots of street art. It was nice and interesting, though not very 'real'.

We got a taxi back to the hotel. We were told to only take taxis that had writing on the doors. If they had writing on both front and back doors, it means they're owned by a company, so they are the best ones. They have a light at the front which tells you when they're free. There are loads of taxis, so it was easy.

Went to *La Recoleta*. This is mainly a large cemetery, which is not a place I would usually visit but it featured in all the guide books and was recommended by our taxi driver. We walked there from the hotel. Passed a few people sleeping in the street, whole families in some cases, which is never a comfortable experience. The only other place that I have passed homeless children is Mumbai.

Found *La Recoleta*, in the middle of a park with market stalls. Was glad the family weren't with me to complain about me liking spooky places and not being 'normal.' I snapped a few pictures, none of which really captured the atmosphere. The cemetery is huge, like a small village of monuments and booths. Some had steps leading down, littered with soiled bags, empty bottles, coated in dust and cobwebs. Some had coffins stacked in view of the doorway covered in white lace cloths. Some coffins were crumbling, threatening to spill their contents, others were pristine, polished oak with shiny fixtures. The booths were white marble, grey granite, weathered stone and black steel gates. There were lots of statues and angels and domes. A little like miniature cathedrals, with the dead being worshipped rather than God.

It was a little incongruous, after passing families of homeless people. I am a tourist here, I don't know what help is available, but at a glance it looked as if the dead have better shelter than the poor.

We saw the tomb where Evita is buried, and several other dignitaries, then we left.

Went to *La Biela*, a traditional coffee house just outside the cemetery, opposite a giant ancient gum tree. It had a motor racing theme due to being a favourite spot in the 1950's for drivers and fans. There was memorabilia on the walls and spanners carved into the chair backs. It had a lovely traditional Argentinian feel, we could've stayed there for hours.

We drank coffee sprinkled with cinnamon, which tasted almost of oregano and ate *'alfajores'*, which were shortbread biscuits filled with *dolce leche*. The cafe was empty when we arrived at 9:30 and was full by 10am –lots of well-maintained elderly Argentinians and young tourists.

Ate a very late lunch in a *parilla* (name for a steak restaurant). Walked from hotel heading south, along narrow streets, littered with blankets reserving sites for the homeless, dog mess, and broken pavements. The houses on either side were a muddle of faded villas with gargoyles and balconies and modern apartment blocks. We passed a burnt out theatre, a derelict mansion, and tiny newsagents. It felt real, interesting and full of life. Buenos Aires is growing on me – perhaps you need more than a day here before you notice it properly.

Arrived at *Chiquilin* in Calle Sarmento. Peered in window and it looked clean, so went in and sat in a corner table, under oil paintings and bottles of wine on shelves below the low ceiling.

Ate more steak than the whole family would normally eat at home. All the restaurants here have an abundance of waiters dressed in black and white, most of whom seem to either speak English or understand my very bad Spanish.

On our last day we paid for a tour out of the city, booked through the hotel. It was brilliant. We wanted to see *La Pampas*, the cattle rearing plains of Argentina.

As it's 'low season' it was just the two of us and a man in his car. He drove us out of the city, explaining things about the buildings as we passed them, so we started to understand a little more about Argentina.

He then took us to a town and a ranch, introducing us to various people and showing us different places. It was all very friendly, it felt more like an acquaintance introducing us to his friends than a paid tour guide. It was also nice because, unlike on other tours we have done, we weren't taken somewhere random (like a jade factory) and then left in awkward silence while the owner waits for us to buy something that we don't really want. This guide didn't even take us into the shop part of the places we visited – he wanted to show us things, not sell us things.

As we left Buenos Aires, we passed some poorer areas, they looked like the favelas we saw in Brazil, though maybe not quite as poor. Marcello told us that they were mostly occupied by immigrants from Peru, Paraguay, Chile. He said they work hard, often in construction, and are gradually moving to different areas. I asked if the homeless people that we saw on the streets were also immigrants, but he said that no, they were probably Argentinians. Economics are very hard here, due to the very high inflation. Everyone is hopeful that the newly elected government can turn things around in the next couple of years.

Marcello also told us about the gauchos that we'd be seeing. They are mainly men who work with cattle. They wear either hats (cowboy hats) or berets. The ranches, which are called *"estancia"* breed cattle, plus horses for working, polo and racing.

We went to the little town of San Antonio Areco. My favourite bit was the gaucho bars, I felt like I had walked into a cowboy film. They are still used today, though they've preserved the historical features. There was a post outside, for tying up the horses. Inside, the walls were shelved to the ceiling and full of ancient bottles of liquor, soap, shoes, tins of tea – all the things that the gauchos would have come into town to buy.

The counter used to have bars all along it, with little windows for the drinks to be passed through, a bit like the railings or glass screens that you get in banks and post-offices today. This was to protect the staff and stock from the rowdy gauchos in an age when alcohol was more expensive. Is this where the term 'bar' originates from?

The floors were tiled, there were ceiling fans and even an old fashioned till. You could so imagine a cowboy walking in and shooting all the bottles.

We also saw silver smiths at work. They make lots of horse related things – cups for polo matches, silver versions of the things that gauchos carry, horse ornaments. The gauchos carry knives (you can buy them in silver sheaves) and *boleadoras*. These were originally stones, wrapped in leather at the end of ropes. The gauchos would throw them, lasso style, at the legs of ostriches, to catch them. You can now buy silver versions, the stones in leather replaced with ornate silver balls.

We saw a chocolate shop. They make the chocolate themselves from cacao, so we saw the beans and husks – which were much bigger than I expected, almost the size of coconuts. The bean is inside and they heat it first, to separate the cacao and the butter (which is white, but hard – more like chalk than butter). They then add milk and sugar to make the chocolate. I would've liked to watch the process with the bean, but we weren't taken to see that bit, we could only watch them work with the melted chocolate, through a glass panel.

A traditional drink in Argentina is called *'mate'* (pronounced 'mah-tae'). The straws have a filter and people walk around drinking it. It's a herb, like a bitter tea. You can buy the drinking straw/filters and flasks just about everywhere, a whole range of prices for the same product.

So, after visiting the little town, we drove out to *La Pampa* - the grassy plains, and to a ranch. The road to the ranch was a dirt track, but still really wide (four lanes wide). ALL the roads in Argentina seem to be very wide.

The ranch we visited was called *Portenia Estancia*, and was used for a film with Antonio Banderos and Emma Thompson.

We were shown around the house and gardens, and given snacks and lunch. Again, it felt more like we were guests than tourists, people were very friendly and hospitable. A gaucho, Fredisco Pereyra, took us riding. We were given polite, slow horses as neither of us can ride.

We saw lots of cattle, pigs, horses, dogs. Mostly we saw grass – as far as you could see, stretching across the great flat plains. There were lots of clumps of pampas grass, which I assume is where it got its name (It's huge, you could fit several of England into the space.)

Lunch was at a long table in a room with a fire at one end. There were flowers on the table and we were served meats and salads, then pancakes with dolce latte and bananas. Along the table were people with other tour guides, so we listened to a range of languages and chatted with different people.

After lunch, the gauchos played the guitar and sang some folk songs (which actually, was very tuneful, so was nice rather than embarrassing) and we were shown some traditional dances.

The national bird of Argentina is *rufous hornero*, we saw lots of the nests. They look a bit like *house martin* nests in England and have a little hole which always faces north (because here, north is warm. I never got used to that, in my mind, north is cold). The gauchos use the bird nests for orienteering, even if there is no sun, they can see which way is north.

Came back tired but happy.

The film (which shows the estancia we visited), 'Imagining Argentina' is a bit odd. I think the people at the estancia were slightly embarrassed by it, and I wonder if they had realised before it was released what it was about, as it didn't show Argentina in a very good light. It's not at all the sort of film I would usually watch, as it was horribly violent and a bit weird, but it was interesting to see places that we visited. It shows the story of Argentina during the late 1970's, when the regime refused to allow any opposition. It was a time when lots of people went missing, they became known as 'The Disappeared'.

I had no idea, before we visited Buenos Aires, of any of the history. In my guide book, it said that every Thursday there is a procession of women outside *Casa Rosada*, protesting about The Disappeared. They are *still* waiting for information about their sons, husbands, sisters. I didn't go to look, so I don't know if the women are there are not. But that so many people disappeared, is terrible – estimates of 30,000 people went missing between mid-1970s and 1982, when the regime collapsed following the war over the Falkland Islands. It reminded me of stories about the old Soviet Union.

As I said, I had never heard, I had no idea what was happening. It is very easy to ignore the circumstances in countries that don't affect us. But the world is small, these places are accessible, the people are the same as us.

Argentina still has political problems, especially with their economy. But it has excellent natural resources and an intelligent, educated population. Buenos Aires is like a faded Paris. With the right governance, it could be a very different place in the near future. The new government seems a sensible one.

It has been a lovely trip. If ever you come here, the two things you MUST do are eat *alfajores* with your coffee and visit a *parrilla* (the Argentinian version of a grilled meat restaurant. They cook roughly a whole cow at a time).

I would also recommend that you try to avoid coming with someone who only knows some of the words to, *Don't Cry For Me Argentina*, but who sings it every time you pass a monument to Evita. There are lots of these monuments in Argentina, trust me.

Uruguay May 2016

Yesterday we went to Uruguay for the day.

We bought the boat tickets online, which was a bit confusing as we knew there were two boats – one which takes an hour and one which takes three hours – but the timetable and prices didn't seem to correspond. Our Spanish was only *almost* good enough. Managed it eventually. We paid the equivalent of £75 each for day return tickets.

Walked to the boat terminal through a freezing cold city. I wish I'd packed my big coat. We went through passport control and immigration, then sat in a large waiting room for an hour. I now have extra stamps in my passport. At one window the Argentinian official gave the exit stamp, then you shuffle along to the next window, where an Uruguayan official gives you an entry stamp. Kinda cool.

The ferry was clean and comfortable. I needed to use the loo on board and was expecting the usual stinky boat toilet, but it was spotless, very clean. The gang-plank in Uruguay was a bit of a challenge for some of the elderly passengers, so Husband did his gentleman bit and helped a few old ladies (while I stood ready with my camera in case they fell in the water. No, not really!)

We walked straight out the ferry terminal, turned right at the first cross roads, walked about ten minutes and arrived in the old town. Very easy, despite Husband telling me that none of the road names matched his map. (There were signs showing the way, we didn't need a map.)

The old town was brilliant, it felt like being in the Caribbean (but a lot colder. May is Winter). There was water lapping on the shore, lots of greenery, cobbled streets, old buildings. Perfect.

We sat in a street cafe in Colonia and drank cappuccinos sprinkled with cinnamon. Music from the shop next door, dappled sunlight through the trees, vintage cars driving past. Double perfect.

There were also lots of stray dogs. Not so perfect. But they seemed mostly well fed and healthy, so we avoided them in case they were rabid, but they weren't threatening.

The vintage cars seem to mainly advertise the buildings they are parked outside. There were lots of them. Colonia is a world heritage site, so I'm not sure what was 'real' and what was for tourists. It was nice though, and very peaceful.

There was an old church, with white-washed stone walls, icons and echoes. Outside was a square with ruins, noisy birds in the palm trees, sunshine and the ever constant sound of waves lapping. Everywhere smells of wood charcoal.

We ate lunch in a little Bistro facing the water. There were signs up saying you should book ahead, I think it gets very busy here at weekends and in the summer. It was very clean and the food was nice.

The prices here are all in Uruguayan Pesos, Argentinian Pesos and US dollars. Or you can pay with credit cards. I wasn't sure if the language was Spanish or Portuguese (it's Spanish) but as both sound exactly the same when I speak them, it didn't make too much difference. Most people spoke at least a little English, some were fluent.

The girl who served us in the cafe was completely fluent in English, she could calculate prices in three different currencies, she was well presented and clearly intelligent. Plus, the cleanliness of the country is much better than England. It was the same when we went to Brazil; I expected small rural cafes and public toilets to have slightly dodgy hygiene, but they were always scrupulously clean. Public toilets in England are usually disgusting. I think travel is good for me, it challenges my preconceived ideas. The world is smaller than I think, lots of countries do things better than we do.

We strolled some more. I loved being near the coast. Lots of green plants and seed pods had washed ashore.

Looked in a couple of gift shops and I bought a cushion cover for my collection. It's made of cow hide, which seemed very appropriate as they raise a lot of cows in Uruguay, on the plains that join Argentina.

Got the ferry back to Argentina. A really lovely day.

Kraków June 2016

Poland was unexpected. Why has no one ever told me what it is like? Husband had a work trip in Warsaw, so we decided to come to Kraków the weekend before, have a romantic weekend. Before I came, I had this image of post Soviet Union countries all being very similar – lots of flat-roofed, concrete buildings, all very ugly and sinister. I came to Poland for the experience, to see with my own eyes what I had imagined. It turns out I had imagined wrong!

First we flew to Kraków. We flew with easyJet, which I quite like actually. Check-in was quick (you did it yourself but there were people to help if you got stuck) and you didn't pay for anything you wouldn't use. I paid £6 on board for a cheese roll and a drink. It was a nice cheese roll.

We arrived in Kraków and got a taxi to the hotel. I was interested to watch the city through the taxi window – was more like Bruges than Tower Hamlets. There was a river with floating restaurants, a castle, cobbled streets, lots of cyclists.

The following day we walked around the city. I wanted to go to see where Schindler's factory was (as in Oskar Schindler, who saved so many Jews in the war). We walked through the Jewish Quarter, and saw lots of old buildings, houses with window boxes of flowers, synagogues, Torah schools. Before the war, a quarter of Poland's population was Jewish.

You could then walk across the bridge, over the river – the same route that the Jews would have had to walk when they were told to leave the Jewish area, their homes, and go to live in the ghetto.

There were about 20,000 Jews squashed into a few streets. Obviously the fences had gone, but many of the streets were still named *Getta* and you could see the old chemist shop, which is now a museum. The square, where people were sorted –

allocated into houses or trains to the camps – now has statues of giant metal chairs. Empty chairs to show the lives that were stolen. Some of the chairs were normal sized and near the tram stop. Husband sat on one. I worried this was disrespectful, but apparently the sculptures were planned like that, to show that anyone could have been taken.

Schindler's factory, a few minutes walk away, was just a factory. Here there were lots of concrete buildings. There were photos in the factory windows of the Jews who had worked there and the inside is now a museum and an art gallery, which I didn't fancy looking at (not very keen on museums). I picked up a leaflet about a tour to *Oswiecim* (which is better known by its German name of Auschwitz). Decided visit would be traumatic, and not really the right thing for romantic weekend away with husband, better to go as a separate trip in the future.

Went to old part of Kraków. This is beautiful. Cobbled streets (glad I wasn't wearing heels), horse and carriages, ornate churches, weddings (with the bride and groom wearing very synthetic clothes which looked almost like costumes), Prussian architecture, trams, sunshine. There were little markets full of breads and pickles and crafts. Really, it was *so* like going to Bruges at Christmas time, but with sunshine!

The churches were dark, full of candles and gilt and oil paintings. I'm not sure what they were used for during the communist reign – whether religion was outlawed.

There were street entertainers, ice-creams, people with designer dogs. And always, just under the surface, in the back of your mind, the city's troubled history. So much suffering. I don't know how long it takes to forget things like that.

We walked for miles. People in Poland do walk, the hotel and Tourist Information told us we could walk to places, which we could, but it was a long walk. Most other countries would've put us into taxis, even though we prefer to walk. It might be why, unlike when you sit and watch people in London, very few people were over weight. I got sore feet.

We caught a train to Warsaw. The station was more like an airport terminal, with all the cars parking on top. You then get a lift down to the correct platform (yellow timetables show you which platform you need, though our taxi driver also told us). We had bought our tickets online before we left England.

The train arrived on the platform forty minutes before it left, with the doors shut. Lots of anxious people positioned themselves near the doors, worried about luggage space (our seats were pre-booked). It was fine.

The train was clean, efficient and comfortable. It cost about £40 from Kraków to Warsaw and took two hours. Watching the countryside as it whizzed past the window, it wasn't so different to English countryside, though the buildings were different – especially the churches with onion shaped domes on top.

Delhi

Slept well. Breakfast in hotel. I'm trying to only eat hot cooked food and no meat (because I'm told, Indians eat very little meat, so the whole process from animal to table is likely to be less 'safe' than in England). It was hard to resist bacon and a wonderful array of pastries. I did have some milk in my coffee, but didn't eat the butter, which although was pasteurised had been left on warm table, not in chilled cabinet. Am possibly being too fussy. Husband ate everything.

We walked around the old part of Delhi. A few years ago, in Mumbai, I bought an Indian tunic and trousers (the trousers – baggy at top and tight at ankle are called *'salwar'*. The tunic is called *'kameez'* and the veil/scarf is called *'dupatta.'*) I felt bit of a wombat in the hotel, which is full of Westerners, but on the street it felt much more comfortable to be dressed the same as everyone else. The clothes are also very comfortable, as the fabric is light and the veil can be used as a sunshade over your head. It also covered my bag rather neatly – being aware of pick pockets is part of being in India.

We saw the Red Fort, a big mosque and a market. Best was the market, teeming with people, noisy with traffic and shouts and loud speakers from Hindu temples. There was a constant smell – spices and diesel fumes and sweet food and urine and incense, all in a tangle. The traffic was mostly on the road, but motorbikes and tuk-tuks sometimes avoided lights by driving along paths, so you had to be alert. It was wonderful and foreign and intense.

There was some kind of parade, with a few lorries with loud speakers and people shouting slogans. No idea what it was about. Some young people on one lorry shouted at us to take their photo, so we did, which made them all laugh. I had some sweets in my bag. I took a handful out to the lorry. The teenagers reached for them, long brown fingers and bangled wrists. They all shouted *"Thank you, thank you"*, and I made it back to the path without being squished under a lorry. It was a nice moment. Travel to different cultures is often like that – loads of difficult things to get used to and the occasional special moment that makes you glad you came.

We booked a tour through the hotel to *Huymayun's Tomb*. It was a short drive away and we went in a couple of minivans.

Huymayun's Tomb was built before the Taj Mahal. It was lovely. There was a beautiful domed building, which the Persians had taught them how to build. Apparently, to build a huge dome, you need a smaller one inside so it doesn't collapse. Persians were rather good at building them.

The gardens are an integral part of the monument. They reflect 'paradise' and have water and trees and birds. Peaceful. There were lots of stars, which some tourists thought were the *Star of David*. Our guide told us that as the Persians were Muslim, they wouldn't allow any depiction of living things, so the Indians used geometric patterns, which included the stars. They have no link to the Jewish star – just as the many swastikas have no link to the Nazi symbol.

We drove back via India Gate, which is inscribed with the names of Indian martyrs. Opposite, at the end of a long wide road, is the president's residence, *Vijay Chowk*. It would be magnificent to look from one to the other, but there was too much pollution haze, so was all rather difficult to see. The round parliament building is also there.

We also passed lots of queues outside banks. Each bank has a guard on the door, armed with a stick. There are two queues, one of women and one of men. The government have recently withdrawn some money, with no notice, and people are having to exchange their old currency at banks. They stand so close together that they are touching, stomach against the back of the person in front. I guess so no one can push in. There was some shouting, but we didn't see any fighting. I wonder how long it will remain calm, the queues seem longer every day.

I am taking note of everything I see, so that I can base a novel here: *Clara – A Good Psychopth?* There is something compelling about India.

Cyprus Family Holiday Diary 2016

Saturday
Met Bea and Boyfriend at Gatwick. Ate big brunch in Lebanese restaurant. Males drank beers – *at 11am*.

Flight uneventful. 4 hours.

Paphos airport efficient – and empty – wondered why. I used toilet. You can sometimes tell a lot about a country from the toilets. These were clean but I was slightly perturbed by the signs, which told you to not stand on the seat – is that a thing here?

Bought water, collected hire car – which, for 7 people, is more of a van.

Drive to hotel long. Jay map-read, with relatively little abuse from family.

Hotel (Hilton, Nicosia) nice. Dinner by pool. Hotel has a glass elevator. Rooms nice. Learnt Greek for 'Thank you' – '*ef-harry-stom*'.

Sunday
Late breakfast. Males very late. Nice range of food. I ate too much (meant to be losing weight). Males didn't drink beer.

Swam/read. Weather very hot (might be why airport was empty).

Drove to Nicosia Old Town. Van very wide for narrow streets. Parked (stressful) and walked around. Wandered, by chance, to border with Turkish-controlled northern section. Saw sandbags, and barbed wire, and a young soldier who picked up his rifle as we approached. Decided not to try and chat (wasn't sure my eight words of Turkish would make much of a conversation. Plus thought he might shoot me).

The whole *divided Cyprus* thing seems strange to me. I missed it at the time, so will explain briefly:

After the Brits left in about 1960, the Cypriots were a mix of Greeks and Turks, who lived peacefully alongside each other.

In 1974, *according to the Turkish Cypriots*, a few Greek Cypriots were pressing for the island to be joined to Greece. They staged a coup, backed by Greece, trying to overthrow the government by force. In order to protect the Turkish Cypriots, Turkey sent in their army, who marched down from the north.

This history is told rather differently by *Greek Cypriots*, who claim the Turkish army invaded Cyprus, unhindered by the UN, and have since refused to leave. They now state the north of their country is under Turkish Occupation.

I can offer no insights as to which is the true opinion. Probably there is some truth on both sides and ordinary people, who just wanted to get on with their lives, were hurt on both sides. I can tell you that the border is odd. It looks temporary, like something students have erected as a dare overnight – but with armed guards, who also look like students. The country is now divided, north and south, with what is called 'the green line' running through the middle. This is patrolled and fenced, with passport border controls and military and signs telling you not to take photographs or enter certain zones. It is odd.

However, for a marriage, I can see that a *'green line'* has certain benefits. Tried to instigate a green line in hotel room (when in Rome...etc) It didn't work. I clearly also need Turkish soldiers.

The old town in south Nicosia seemed a bit run down. Not sure if this is because we were seeing it mid summer (when sensible people are elsewhere). There was a strange mix of very expensive shops right next to very cheap shops. We wandered round for a while, then ate dinner in a boiling hot kebab place (which said it had air conditioning, but if it did, they hadn't turned it on!) Husband worried about the drink/driving laws half way through a *Keo* beer, which boys kindly finished for him. We were given tiny pots of bitter yogurt for dessert. Most of us passed them straight to Boyfriend.

Monday

Breakfast at 9. Ate loads again. Then waiter appeared with fresh pastries so ate those too. Diet not going well.

Sandwiches by pool. Looked around hotel and discovered there's a bar with free drinks and snacks. Males view this as a challenge.

Drove into Old Town. Found easier carpark. Walked up to the 'green line' and showed our passports at border control. Walked through a deserted bit of road – the 'buffer zone' – (wondered if the people who owned houses there had been compensated) – into the Turkish section of Nicosia. It was VERY different. Almost at once we were in bustling lanes with crafts and trinkets spilling into the paths. It was exactly like being in Turkey. I bought some gifts, which I paid for with Turkish Lire left over from a previous holiday (Husband so pleased I had kept them in my purse for a few years). I could have used Euro. Saw minarets of mosque.

Went to *Büyük*, which used to be an inn, is now a market. Males delighted I had found more lace and needlework to admire. Had drinks and sandwiches in the shade. Very hot.

Back through border, didn't get shot. Drove back to hotel (slight detour).

Husband decided we would eat in typically Greek restaurant listed in guidebook. Did not turn out as planned: Found correct hotel, but had trouble locating actual restaurant. It turned out to be next to the pool, which was very pretty with urns and arches and flowers. It was also shut (despite him phoning ahead). We were told they were serving the full menu in the bar. They weren't.

Phoned another restaurant from guidebook, and were assured they were open. It was shut. Our call had been diverted to a different restaurant, in the same chain (but they hadn't mentioned that). This was a challenge to find.

Bea used clever phone to mark exact position on map. Jay then directed us straight to marked position, which turned out to be a carpark in a dodgy residential area.

Finally drove to correct place.

Dinner was actually very nice. *Cafe La Mode*. Good food.

Returned to hotel. Hot chocolate and cards in lobby.

Tuesday

Big breakfast again (diet not what I was hoping).

Swam. Everyone in danger of burning, sun very hot.

Checked out of Hilton. Reception gave gifts to the females – nice thought, nice box, not entirely sure what it is – I think metallic pomegranate; or tomato.

Driving through the border into Northern Cyprus was fine (once we found it, *it is not signposted*). We bought 3 days of car insurance, because Cypriots won't cover driving in the north. On the way, we saw a huge Turkish flag on the hills. Somewhat confrontational for the Greek Cypriots one might feel…

Arrived in Kyrenia. The hotel, *The Colony*, seems nice and is a short walk from the harbour, which is beautiful.

3pm lunch on hotel roof. Slow. Great view of mountains behind Kyrenia. Could see outline of castle my sister wrote about in her blog (which describes how high it is, so I am not tempted to visit).

Males drank 1L glasses of *Effes* (local Turkish beer). Am thinking whole afternoon will be slow.

Walked round harbour. Pretty.

Walked to Roman amphitheatre. Slightly renovated (the plastic chairs were a giveaway).

Ate in Italian restaurant overlooking harbour. View magnificent, food shabby, service careless. Hoping none of us have food poisoning.

Walked around town. Saw some stalls selling things they had made, or had found (looked a bit like an attic clear out in some cases). The people looked so poor in cheap synthetic clothing, and were trying so hard, straightening things made from beads to try and present them better, I felt uncomfortable. Husband gave me some local money so I could buy bracelets and scarf – not quite sure what to do with them, but felt better for having bought them. (Part of trying to live by the Micah verse: *What God requires is this: to do what is just, and to love kindness, and to walk humbly with your God.*)

Wednesday
Nice breakfast, huge choice. Waiter was from Ukraine, and had rings on his thumbs (those facts are unconnected). Learnt 'thank you' in Ukrainian - *'jack-queer'* – not unlike the Polish, *'chink-queer'*. (Spelling my own, in case you were wondering.)

Family swam/sunbathed. I wandered around the lanes of Kyrenia. Pretty town. Saw tiny shops, an abandoned church, a mosque, and lots of cats and dogs who wandered freely and seemed content.

Pizza lunch on hotel roof. Then most of us drove south, to Salamis – this was Emm's choice, strangely. Either due to latent historic interest, or because it features in certain computer games. I expect it was for intellectual reasons.

Salamis is old Roman/Hellenic city. Lots of random walls and pillars left. Very relaxed rules, we could walk where we liked (later read Ruth's blog, which warns of snakes, but we didn't see any).

Toilet incredibly clean (in case you ever visit). Apparently Barnabas (New Testament character) lived there (in Salamis, not the toilet).

Drove to Famagusta, which is relatively famous having once been a popular resort, and then completely abandoned during the civil war/Turkish invasion. Eventually found the part that has been fenced off (after lots of stress-free U-turns by good natured husband).

Famagusta is weird. The deserted area runs right to the seafront, with fences and warnings going into the sea. What a waste. We could see houses, boutique hotels, shops, all left to crumble into ruin. Lots of barbed wire, and notices warning people to keep out, that photos were prohibited, soldiers with guns – right next to kiosks selling cold beer, ice-cream and flip-flops. I cannot believe it has been like this since 1974 and nothing has changed. No wonder people are angry. What a waste.

Didn't get shot/arrested. Drove back to hotel.

Buffet dinner in hotel. Not especially nice.

Thursday

At 12:00 we checked out of hotel. Well, Husband checked out, it takes a long time for seven people to all arrive in the same place at the same time. About an hour in fact.

Drove for a few hours, doing a slight detour to Mount Olympus.

Journey enhanced no end by Husband taking photographs of everyone for a very long time in the very hot sun.

Eventually arrived at *Annabel Hotel*, Paphos. Jay did a better job of map reading than yesterday (when we were suddenly aware he had fallen asleep).

Hotel seemed very nice, though crowded with English people. It has beautiful pool area with plants and lazy rivers and pillars and rows of sun beds. There's even a pool bar, where you can sit on stools in the water (for people who like to drink with a wet bottom). A few steps led to the beach, and a promenade you can walk along for miles, towards touristy shops or other hotels. Seems lovely.

Pathos has a beach front full of shops and restaurants designed for tourists. Most of them seem to be English. We ate in *Bacchus*, a Bistro overlooking the sea. They were very friendly (the old man who enticed us in gave us his home-grown cucumbers to try). Food was a bit rough.

Drank cocktails in bar.

Friday

Breakfast at 9. Everyone surprisingly awake. Apparently, if you have a room overlooking the restaurant, it gets noisy from 7am. Breakfast was busy, but had a huge variety of food to choose from.

Nice lunch in cafe opposite hotel – a fraction of hotel prices. (Am assuming we did something between breakfast and lunch, but I have no record of it.)

Swam in sea, which was cold and had big rocks near the surface, so you had to be careful. Played 'netball' in the pool and didn't get shouted at by attendant (we sometimes have rather unhappy relationships with pool attendants on holiday).

Chinese for dinner. Very nice, though slightly strange being in a Chinese restaurant where no one, at all, was Chinese. Perhaps the cooks were.

Saturday
Breakfast a bit 'old' – had been there a while I fear. Not everyone made it to breakfast due to extensive clubbing the night before (will remain nameless, but they know who they are).

Swam/read on balcony. Pleasant.

Lunch at *La Place Royal* opposite hotel again. Emm dropped a chip and a whole deluge of ants arrived (waitress swept them away with a broom). Big telly was showing Olympics.

Husband and Boyfriend played table tennis (obviously inspired by Olympics).

Drove to Pathos old town. Guide book showed bustling markets, interesting churches and mosques, historical sites. This is not what we saw:

Firstly, we got lost trying to leave town, as there were random one-way streets and closed roads not marked on the map – apparently – Jay was map reading. Found some ruins, with St Paul's pillar, by chance.

This was where St Paul was tied when he was whipped. I have to say, this story does not appear in my Bible, where his trip to Pathos was relatively smooth, but perhaps I missed it. There was a pillar, clearly labelled, so who am I to doubt its authenticity?

Finally made it to Old Pathos. A large sign directed us to parking, but we realised, just in time, that it was pointing to a steep flight of steps, so didn't drive down there. No other cars in carpark (which perhaps should have been a clue).

Wandered around. It was very hot. Everywhere was deserted. There was a gun on the floor, and sounds of chanting from the church. The shops had mannequins straight from a horror movie, all the roads had been dug up, cafes and market were all deserted. A few isolated cars and bikes passed us – we began to think they were all driven by the same few people. It was very weird. It also made for a perfect story, so I wrote one – I didn't have to use much imagination!

Decided we would visit again another day. Returned to the seafront. Arrived back at Annabel Hotel. Husband drove up to the barrier and spoke into the intercom:

D: Hello - Guest-e-o (why??)

Reply: Hello, welcome.

D: Welcome (why?? Why repeat welcome?)

Silence, then:

Reply: Are you a guest?

We all refused to walk in with him.

Jay informed me that: "Physics is all the interesting parts of maths."

So much I do not understand in that statement.

Went to Democritos, which promised to be a traditional Greek restaurant, with music and dancing. There was a good menu, a pretty atmosphere, and live music by some talented musicians. Had a very nice selection of starters to share. And then the dancing began... I have to say, Greek dancing is somewhat repetitive by the time it is in its fiftieth loop of repeated steps.

A man came and balanced glasses on his head. Lots of them. He wore a badge declaring he was a *Guinness World Record* holder – was tempted to ask him what for. He asked for volunteers to add glasses, and then put his hand up their skirts. Emm and Jay decided he was a pervert. It was a very long evening. I think perhaps Greek restaurants are something you only need to experience once in your lifetime.

It has been much discussed since. At the time, I was just bored – I now realise how lucky I am that Emm and Jay didn't get up and punch the glass balancing man. (I much prefer the bored option.)

We checked out of *Annabel Hotel*, Pathos, and drove along the coast to Coral Bay. We had rented a villa for the last week of the holiday. Bea and Boyfriend had left to return to work, so it was just Emm, Girlfriend, Jay, with me and Husband. We drove there via a supermarket. Parking is always stressful, but foreign supermarkets are usually interesting. This one was fairly standard, disappointing.

The villa, was fairly basic, and very brown – but will be fine as long as nothing breaks. It has air conditioning (essential) but only in the bedrooms – so I decided pretty quickly that home-cooking was not on the menu. (I was being considerate to the others, not wanting to heat up the villa.)

Coral Bay is a mix of beautiful coastline and trashy restaurants. We ate in a 'traditional' restaurant that wasn't traditional at all, just over-priced and full of 'Brits Abroad'. Hope we find somewhere nicer tomorrow.

Monday

Woke late after a terrible night. Lazed around, swam/read.

Found washing line (most exciting feature of villa) and hung up classy fluffy expensive beach towels that we bought in the supermarket. (The expensive bit is true.) Ate stale bread for lunch.

Drove to catacombs. Quite interesting, though spoilt by all the litter. One cave had a pool of water (hard to see in the dark) which Jay washed his muddy shoe in, and then worried might be a leaking sewage pipe. Afterwards read guidebook (why does my family always read them after the visit?) and discovered that actually it was miraculous water. All hoped it might improve his rather ugly feet, but no change so far.

Drinks in McDonalds (so nice, mainly because it was cool in there).

Stopped on way back to villa to photograph banana plantations. This area has lots of them. It was interesting because you could see the various stages, from flower, to tiny beginnings to full bananas – which were then covered in blue plastic bags. Never found out why.

Walked from villa to beach. Husband claims this is a 7 minute walk. It isn't. It is 10 minutes of *fast* walking to the top of the cliff. Beach crowded, sea nice – not cold, wonderfully blue, with gentle waves.

Dinner at *The Old Cinema Tavern* next to the church in Pegeia square. It was very nice, traditional Greek food (without the dancing or pervy glass-balancing man). It was recommended by the woman who works in the supermarket.

{Top travel tip: Forget guidebooks, just ask the woman who works in the local supermarket for places to eat. They will be better, cheaper, and more traditional than anything you'll find in tourist guides!}

When we finished our meal, they brought us plates of fresh fruit and shots of zivania. This was a little like drinking paint stripper.

Drove back to villa. Saw the glasses-balancing man doing his act (complete with "hand up volunteers' skirts" routine) in a different Greek restaurant. Evoked an extremely strong reaction from both boys. This is how wars are started. So glad we hadn't chosen that particular place to eat.

Arrived back at villa, and Husband set off the burglar alarm.

Tuesday

I read the book of Acts, about Paul visiting Salamis and Pathos 2,000 odd years ago. Pretty cool to read about places we've visited ourselves.

Stale bread and cereal for breakfast. Husband tried to educate everyone in early eighties music and played *Alan Parsons Project*. Loudly. Not sure everyone appreciated it. I washed my extra-expensive quality fluffy towel with tee-shirts. Tee-shirts now covered in fluff.

Bought a selection of pastries for lunch. Olive bread a challenge due to olive stones. One pastry seemed to contain toothpaste – wasn't popular. Also, we keep having ants in the kitchen.

Went for drive. Fantastic views of Pathos and coastline from hills. Walked along deserted hills for a while, then came to some leather chairs under a sunshade. Really – there they were, a complete leather three-piece-suite, in a deserted wilderness – with a sunshade. Bizarre.

Dinner in *'Imogens Tavern'* in Kathikas (another recommendation from supermarket lady). Sat at tables with chequered cloths and candles, under vines and fig trees. Not bad at all.

We were slightly put-off by the weather, which was cold. (*Cold!*)

Wednesday

Breakfast. Didn't swim, instead went back to Old Pathos. It was full of tourists, and completely different to the ghost town we had visited before. We walked around the market, which had lots of lace, leather goods, local food and wine, and fake designer handbags. I bought some gifts.

We bought pastries and rolls from the supermarket, and then everyone played cards (while I wrote a story).

We drove to look at a shipwreck. Husband had Googled "Shipwrecks in Pathos" and found the exact location, which he marked on the map. Jay then left the map in the villa, but Husband hardly mentioned this.

The coastline was interesting, with lots of caves. We found the wreck. Apparently, it hit a rock out at sea, and then veered off course and hit the shore. It was hard to understand *how* such a massive boat could have managed to not notice the land until it crashed.

Went back to *Old Cinema Tavern* for dinner. Girlfriend and I shared the 'mini mezze' and Husband and Jay shared the 'full mezze'. The males planned their eating strategy. Jay took photographs of each course, and each empty plate. I am not sure how interesting the empty plates will be in later years, perhaps it's a physics-related thing.

Thursday
Lazy day.

During the afternoon, everyone built sandcastles on the beach, and I tried to walk – but it was a fairly small bay, so rather dissatisfying. I then walked around the new houses being built near to the villa. Cyprus has a lot of new houses, whole avenues of brand new houses. It was slightly strange.

Friday
I made pancakes for breakfast. There was something wrong with them.

We went to 'The Tombs of the Kings'. The guidebook said the best time to visit is early morning, we went at noon. It was unbelievably hot. We wasted some time looking at rocks with holes in them, which weren't the tombs. By the time we found the tombs, we were too hot to be interested. Jay said he would pay his admission fee simply to be allowed to leave.

We went to McDonalds, which was stressful due to lack of parking. Bought a drive-thru, and took it home for lunch. Cold chips are rubbery and unappetising – but perhaps I'm too fussy.

Swam/read.

Went to the Chinese restaurant in Pathos for dinner (the one which doesn't have any Chinese people).

Saturday
Last day. I feel quite affectionate towards the brown villa now, despite the uncomfortable beds.

Went to a museum showing the struggles of *'Eoka'* – the fight for Cyprus to be independent. The museum however, was not very interesting, and consisted mainly of the same newspaper articles copied many times over. But it used up the time nicely.

As we drove back, we stopped to look at Potoma Bay, which has very blue water.

Husband and I went for a drive and stroll around the area, looking for signs of 'normal' Cypriot life. We saw families eating in their gardens, olive trees, urns of flowers, amazing views down to the coast.

The others went back to the beach, for more sandcastles.

Our last dinner was at *Old Cinema Tavern*. We like it there, it has nice food, friendly service, and a relaxed atmosphere. We said goodbye to the owner, and he presented us with a bottle of wine. How lovely.

It's been a pleasant two weeks. Everyone has seemed happy and relaxed. Husband gave his: "I think this will be the last family holiday ever" speech, which he has been saying since 2011. Perhaps this year, he is right...

Mumbai

I am writing this in Mumbai.

We arrived late Wednesday night, having woken early that morning (left home 5.45 am), so I was tired. We had to go through different immigration, as I was travelling on a tourist visa, and husband had a work one. The woman at the desk was very pleasant, and when husband pointed out for the sixth time where he would meet me, she laughed. When he went off to his work visa desk, she commented that he seemed very worried about me.

"Yes," I smiled, "he thinks I'm incompetent."

Immigration officer then asked for my visa. I gave her the print out with the hotel details on. (They look the same, both printed from the computer.) She politely asked if I also had a visa.

She then asked where I had come from. I was surprised, but gave my full postal address. I even remembered the postcode, which often defeats me, so felt rather pleased with myself. Immigration officer looked confused and asked for my boarding pass. It was somewhat crumpled, but I dug it out from the bottom of my bag, then realised my mistake.

"Heathrow!" I said, "You wanted me to say Heathrow, not my address, didn't you!"

Immigration officer continued to smile. We then had trouble making the fingerprint machine work (but I don't think that was my fault).

Eventually I was allowed into India. I think Immigration Officer went for a tea break.

We're staying at the *Taj Mahal Palace Hotel*. It's beautiful. There was a mix up with our booking (also not my fault) and as a goodwill gesture, they upgraded us to a suite. The hotel really is beautiful. There are flowers and candles everywhere, and the corridors are all open, with lots of carved lattice work.

When we returned yesterday evening, there were patterns of flower petals everywhere, so pretty. (Romantic husband referred to them as "vegetation on the floor.")

Walked to Gateway to India. Lots of people there, some were catching ferries across the sea. It was previously owned by Portugal, (the Portuguese for good is "bom" and it's a bay, hence was called "Bombay").

We went to a market and bartered for some trinkets. I am not very good at bartering, especially when the crafts are actually very pretty, and the price seems to be low to start with. Tradesmen smile a lot when I shop (and tell me not to bring my husband next time, because he's cannier than me!)

Wandered around the city. I love the faded colonial buildings covered in vines, the huge plants, the colour everywhere. Every sense is bombarded, so much noise and smell (not always pleasant), and so hot. We met some friends for lunch. They said that in a couple of weeks the rain will come, sometimes raining for several days continually, which cools everything down.

Mumbai is very different to Delhi (where I set my book *Clara*) but both cities have the same busy feel, the same muddle of colour and sound and scents, the same mass of humanity.

Day 2

So, deciding to be brave, I went to the red-light district of a Mumbai slum (for more research ready for writing *Clara*). Husband was working, so I contacted Tearfund, and they arranged for me to visit one of their projects. Beforehand, I was very nervous about going on my own, but I am so glad I did it.

I was met by Sam, who is the director of Sahaara. We've never met, so it was a little like a spy story: "I will be under the arch with a pink carnation in my buttonhole." (Well, actually, he just told reception who he was and we met in the hotel lobby, but you get the idea.)

We then got a taxi to *Turbhe*, the area of the slum he works in. We chatted in the car, and I could check on a few things I've included in my novel (which is set partly in the slums of Delhi).

There was one scary moment, when the taxi driver missed the turning, and so reversed, along a 4-lane motorway, back to the exit. I held on tight and prayed. We didn't die.

As we walked through the slums, it was all very similar to places I saw when in Delhi: Homes made from scavenged materials, uneven walls, unglazed windows, corrugated iron roofs, open sewers. The hard mud paths were litter-strewn, in a couple of weeks they'll be quagmires of wet mud. Roads were pot-holed, narrow, stalls and heaps of rubbish making obstacles for vehicles to inch around.

At one point, the road was blocked as a lorry driver was asleep, curled up over the steering wheel, oblivious to the honking from other drivers who were unable to pass.

We first went to a building (actually, it was really just a narrow room) which is a feeding centre/education room. In May, everything closes (due to the heat) but they were still providing a midday meal for the children of sex-workers in the area.

They had two gas burners, one with a pressure cooker of dhal, one with a vat of rice. There was a bowl of hard boiled eggs, which they must've cooked earlier. No work-surface (no idea how they chop vegetables – they must do it in their hand, on a plate balanced somewhere). No sink, no running water. There were cupboards, some of them very high.

At one point a woman climbed, a foot on a shelf, other foot on the top of a cupboard door, to reach plates from a top cupboard. Metal plates were stacked on a drainer. They were washed in a bucket on the floor, the water fetched from an outside water butt. Water is piped into the slum once in the morning, once in the evening, and people fill containers to use throughout the day.

The children arrived. Black-eyed, smiling, interested to see a big white woman sitting in their room. (I feel huge in India. Everyone is smaller than me.)

These children were growing up in an environment where prostitution is the norm. Sahaara is educating them, so they don't have to follow their mothers into the same profession, they will have choices in life. Previously, they found that some children arrived only for the food. They made a rule, if the kids don't attend lessons, they can't eat. People complained, but now they all come to lessons. Seems a wise decision to me – if we just feed the poor, they will always be poor. (This is why I like Tearfund/Sahaara – they sometimes make unpopular decisions if it is for a greater good.)

They showed me the toilet, a room with a drain, a bucket, and a ladle. Absolutely no idea how it should be used (thankfully, was just a morning visit, I didn't need to use a loo). Sam told me that families are more likely to have a mobile phone than a toilet. There was also a fridge (not in the toilet, just in the room).

While we were there, the power went out. This happens every Friday. There isn't enough electricity, so different areas have no power for certain times during the week. They never know how long the power cut will last, sometimes a few hours, but when I was there it came back on after about 30 minutes. The fridge whirred back into life and the ceiling fan stirred the warm air. Would make the fridge pretty useless for anything other than drinks though.

We walked through the red-light district. The houses here were slightly better, I guess it pays well. Each little house had 3 or 4 women outside, just sitting on chairs or on the floor. I thought they were sitting in the shade, chatting to each other. (Later I realised they were soliciting customers – am a bit naive about such things.) Sahaara has a second centre in the heart of the red-light district.

Here, they chat to the women, teach them skills like sewing, hairdressing, making things from junk; enabling them to have other life choices if they want to choose a different career. Sam said it's about caring for the women, showing them that God loves them, that they have worth, that they matter.

Usually the centre is shut during May, but they opened it to show me inside. When they saw it was open, a couple of women came in, to see what was happening. We chatted, and the women asked me to pray for them. I'm not sure how it rated as a prayer – I felt it was more of a lucky talisman than talking to God, but who am I to judge what was in their hearts?

Then we left. As we walked back to the feeding centre, I saw one of the women, sitting outside her brothel. We smiled and waved at each other – friends – but with lives in different worlds.

These women were young enough to be my daughters. Caring about them was easy.

Back at the other centre, about 35 children sat on the floor. One child said grace (I think it was in English, which seems bizarre, as they all spoke Hindi. But I was tired, brain was fuzzy by then, so maybe was imagining it). They ate from the tin plates, no cutlery, scooping the food with their right hands. The women were busy, one dishing up the food on plates, the others taking it round to the kids.

I nearly offered to help, but then I realised, it was like Lunch Club at home. Everyone had a role and knew what they were doing, the last thing they wanted was some big foreign woman getting in the way!

We got a taxi back to the hotel, and Sam delivered me safely to the lobby. I was so glad I had been, met the women, seen the children. It makes it easier to support the work and talk about it to others. Everyone has a different story. Some of the women would have been trafficked as children, some had gone into prostitution by choice, because their options were very limited. Sam said they work with everyone, the prostitutes, their children, the pimps. They all need to be cared for.

It would be easy to judge, but their lives are tougher than ours, we are not so very different inside. If a woman with an extra room finds she cannot make enough money from rent, she may well decide to go back to her village, to buy a young girl, to act as her pimp, so she can feed her own child. Not because she is more wicked than you or me, but because she has grown up in a harsher place, where survival means hard choices.

Sahaara is trying to show that God loves them, wants a better life for them and their children, and is teaching them the skills so they can make that choice. But the decision has to be theirs. All Sahaara can do is give them the choice. All we can do is help to provide the resources, and pray.

Austria 2017

Day One : Munich to Austria
Car arrived 5am. Everyone ready – unexpected – maybe some of them didn't sleep.

Flew Heathrow to Munich, all went smoothly, and everyone managed the automatic barriers.

Collected minivan, and drove Munich to Salzburg. Jay made redundant from map reading due to rather efficient satnav.

Arrived at Sheraton at Fuschlsee, a lake near Salzburg. Staff at reception predominantly female, wearing national dress, which does make them very buxom. Impossible to avoid mainly noticing bosoms.

Dinner in the expensive hotel restaurant. Lots of antlers on walls, candles, flowers. Nice meal, but tired (me, not meal).

Everywhere here is SO pretty.

Day Two : Hallstatt
Nice breakfast, though I had problems with coffee machine and covered surrounding area with milky froth – rescued by very nice waiter who collected me a mug of coffee.

Drove to Hallstatt. Traffic terrible and nowhere to park, so we abandoned Husband and car, and walked into town. It was full of Chinese people, really full. Coach loads of them. All the signs were written in German and Mandarin, so clearly a regular occurrence. Also full of extremely expensive souvenir shops. Followed signs with a skull on them up a mountain (Jay in flip-flops, but still faster than people in hiking gear). Signs took us to a cemetery.

Found Husband (not in the cemetery) and ate lovely homemade pizza for lunch. Read guidebook to try and find out significance of skulls and cemetery. Read that apparently, cemetery is very small – due to being half way up a mountain, so when it was full, someone had the good idea that they could dig up the old corpses and replace them with the new ones. Honestly, this was the solution they decided on! Did anyone object? Was there a committee involved? Anyway, this is what they did. While the bodies were waiting to be buried, they decomposed, and the bones were bleached by the sun. The skulls were separated from the other bones, and they are displayed in a side chapel.

We HAD to go back and look.

There they were, bones stacked neatly, skulls decorated with the name and patterns. Brilliant!

The rest of Hallstatt is also interesting – lots of cute cottages clinging to the mountainside. Too many tourists and over-priced shops, but well worth a visit.

Walked around a mountain lake, *Vorderer-Gosausee*. So beautiful – lake, trees, glacier, mountains.

Dinner in *Fuschl*. Parked in large town car park, which we returned to after dark, and so didn't know how to pay. Husband set off in the dark to investigate, we sat in car.

Arrived safely back at hotel, despite best efforts of suicidal deer on dark road.

Nice day.

Day Three: Salzburg

Only table big enough for seven of us was outside, which was good due to sunshine, and bad due to wasps. Austria is not great for vegetarians, and even menus marked as 'vegetarian' sometimes contain fish.

Drove to Salzburg and parked in a car park dug into the rock. Car parks here are well-signed, with each one telling you exactly how many spaces are left.

Walked around historical part of Salzburg. Saw where Mozart was born (building now a Spar supermarket, which seems wrong). All the shops sold lots of Mozart souvenirs.

Especially small round chocolates. Did Mozart eat small round chocolates? Jay assured me this was not covered by music A level (which seems a shame).

Saw a lot of traditional Austrian dress – the boob-enhancing white blouse under pinafore dress for women, and lederhosen for men. I understand why people in tourist shops/restaurants would wear this, but not really why so many other people do. Especially lederhosen. These are leather shorts, and I'm guessing there's not much 'give' in them – I saw a lot of men attempting to walk without moving their legs, they had a sort of shuffle. Not a good look. Also not sure if you can wash them...

Went to Residenzplatz – saw horses and fountain and cathedral. All very pretty, though the cathedral feels more like an art gallery than a church – was interesting and grand, but did not inspire me to prayer. It also had some very spooky cherub faces in the ceiling.

Saw a bridge and steps that I recognised from *The Sound of Music*. Suggested family could reenact some of the scenes, but they were unkeen. Went to Mirabell Garden (*"Do! Doe, a deer.."*) and saw some excellent gnomes. I think they represent the children of the owner – I might copy this idea.

Walked across a bridge covered in padlocks put there by people in love. Sweet idea, but what happens if you fall out of love? Do you sneak back with a metal cutter and remove your padlock?

We walked to a viewpoint near castle, and the convent Maria Von Trapp left. The chapel was open, so I went inside. That church DID feel like it had been prayed in, I preferred it to the cathedral.

Walked back past the cathedral. Saw a sculpture outside, which was an empty person (I later learned it was a copy of *The Cloak of Conscience* by Anna Chromy and is called *Pietà*, or *Coat of Peace*). Next to it was a beggar – another unseen person, which felt significant given her position – an invisible person next to a sculpture of an invisible person. Perhaps that's why she chose that spot to sit in. I gave her some money, which I don't usually do, and held her hand – I wanted her to know she was 'seen'. We all need someone to see us.

Followed Jay for a long way – a very long way in hot sun – to *Lindhofstraße 7*, to a beer garden the boys had discovered last summer when inter-railing. It was brilliant.

There were shelves of pottery beer tankards, which you could dip into a dodgy looking fountain, to increase the head on the beer. You paid a man, took your ticket and tankard to a man with a barrel, and he filled it with beer. You then sat in the garden, under the trees, next to the brewery. You could also buy olives, pretzels, sausages, but most people were just drinking. Great fun.

Day Four – Fuschlsee near Salzburg
Breakfast 9 am. Managed to sit inside today. Sheraton provides a good selection for breakfast. We didn't break the coffee machine today.

Choices for activities today were: walking, rowing, golf, cycling, swimming. We, of course, had a voting system (20 votes per person) and made an Excel spreadsheet. Sometimes I wonder how I came to be part of this family. Anyway, rowing won.

Hired two boats (€10 per hour) and set off across Fuschl Lake. Made it to a jetty with a fish restaurant and had drinks. Had to walk across a scary floating jetty and down a plank of wood. I don't generally do well with activities that involve balance. Used washroom – all public conveniences in Austria seem to cost 50 cents. Rowed back. It is harder than you might think to row in a straight line.

Family played golf (not me). Then we met for hideously expensive drinks in pretty hotel bar.

Had trouble booking anywhere for dinner, as it's Assumption Day and everywhere is closed (would've been nice if hotel had warned us). Ate in The Grill at hotel. Nice food, very friendly waiter.

Day Five

Nice breakfast again.

Drove to *St Wolfgang* and caught tourist train up mountain. Tickets so expensive Husband wouldn't tell me the price.

Mountain very cold at the top. Brilliant views, though one side was covered by cloud.

Drove to *Bad Ischl* to a coffee house recommended by Trip Advisor.

(When in Austria, you HAVE to visit a beer garden, a coffee house, and run across an Alpine meadow singing words from *The Sound of Music*. It's the law.)

Really nice coffee, really grumpy waiter. We wanted lunch, and when we asked if the menu had any vegetarian options, he told us to go to the cafe up the road! Used the washroom, which had a strangely placed mirror, right next to the toilet – I could not see any purpose for it, do people check their make-up while sitting on the loo? Very nice coffee though…

Saw some red phone boxes. One was filled with bookshelves, and was a 'book-swap' place. Nice idea.

It's our last day in Austria, so I bought a cushion cover for my collection. Tomorrow we drive to Slovenia. Now, I just need to find a meadow to run across…

Austria is wonderful. The air feels clean, the mountains are beautiful and the people are mostly very efficient *and* very friendly – they even like dogs. I would like to live here.

Slovenia 2017

Ljubljana, Slovenia

Arrived at *Grand Hotel Union* (yes, that is the correct order of words) in Ljubljana.

(This is pronounced libby-ana. But Husband insisted on calling it Lubbily-Jubbily, and now it is REALLY hard not to. Which will be embarrassing when I'm telling friends about the holiday.)

Hotel is in the old town, which is lovely. Weather hot. People speak good English (which is lucky, as we are having trouble with even the name of the city!)

We wandered around looking for somewhere to eat. Husband tired after 8 hours of driving. Ate in an over-priced cafe in a square and watched the world go by. Lots of young people. Old part of the city is pretty, and full of bars and cafes and street artists. There are famous bridges, interesting statues and lots of people. For a city I had never even heard of, it is surprisingly well-known amongst tourists.

Breakfast was in a huge room – busy, but a good selection of food. It was very different to the Austrian buffet (for example, there they had slices of melon and a fruit salad; Slovenia offered whole peaches and apricots and plums, which you peeled and cut yourself). Coffee was rough.

The whole hotel has a sort of faded prettiness, but it somehow feels less 'classy' less 'safe', than Austria. I like it, but feel more cautious.

Family made a plan for the morning. We wanted to see the Dragon Bridge, the Cobblers Bridge, a church, and a market. So Husband decided we would go to the castle. (Not complaining, just saying.)

Actually, to be fair, the walk to the castle did include all the other stuff. The Dragon Bridge is from the legend of *Jason and the Argonauts*. The market doesn't sell cushion covers, but has the biggest tomatoes ever.

The way up to the castle was by funicular. You can either queue for 15 minutes to buy the tickets, and then queue again for a further twenty minutes for the next funicular to arrive; OR one person can queue for tickets while everyone else queues for the next car – hence avoiding time standing in hot sun. But stroppy Slovenian women who didn't think of doing that will hiss at you.

The castle is boring. Most castles are boring – but males have a strange need to visit them, in the same way as they HAVE to climb towers. This particular castle was also very full of tourists. (It was probably nicer under communist rule – if somewhat less friendly.)

The castle used to be a prison. Some cells had a window, and the best views of the city. Other cells did not. I don't think I would've survived 10 years in a stuffy stone box. If you do visit, then the water costs less in the gift shop than from the ice cream lady in the courtyard.

The walk down from the castle is along a slippery gravel path. It has good views, but you can't look at them or you'll trip over a root and plummet to your death. Probably.

We ate lunch in a *BackWerk*, which is a sort of ethnic Costa where you make your own coffee from a machine (but it has nice sandwiches). It's too hot for food really.

We walked to Tivoli Park, via a couple of churches and an ice cream cafe. The churches had a lot of gilt, the ice creams were nice. Saw the Parliament building, which is a boring square building, but has interesting sculpted figures around the door. They represent the Socialist ideal, of everyone striving together.

The park, when we had slogged there through the afternoon heat, was not worth visiting, I thought. But perhaps I was just too hot.

Ljubljana is pretty, it reminds me of Bruges. It is nice to visit for a day, but it felt weirdly insubstantial. If you took away the cafes and chocolate shops, I'm not sure what would be left. I never managed to see the 'real' part of Slovenia.

Dinner was at *Julija*. Jovial waiter and nice food, followed by blackberry liquor shots.

Croatia 2017

The Drive to Croatia:
Checked out of hotel in Ljubljana and drove south.

Stopped at *Predjama Castle* in Slovenia – a fortress built into a rock. Parking was an adventure (car parks in Slovenia rather more casual than in Austria). We paid (I chose to not look at price because Husband had decided we were going in anyway – due to the whole male/castle/compulsory visit gene, which females don't inherit.)

However, having moaned about the castle in Ljubljana, I have to admit, this one was really interesting. They gave us portable recorded guides, which were brilliant, as you could skip ahead to the bits that were interesting – like the torture chamber, and the secret tunnels through the rocks which meant that when the castle was under siege, they could sneak out to top up their food. All the boring bits could be skipped.

The castle was not a happy place, but they have turned it into an interesting museum, with several rooms furnished, and it is well worth visiting. If you happen to be in Slovenia.

We didn't buy sandwiches at the castle (a mistake) and decided to stop for food during the journey. Big row (which only families can have) about whether to go to a McDonald's in Croatia, or stop for food sooner. Nearly stopped at a supermarket, but this was strongly vetoed by Jay, who objected to eating food bought from a shop with broken windows. I just love my family sometimes. We ate at a McDonalds in Croatia.

The border crossing had queues, but we were waved through with our EU passports (not sure what will happen when Brexit has happened). As we drove away, we saw miles and miles of stationary cars waiting to cross the border OUT of Croatia. Decided we would leave very early next week.

Croatia reminds me of Turkey. Lots of dusty agriculture.

We're staying at *Lone Hotel* in Rovinj. It's a contemporary hotel, with lots of art that I don't quite understand. Family seem happy, though somewhat perturbed by glass wall in bathrooms. Husband, who knew about these in advance, had brought rolls of brown paper and *Blutac* (we have a mix of family and friends in various rooms). Family strangely unimpressed by his forward planning (especially Jay, who had been persuaded to carry it through three countries).

Dinner was in hotel restaurant – very trendy, and very lacking in actual food. My "steamed tuna and avocado" was seared (raw) tuna with shavings of avocado. Tasty lemon and ginger sauce, but not exactly filling. Boys have offered to find future eating places for rest of holiday.

Family went to explore hotel's night club (am sure they were pleased Husband decided to go with them). I went to bed. There's a thunder storm, so watched lightning across the sea for a while. Tomorrow we'll explore Rovinj.

Sunday 20th August

Breakfast was another buffet – a huge selection in a gigantic room. But some food seemed a little 'old' – perhaps because we were fairly late getting there – and there were ants.

Lots of food to keep our vegetarians fed though (which has been quite a challenge this holiday). There was also a very low table, at child height, full of cakes and pastries. A small boy was happily stroking everything. Clearly a nice idea, planned by someone who is not a parent.

Walked into Rovinj (15 minutes along the coast). Lovely town – old buildings scattered on a hill, stretching out to sea. It felt like an Italian town, and Son-who-knows-stuff told me that it was originally built by the same people who built Venice, hence the similarity. I loved it. It was full of tourist shops and cafes, but all around were signs of real life – washing strung high above the street, craftsmen working, fishermen. It has more of a soul than Ljubljana had.

Took bread and cheese back to the hotel and ate in the lobby bar. They have shiny black tables, and provide white marker pens, so you can doodle while you sit. Young children had drawn pictures, some people had written rhymes. My family wrote mathematical formulas (how sad is that?)

Everyone did their own thing for the afternoon. I ventured down to beach, and sunbathing daughter agreed to swim with me. Very stony beach, hurt feet. There was a lifeguard's chair, but the only person near it was in a wheelchair, which didn't inspire confidence, so I didn't swim out too far.

All the guests have been provided with room key cards and a towel card — so you can collect swimming towels when you need them. Both cards look very similar, which is causing some people problems.

Walked to *MaliRaj* restaurant in Rovinj. It was down a narrow cobbled street, and someone had put tiny candles in the wall crevasses — very romantic. The streets are cobbled, and very slippery. (I assume worn smooth by thousands of feet, but it is possible a grumpy old women sneaks out every night and polishes them, hoping to make tourists fall over.) The streets are also steep and uneven, so leave your heels at home.

Mali Raj is a fish restaurant — real, fresh, head-attached, caught this morning, fish.

Dessert was pancakes with ice cream and sour cherries. Delicious. I popped to use the loo and peeked into the kitchen. Grandma was sitting on a huge chair, and they were passing her things to dry up. I like this place. At the end of the meal, they gave us grappa shots. (Pretty foul, but a kind thought.)

Walked back through crowded streets full of music, dancing in the square, street artists.

Hotel Lone has lots of activities you can book. Tomorrow people plan to cycle, or kayak, or go to the gym. I might just sleep and read and eat ice creams.

Monday 21st August

Breakfast at 9am again. Lots of the 'hot' food wasn't.

Husband hired a bike and cycled, I went to the gym.

Lunch in Rovinj at Sergio – a pizza place the boys found. We had to wait ages for a table, but it was very nice pizza. It's on a hill on the old town, down a narrow cobbled street which is terribly pretty to look at and terribly difficult to walk on.

Spent afternoon relaxing.

Walked back into Rovinj for dinner, to almost the exact same place as the pizza restaurant. Ate dinner in *Tipico* – a cosy restaurant with an open kitchen, so we could watch them work. I had stuffed courgettes, then chocolate cake and semi-freddo. All delicious.

Tuesday 22nd August

We hired bikes and cycled along the coast. There's a gravel path, so it was hard going in places, but the views are fabulous. Lots of coves with local people swimming, and the cliff tops are a huge park, with trees and paths. There are climbers on the cliffs, boats on the sea, tiny islands, sunshine, pine trees – lovely.

Drove to *Restaurant Maslima* for lunch. Sat under olive trees. Lots of mosquitoes in Croatia, so bring repellent.

Went back to hotel. We walked into Rovinj later for dinner.

Wednesday 23rd August

Decided to walk to a bay to swim. We walked a long way (all the bays were quite crowded). Found a nice empty spot and settled onto the rocks, then noticed the sea was FULL of jellyfish. Tiny transparent globs of jelly. Didn't swim, went back to hotel pool, where we read and ate ice-creams, but didn't actually swim.

I later learned these jellyfish are also called "walnut sea jellies". They are native to America, and often transported via ship ballast. They reproduce rapidly, and cause huge problems to ecosystems as they eat plankton, which upsets the food chain for bigger fish. Big problem for fishing-based industries. However, they do not sting, so later we swam quite happily in water infested with them. It's a little odd swimming with jelly, but not harmful.

After lunch, we went to Pula. Always stressful trying to find somewhere to park.

Huge Roman amphitheatre, which is very hot in the midday sun (just thought I'd mention that). There are some interesting chambers underground, where you can imagine the prisoners and animals being kept. There were also lots of pots. Not sure why lots of pots are interesting, but they seem to be a feature of Roman monuments.

Whenever we go on holiday, Husband wears a hat we are all very rude about. Pula had a whole family, all dressed the same, all wearing same hats. Perhaps they get lost a lot and it makes it easy to identify them. We sent Husband over to join them.

Pula also has Hercules Arch, which I was keen to see. Family led me to a variety of arches. The one I think actually IS Hercules Arch appears to be incorporated into a modern apartment complex. It is certainly less spectacular than I was expecting.

Tried to have coffee and cocktails in a pretty square.

Managed to have beers and nasty wine in a mosquito infested alley. Husband (who has been trying to learn a few words of Croatian) wished them *"Ooga dan dan,"* when we left. They looked confused.

Ate in *Sareni Papar* restaurant. This was great, if slow. We sat looking at the chequered table cloths, and rather spooky pictures, waiting for our meal. Lovely stuffed peppers, served straight from the oven in a boiling-hot baking dish, which was plonked straight onto the table. It felt like eating at home. (Stuffed veg are, apparently, a feature of Croatian food.) Husband said: *"Ooga dan dan,"* to friendly waitress. She looked worried.

Blokes drank 1L glasses of beer, sang all the way home (surprisingly tuneful) – and then happily walked to the wrong hotel. A nice day.

Thursday 24th August

We decided to hire a boat and sail around the little islands we can see from the coast and swim in places that aren't full of other tourists. Family remembered our holiday in Malta, where they composed a song entitled *"A Speedboat Driven by an Accountant"*, so Husband decided to hire a boat with a skipper.

Had a brilliant day. The skipper (I never asked his name – isn't that terrible) was a sports teacher during term time, and he kindly took us on a little tour. He told us that his grandfather has lived in the same small village his whole life, and has lived in six different countries : Austro-Hungary, Italy, Germany (under occupation), AngloAmerican, Yugoslavia and now Croatia. That is weird.

We stopped in little bays to swim a couple of times. All the water seems to be full of the 'walnut sea jelly' – the clear non-stinging jellyfish – you get used to them after a while. The water is beautifully clear, and fish flash away as you swim. People who can dive (not me) dived from the side of the boat. At one point the skipper drove with enough speed for Husband's hat to fly off (which was very funny. I never liked that hat.)

We spent the afternoon lazing around, then walked into Rovinj for espressos and ice creams. We looked around the market, and I saw lots of wonderful things to buy that I would never be able to transport home. They had crafts, and bottles of olive oil, and meats and spices, and crockery and lavender – lots of lavender.

Dinner at *Tipico*, Old Town again.

Friday 25th August
The family hired kayaks. I sat by the pool with Husband .

Ate dinner at *Tutto Bene*. They don't have vegetarian options on the menu, but will cook them if you ask. Lovely table outside, friendly waiter, nice food. Though I was too warm to properly enjoy it (I think my seat was next to the kitchen window, and the extractor fan was blowing at me.)

We packed. Early start tomorrow to try and avoid delays at the border.

Saturday 26th August

We left Lone Hotel at 5am (this was to try and avoid long queues at the border). The night manager looked nothing like Tom Hiddleston (shame) but he *did* give us all a packed lunch, as we would be missing breakfast. Isn't that nice? I've never been offered that before when we've had to check-out early. It has been a really good hotel, with lots going on and good facilities.

The border crossing was fine, no queues at all (unlike the 4 hour ones we saw later in the day when arriving.)

Stopped at Services when we were in Italy. *Completely* awful. We arrived at the same time as several coaches, and the lines for the washroom were crazy. Gave up in the end.

Arrived in Marriott Hotel, Venice at 9:30am. Left the hotel at 11am, and caught a bus to Venice (€3 return ticket).

Walked around the city, which was way more crowded than I remember it being a few years ago. It's still beautiful. We drank coffees and beers and ate lunch and ice-creams, and wandered around taking photographs.

We caught the bus back to the hotel, and Husband drove to buy petrol.

We ate dinner at *Al Quadrante*. It was cheap and nice, but the service was really slow. As we were only 100 yards from the hotel, Bea and I left early so we could sleep. It was a long day.

This was a brilliant holiday. I enjoyed every single day. We had heard lots about Croatia before we visited, and most if it was true. The "everything's very cheap" part was not true – I guess it doesn't take long for prices to match the number of tourists. We only visited a tiny area, so I hope to explore more of Croatia in the future.

Tokyo

Arrived in Tokyo after a week of obstacles: dog kennels all full, no one able to cover Lunch Club or children's work, house being painted (will not comment on the wisdom of deciding to arrange for renovations to coincide with a trip away). However, we did finally make it to the airport (after a brief return to the house because one of us forgot to put on shoes and suddenly realised they were wearing slippers – but we won't comment on that either).

The flight, with BA, was about 11 hours, which is way too long wherever you're sitting, but if your seat happens to be right next to the toilets, is even more unpleasant. The highlight – which almost made it worth it – was a brilliant view of the peak of Mount Fuji as we landed.

Finally arrived at *The Westin* in Tokyo. Hard to keep track of time when travelling, so several days had merged into one long one. Hotel was nice, dumped bags and went for a wander.

I have never been to Japan before, and had fairly low expectations. Tokyo is unexpected. It reminds me a little of the Stockholm I visited 20 years ago, in that it appears to be very clean and functional but with ugly buildings. And massive flyovers. Things are designed to work efficiently, not to look nice. Perhaps in a city this is sensible – I'm not sure people who work in London are particularly enamoured with the time it takes to edge your way around Trafalgar Square.

We went for a quick stroll, to a river near the hotel. The weather is humid but not too hot. We wandered through a little park, where school children were growing vegetables. We saw lots of bikes – many of them electric, and lots had a young child sitting in a child seat at the back. Japanese children are very, very cute.

I can tell you that everyone obeys the traffic signals, the streets are very clean, and everyone has the same hair as me.

This is weird, and feels rather surreal (perhaps not helped by being awake for about 36 hours now). In England, straight dark hair is fairly unusual, but here everyone has it. It is like looking at the back of me all the time. People are also very smart, and I feel scruffy and crumpled. I may have to do some ironing while we're here.

There are lots of men with flags, who wave you around every obstacle (sort of the opposite to India, where a deep hole in the street will be completely unmarked).

We went to the Shibuya district. There's a statue of *Hachiko*, a dog who sat outside the station every night waiting for his master, for ten years after his death. We also saw a famous road crossing, where people were pausing, in the middle, to take photographs – it's one of the iconic scenes of Tokyo.

We wandered around a district which appeared to be full of hairdressers – lots of shop windows filled with photos of women's faces. Checked the Chinese characters, and realised that they were in fact brothels – suggested to Husband that we might find a better area to walk around. (Later, someone told me that they weren't brothels, they are sort of escort services, without the sex.)

Went back to Ebisu district, which is where our hotel is. Wanted dinner, but didn't have the energy to cope with anything unfamiliar, so opted for Burger King. Buying a burger in a foreign language is challenge enough, but a combination of pointing and smiling, plus a very helpful server, managed to buy a couple of burgers. In Japan, "small" means small – I think I had a child's dinner (about 8 fries and a half-sized coke).

We pretty much sussed the underground system, it's a brilliant way to get around Tokyo. Went to bed feeling exhausted but not at all sleepy. The joys of jet-lag...

Startled by Beauty
I turn a corner, and happen upon a small pond, filled with water irises all in bloom, their sword-shaped leaves reaching towards the sky. The pond is edged with azalea and has a backdrop of shaped fir trees. It is beautiful, a tiny spot of perfection.

All around me, people are taking photographs. There are kneeling professionals, aiming long lenses for the best angle, tourists with iPhones, teenagers taking selfies. Everyone pauses, surprised by the beauty, snap a shot. Then they move on. Very few make use of the wooden benches, stop a while, take time to absorb the scene. We have become a species that rushes to record, to collect, to own. But we rarely live in the moment. How many of these photographs, I wonder, will be examined, enjoyed. Or will they too be quickly glanced at before put away? The next event is always more pressing, more important.

This was art. The sculptured trees, the colour, the trickle of water, the flash of bright koi as they swam through lilies. I was startled by the beauty. It is, perhaps, the most beautiful scene I have ever encountered.

****

The Imperial Gardens in Tokyo

We got a taxi to the Imperial Gardens (which was very silly, as the underground is a fraction of the price, safe and clean and would have delivered us to *Hibiya* station in less time. But we're tourists – knowing things takes time). We passed the *Nijubashhi*, which is a stone bridge over the river, and used to be the main entrance. Lots of people were taking photos, so we did too, assuming this was a famous landmark.

We walked to the park entrance, which seemed like a long way in the hot sun, and there weren't many signs, but we found it eventually. We were issued with tickets, which were free, and had to be returned at the end (am not entirely sure of their purpose).

The gardens were a mix of huge walls (the Japanese are very good at walls) and random buildings. We passed a restroom, which is NOT a washroom, but rather a shady area to sit and rest. Most Japanese gardens seem to have them. They have vending machines (everywhere in Japan has vending machines) and seating, sometimes people remove their shoes to enter, and they are generally quiet. I like them.

The gardens were also, at times, startlingly beautiful. I imagine that during different seasons, various areas would become more lovely. It is a garden you need to visit throughout the year. There were several trees that were bandaged and supported by posts, trimmed and encouraged to grow into the desired shape. Trees in Japan are also beautiful.

We went into an old guard's barracks. We had to remove our shoes, and were provided with a plastic bag to carry them. A man seemed to be employed for the sole purpose of taking the plastic bags from the 'finished' bin, folding them, and replacing them in the 'to use' bin. I am not at all why we needed to remove our shoes. The barracks were rebuilt, and had a modern Lino floor. It was where the soldiers lived, not died, so I don't think it had any sacred significance. Perhaps it was for cleanliness reasons – Japanese people are very clean.

***

The following day (after an almost completely sleepless night – jet-lag is horrible) we returned to another park in the same area. This time we went by underground. I am not convinced that Husband read the scale on the map properly, but perhaps I was just tired. After walking for about 6 hours, we found the entrance. I was not really in the mood for wandering around a park, so we went straight to the park cafe for lunch.

We ordered burgers and cokes, using our pointing and gesturing method. Japanese people all seem to be very polite and helpful, and they cope very well with people who speak no Japanese at all. The burger was really nice, very fresh, and served with salad (not the mushy slime you tend to get in the UK). Portions are smaller than in England – it would be easier to be healthier here I think. Lots of areas are for jogging, and we saw several runners.

We then realised we had seen most of the park on our way to the restaurant. It wasn't huge. We wandered around for a while, and found some shady tracks through trees, saw a couple of rest areas (vending machines and seats) and walked to a viewpoint over a river (somewhat marred by the massive flyover). Then we gave up, and went back to the hotel.

Tokyo is beginning to grow on me. The people are very polite, and friendly and helpful. When we are confused, people will stop, and ask if we need help. Everywhere is very clean, and it feels very safe. We saw people jogging around the parks, and they had left a bag with their belongings in, on a bench. Bikes are left unlocked. In restaurants and trains, people will leave their things – even mobile phones – on their seats while they order food or go to the washroom. No one seems to steal here, it is rather nice, how you feel society ought to be. We have not seen a single homeless person or beggar, which is very rare in a major city. Are there no homeless people in Japan?

I look forward to discovering more as we explore a little further.

Travelling Around Japan – A Few Tips
For the foreign traveller, Japan has a very user-friendly transport system.

Everyone knows that Japan has bullet trains. They are quick and easy. They are not the cheapest way to travel though. In 2018, a trip from Tokyo to Kyoto takes about 2 hours and costs about £200 return. It's a few pounds more if you want to reserve a seat. Announcements on the trains are in Japanese followed by English, and an onboard sign shows which station you are approaching. Each carriage has a map of the train, marking toilets, bins and crew positions. The seats are comfy, forward facing, and recline. When passengers disembark, they replace their seat to the upright position (Japanese people are very polite, they don't leave things in a way to inconvenience other people).

Buying tickets was relatively easy. We went to the ticket office, and staff spoke enough English to be helpful. They also told us which platform we needed. Platforms can be confusing, as different ends of the same platform have trains going to different places, but we found that other passengers were willing to help. Carriage positions are marked on the platform, so you can queue in the correct place. Stations have a shortage of seats, so don't go to the platform before you need to unless you enjoy standing.

Local trains stop at more stations, and have less comfy seats, but are still clean. The onboard facilities depend on the train.

Taxis can be hailed anywhere (unlike in Singapore, where there are special places, like bus stops for hailing cabs). When they are available, they have the Chinese symbol for 'free' 空 lit in red lights in the windscreen.

In some places (like *Hakone*) you can buy a ticket that covers trains, underground, and buses. The buses run to timetable, so be at the stop on time. The timetable will show the bus number or letter, which you then match with the sign on the bus stop. If you don't have a prepaid ticket, you take a ticket when you get on the bus, and pay the driver when you leave (though I think this varies, as some have machines for paying). The next stop is shown on a sign at the front, and you press a button to request a stop. I think eating on a bus is impolite, as is blowing your nose. So you might want to sit separately from your husband. (Just saying.)

When you arrive, stations have good facilities. There are often shops and cafes. Tokyo station even has tunnels full of market stalls!

Public toilets are clean, and tend to have both traditional toilets and European style ones. All the ones I found were free to use. They also provide loo paper (some countries don't). ALSO, Japan is the first country I have ever been in, where there is one cubicle designated for mothers of young babies. Inside, in the corner, there is a seat where you can strap a young child. This is SUCH a good idea – why do all countries not have them? Using the washroom with a young child tends to involve either abandoning them in a public place strapped into their buggy where you can't see them, or leaving the door open so the whole world can watch you pee, or attempting to hold them while you use the toilet (which they always see as a time to wriggle unhelpfully). On behalf of mothers everywhere I would like to say, well done Japan!

249

Walking around cities is safe, as pavements are clean and well maintained. Any building work or obstacles have men who wave red flags at you so you notice. Signs are in Japanese, so you need a good map. Roads have crossing points, with lights. Everyone obeys the lights. Sometimes you have to wait for a long time, but they tweet at you when the light is green, which is a helpful indication that you should stop writing emails if your wife has decided to ignore you. (Just saying.)

A Day Trip to Kyoto
Although I know very little about Japan, even I have heard of *geisha*. Which means I have heard of the ancient capital city, Kyoto. When I saw that it was possible to do a day trip from Tokyo, I was keen to visit.

Ate breakfast after another 'not much sleep' night and walked to Ebisu Station. We got the underground to a mainline JR station, and then tickets for the bullet train to Kyoto. We had reserved seats on the way there, but left the return journey open, as we weren't sure how much time we'd need in the city. There was a lot of flexibility, as trains left every ten minutes.

The bullet train was brilliant. At the end of the line, they turn all the seats, so you are always facing forwards. Your seat is comfortable, and reclines, with a pull-down table on the seat in front (like an aeroplane seat). There was a food/drink trolley. Eating on the train is acceptable (in Japan, eating in the street, or on a bus, is considered very bad manners). The journey took about 2 hours.

When we arrived, Kyoto seemed just the same as any other city – too much traffic, lots of tall buildings, people in suits looking busy, department stores. We popped in to the Tourist Information office in the station, and a helpful lady gave us a map and advice as to where we should walk. Her directions were good, but her distances were a little off, as we walked a very long way to reach the old part of the city.

Old Kyoto is a bit like a Japanese *Clovelly* – there were way too many tourists, and it was almost impossible to imagine what it used to be like. As we walked up the main street, avoiding the coaches, the over-priced gift shops, the coffee shops, I began to wonder why we'd come. It was school-trip world, I think every school in Japan was on an outing to Kyoto.

But as we found some back streets that were less busy, and got used to the general bustle, we started to notice things. There were lots of shops hiring kimono for the day, and many of the Japanese tourists were wearing them. I'm not sure why, it's clearly a thing to do. We glimpsed tiny gardens outside tea shops, many, many temples, and streets of two-storey wooden houses on narrow lanes. I saw a geisha hurrying past, but whether she was a real geisha or someone dressed up, I couldn't say.

The guide book said that the main Geisha District was Gion, so we walked there. I know that it is rare to see geisha today, but I hoped to be lucky. We left the main street, and began to wander down the narrow lanes. This area felt more seedy, with clubs and shuttered buildings. I wouldn't have walked there on my own. Then we saw lots of men with cameras, standing outside a small, wooden fronted house, which looked to me like an *okiya* – the house where girls live while they are training to be a geisha. In Kyoto, trainee geisha are called *maiko*. We asked a woman why all the photographers were there, and she told us that it was the debut day for one of the maiko. She was twenty, and had completed her geisha training, and would be taking her first walk as a geisha, which is a big event.

We were very lucky, as while we were talking, she emerged. All the photographers leapt forwards, cameras clicking, pushing for the best view. Then they followed her as she made her way down the street.

I'm not sure what my view of geisha is, as their role is slightly fuzzy. Historically, they were beautiful girls, trained to sing and dance and play a shamisen (a stringed instrument like a guitar). They were very elegant, witty, and trained as hostesses of the tea ceremony. They earned money by entertaining rich men, a sort of ritualised escort. Their aim seems to have been to be taken on as a mistress, so supported as a companion by a wealthy protector. They weren't prostitutes, as they didn't trade sex for money, and were more like concubines, faithful to one man. However, sometimes this was not by choice, and beautiful young girls were trafficked, sold to okiya. Clearly wrong.

Over time, the role of the geisha has changed. After the war, lots of allied troops came to Japan, and they wanted to sleep with geisha, so prostitutes copied their costume and style, and the word geisha became synonymous with prostitute. However, the tradition of geisha continued, and today, they prefer to be called geiko, emphasising that they train in the arts, and are entertainers, not sex workers. I'm not sure if it's the same as being an actress or ballet dancer in western culture (bearing in mind that a hundred years ago, ballet dancers were the scantily dressed girls who appeared at the end of an opera, who posed for the men in the audience, hoping to procure a male protector – yet we do not today think that girls who want to be ballet dancers are sex workers).

I decided to not think about it too deeply, and simply enjoyed seeing a piece of Japanese culture. I glimpsed the white face, meant to resemble a mask, hiding the geisha's real face. A section of her neck, an erotic area in Japan, is left unpainted (like a revealed shoulder can be more seductive than a nearly naked body). Her hair was full of ornaments, and I know that geisha have wooden head rests rather than pillows, so their hair is kept in place at night (which sounds extremely uncomfortable, and I'm surprised they're not all cranky from lack of sleep). Their collar is dipped at the back, to expose that erotic neck, and a geisha has a white collar, whereas a meiko will have a coloured collar.

They wear white socks, and walk on platformed wooden shoes, which also look extremely uncomfortable. The long sash is called an obi, and requires another person to help tie it. Their silk kimono are beautiful, and very costly. In the past, the okiya owned the kimono, which was a way of controlling the geisha, as she needed to remain with the house (and pay them some of her earnings) in order to work.

Human history is always interesting, and so much more complex than we first think. I'm glad I saw a geisha, as they seem like an intrinsic part of Japanese history. But I'm not sure how long they will be here for, there is too much that jars with modern life.

Hakone Tozan

I fancied being away from a city, plus I saw a picture in a guide book of a pirate ship, so we went to Hakone Tozan. The guide book listed all sorts of activities, like hot springs and cable cars and temples (Japan has lots and lots of temples) but all I wanted was a little countryside with a view of Mount Fuji...and maybe a pirate ship. (If I'm honest, I might not have mentioned the pirate bit to Husband.)

We got a train into Tokyo, then the *shinkansen* (a bullet train) to Odawar. There we were able to buy a two-day pass to the Hakone area. We took the local tourist train (Hakone Tozan Railway) to Hakone Yumoto. Here, we caught a bus, which went up the mountain, to Lake Ashi.

Lake Ashi was exactly what I'd hoped. As we arrived, the sun was shining, and there, in the distance, was Mount Fuji. It was very clear, and very exciting. The lake has ferries, which take you to various tourist spots, and one is designed to look like a pirate ship. I could tell Husband was impressed. (Actually, if I'm honest, his only comment was to wonder how they managed to get full-sized ferries onto a mountain lake. Did they build them on site, or were they helicoptered in?)

The whole area is a well known tourist spot, so there were lots of facilities (and luckily for us, not too many tourists). We bought lunch in a 7-Eleven (which is, interestingly, a Japanese owned chain) and ate next to the lake. Then we walked to a view point, across a bridge where you could see koi, up two hundred steps through a woodland hill. There were birds calling, the weather was warm and humid, the air felt green and peaceful. It was all pretty perfect.

We considered hiring a rowing boat or peddle boat, taking the ferry across to a temple, or going to see the hot springs. But really, to simply sit in the sun and listen to the water lapping and the birds singing, was all we wanted. That and a bin for the rubbish – Husband was strangely fixated on finding a dustbin.

We then caught the bus back to Hakone Yumoto. We bought tickets for the Romance Train, which was a slower and cheaper way to get to Shinjuku, where we could go on the JR line to the hotel. A 'Romance Train' is not, by the way, romantic. Kissing in public is considered indecent in Japan, and we saw very few people even holding hands.

Fabulous day out.

I loved Japan – it is one of the few countries that I feel I could live in. Although the cities were, to be blunt, ugly (well – the ones we saw were ugly) the natural beauty is spectacular. But mainly, I really liked being somewhere with people who were polite and helpful, so it all felt very safe.

Camber Sands, UK

Mum said she wanted a week by the sea, and I can write anywhere, so I told her that if she didn't mind being ignored until midday each day, I would take her to Camber Sands. Am hoping we don't murder each other.

Other people's reactions to the news were telling. My children all declined to join us, citing work/parties/washing their hair as plausible excuses. My siblings all advised I take lots of alcohol. My friends all said, "A *whole week?* Gosh!" I expect they were jealous.

We set off on Saturday. The dog filled the whole boot, so I told Mum we could only take what would fit behind her seat. I packed the dog, my stuff (one tiny bag) and the food (quite a lot of bags) and went to collect Mum. Her stuff was already packed, and in a long line down the front path and round the corner and half way to the next town.

Arrived at the cottage in one piece, despite my dodgy driving and fairly useless brain and completely useless SatNav. We have rented a two-bedroomed house from 'Beside the Sea' cottages. It's on a little estate of pastel coloured houses, and is 3 minutes walk from the beach. The house is pretty small (Mum suggested we could empty a cupboard for big smelly dog to live in) but it's very pretty. It also – most importantly – has a shower with decent water pressure, an outside hose (for rinsing big smelly dog) and two washrooms. There are also a few luxuries, like a Nespresso machine (am on my 4th coffee this morning and the world is buzzing) and Netflix. The owners have included helpful things like capsules for the dishwasher and hand soap for all the sinks, and we arrived to cake and biscuits and a bottle of wine. All very nice.

After a quick cup of tea, we walked to the beach. In the summer months, the only part of the beach where dogs are allowed is accessed via sand dunes. Dragged Mum over one the height of Snowdon but we made it to the beach. Tried to take selfies – realised neither of us were very good at this, and we now have several photos of our feet, and the sky, and the dunes. Both dog and mother went completely nuts and insisted on paddling. Mother told me she thought I was completely ridiculous to be wearing wellies on the beach in June. But I have lived with Husband for too long. And I hate sandy feet.

Sunday:
I took the dog for an early run. The tide in Camber goes out for miles and miles, so we had a good walk. The only other people out there were fishermen digging for lugworms. I worried a little that the tide might come in and we'd get cut-off, but there were no warning signs (only about riptides for swimmers) so we walked 27 miles out to the sea and back. Kia chased seagulls and brought me dead crabs and stones to throw. (I didn't throw the dead crabs, in case you're wondering.)

Met Mum and we walked to the little wood and brick church on the main road, next to Pontins. People seemed friendly, and there was coffee and cake afterwards, which Mum stayed for as she likes chatting to strangers; and I didn't, as I don't.

We had lunch at The King's Head in Playdon. I've been there before, and it never disappoints. It's pretty and cosy and the food is lovely. Spent the rest of the day walking and reading and watching Netflix.

Monday
This morning I walked along a footpath towards Rye (I couldn't face even more sand and wet dog, I figured one trip to the beach a day would be fine.) The path went past fields of chubby lambs and great pools of deep water with fishermen next to them, and was lined with poppies. Camber seems to have lots of poppies in

June. Came back to write this, and will now do some work. So far the week is going well, and we are both still alive.

***

Well, you'll be pleased to know I have managed to not murder Mum, so far... In fact, we're having a rather nice time, here at Camber Sands. The little cottage we've rented is turning out very well, everything works, and there are a few novelties. I am enjoying the Nespresso machine, Mum was unexpectedly taken by the spy-hole in the front door. I haven't liked to ask how often she stands there spying on the neighbours. Even the dog is happy, as she simply adores the beach.

The beach is great, though we did have a near-disaster yesterday, as we hadn't realised the tide was coming in, and we were walking along a sandbank, completely oblivious to the water rushing in between us and the beach. The water wasn't deep, and we'd noticed in time to wade back to the beach, but it was bit of a shock. None of this was helped by a particularly bouncy dog who thought it was great that I was finally joining her in the sea.

Today we had another disaster – not our fault – as we decided to go to Rye for the day. I hate driving, and find it particularly stressful driving through towns I don't know, trying to find a carpark. And I know Rye has lots of one-way streets. There is a map in the cottage, but it doesn't show the one-way streets AND it has South at the top. So it's all backwards. (I find this completely irritating – *who* would draw a map with South *at the top*???)

Anyway, when Mum suggested that we could catch a bus into town, it seemed like an excellent plan. I took the dog for an early walk (ignoring her when she pulled desperately towards the beach path, as I didn't want her to get wet, so she had to settle for the fields) and checked the timetable at the bus-stop. There are buses every hour, so we planned to catch the 11:13 bus, wander around Rye, have lunch, and catch a bus home early afternoon. Perfect – or so we thought.

We allowed plenty of time to walk to the bus-stop, so were there about 11:05. We stood at the shelter, and I worried they might not take notes or cards and I didn't have enough change. At 11:13, there was no bus, but Mum, who catches a lot of buses, assured me they are often a few minutes late.

At 11:50 the bus arrived. Happy days.

Mum and I stepped onto the bus. The driver said, "I can only take one of you."

We stared at him. I nearly asked which one – but decided it wouldn't be polite. The bus was full of people, and the driver refused to take any more. Bus then sped away, and we walked back to cottage. The dog was pleased to see us.

We ate in a pub in Camber instead, and had a nice time, and will take the dog on the beach later. But it was a bit of a shame, especially as until recently there had been more buses, so we'd have got a seat. It must be infuriating for people who are local, to have the bus to Rye full of holiday-makers. Perhaps the bus company will reconsider the cuts for the summer months. I hope so.

***

I prefer Camber in the winter, when you can walk the dog along the whole beach, but it's cold. Even in the summer, it always seems to be windy.

We had very good weather. It was always windy, but it was dry, and warm in the sand dunes. On Friday, the main road was quite busy, which gave a taste of how it must be in high season, when I imagine it would be fairly difficult to cross the road if you're a slow walker (which one of us was).

The beach is flat and sandy – so great for kids wanting to build sandcastles or old ladies who like to paddle, or dogs who want to dig and bounce through waves. The carparks all seem to have toilets, and there are plenty of bins.

However, the tide comes in unevenly, so you have to watch out so you don't get cut-off. This can be dangerous for non-swimmers. And there are rip tides, which are dangerous for swimmers. They now have life-guards on duty (which I've never seen before) and signs telling you the tide times and where is safe to swim. One day there were jellyfish in the water, but I have come to Camber many times, and never seen them before, so perhaps we were just unlucky. Another hazard, is towards the Rye end, where at low tide, some of the sand is oily. It is the wet sand, and your feet sink into the sand and then come out black, which is very unpleasant, and bit of a worry with the dog, who was most unhelpful about being taken into the sea to be washed. I still maintain that wellies are the best footwear for a beach.

The marshes around Camber are beautiful, and there are paths and cycle routes through them. You can hire bikes in Rye and Camber While we were there, they were full of poppies and chubby lambs and water birds.

So that's it, a quick review of Camber Sands. If you would like to also borrow my mother to take for company, I'm sure that can be arranged.

Portugal 2018

August 2018
One week before we leave, and most of Europe seems to be covered by a heatwave. England is hot and dry. The family decided it would be helpful to check the weather in Portugal:45°. This has caused Bea some angst, as her primary reason for holidaying is to get a suntan, and 45° is too hot for sunbathing. The boys were extremely sympathetic and offered much advice.

Emm assured her that she could buy a suntan from Boots, and that he'd always felt that orange was her colour.

11th August
For once, we had a civilised flight time, and set off in the taxi for the airport. Bea was meeting us at Heathrow, and Jay kept her updated on our progress. He sent her helpful messages such as: "Leaving from Gatwick," "They are now calling our flight," "We are boarding now," "Byeeee..."

Luckily after twenty years of brothers, Bea ignored him, and met us at the bag drop. We went for breakfast.

I like having a daughter, we can share 'girl stuff' together. I told her that I wanted to buy a travel hairbrush, and she told me she has one that has the main part with the bristles, but no handle. I'm fairly sure this is a dog brush.

Flight was fine. Emm (Factoid Boy) sat next to me and told me lots of facts about Portugal. Some of them were very interesting.

Collected car, drove to Sheraton Hotel. Husband got us upgraded to a suite. The hotel has a glass lift (quite noisy when Bea and the boys went up in it).

Walked to metro, and caught a train to the old town. We had ice-creams in Freedom Square, Emm ate custard tart, as that's a local dish. We wandered around, and then spent six hours trying to find a restaurant on Trip Advisor. Jay recommended a steakhouse, Bea didn't feel that boded well for vegetarian options.

Eventually, booked a table at *A Despensa*, a lovely Italian restaurant. Great service/food/atmosphere. Confusingly labelled toilets (the gender was only marked inside the door).

Metro to hotel.

Bed. Slept well.

Sunday 12th August

Woke 7am. Weather cloudy – hope no one notices.

Metro into Porto, and walked down to the river – very pretty. Most restaurants here seem to be fully booked or closed, but we found somewhere nice for lunch.

After lunch, crossed the bridge, and saw a boy who was standing on the balustrade, as if about to dive into the river. The river had quite large boats, so I wondered if he'd die. Several people stopped to take photos, and his friends wandered through the crowd collecting money. I think it was a scam, as he never jumped, and later a different boy was standing there.

The Gaia side of the Douro River is the north side, so has less sun, and it's where all the port cellars are. We toured Calems. This was brilliant. The tour-guide looked like she was about 12 years old and she was very witty. Portuguese humour is very similar to English humour. We tasted three types of port, and chatted to a merry couple from Angelsey.

On the way out, we walked through the shop, and everyone bought some bottles of port (it was cheaper than in the UK).

Portugal is one of the main cork growing places in the world. They are trying to increase the popularity of cork by using it for products other than wine stoppers. So as we walked around, we saw lots of shops selling postcards made of cork. We all bought one for our mothers/partners who are back in England. We passed a postbox with a fun sculpture next to it, so took lots of photos and posted our cards. Then we worried that the postbox was just part of the sculpture, and not a proper postbox at all. Tried to retrieve cards, but it was impossible. All the post-offices in Portugal seem to be yellow – so why would there be a red English postbox? I fear we may never see those cards again.

Caught Metro. I somehow managed to get separated from the others, and didn't know where I was going, or where the hotel was. Felt abandoned. Bea sent me a message, telling me where to get off.

It was raining (*raining!*) so we got taxis back to the cathedral. (We popped in to the cathedral earlier, but I didn't mention it because I didn't like it.) Husband and I were in one taxi, the kids in the other, and our driver was very concerned that our 'children' were on their own. I decided not to tell him how old they are.

We walked to several fully-booked restaurants. Eventually found one with okay (ish) food and okay (ish) service. No one got food poisoning, which is the main thing.

Walked back to the metro in the rain.

Monday 13th August
A terrible night's sleep.

Went down for a Sheraton breakfast, which was rather brilliant – it caters for all of us. I have fruit and pancakes, others have eggs, some people (no judgement) have fruit and pancakes and bacon and cheeses and eggs and pastries and salmon and mushrooms and…

Metro into Porto (hotel is really a business hotel, so although it's comfortable, it's a long way from the 'touristy' stuff). We walked past the postbox sculpture where we posted our postcards – have a sense of doom about those cards.

Saw a shop which sold tins of sardines. Just tins of sardines. The tins were brightly coloured and dated, right back to the early 1900s (I am hoping the sardines inside did not also date back that far). They were intended as gifts, due to Portugal being a centre for sardines, but at 7 euro each, they were a bit too expensive a novelty for me. Shame, Mum likes sardines and her postcard is probably lost forever.

Pizza lunch in a café that had nice pizza, but no light in the ladies loo. As in, no light – not a missing bulb, there was no fitting; which with no window either made for an interesting experience.

Went on a 'free' walking tour (you pay whatever you feel the tour was worth, at the end). Met Pedro, our geographer-turned-tour-guide. He was interesting, with some good sarcastic humour, though not especially friendly. Part of the tour was to a student café, which is called – in Portuguese – 'Head lice café'. Pedro can say "head lice" in 26 different languages. Useful skill.

We also saw two churches, built almost – but not quite – touching. The Catholic church doesn't allow churches to have adjoining walls (why?) so between the two churches was a narrow house. This is possibly the inspiration for Sirius Black's house in the Harry Potter stories, as J. K. Rowling lived in Porto for a while. We saw the queue of people waiting to pay to go in to the bookshop which is thought to have inspired her moving staircases, and the Diagon Alley shops.

J. K. Rowling has clearly been good for Porto. So too, is Ryan Air, as apparently before they began cheap flights to Porto, no one ever visited the city. This might actually be true, because many of the nice restaurants were fully booked, and it was often hard to find somewhere to eat.

There are more tourists than the city is quite ready for. The prices are also low at the moment – how long before they catch up with demand, I wonder?

Pedro told us that there is still some poverty in Portugal, a remainder from the days when it was a dictatorship, and people were encouraged to have big families, little education, and mainly farm for a living. He said the statue of a blindfolded Lady Justice, with her folded scales, show how the law courts functioned under the regime. Portugal had a peaceful revolution, and it's now a democracy. It is also very hot, and a 3 hour tour was slightly too long for me.

We went to McDonald's to recover. It used to be the Imperial Restaurant, and has chandeliers and art nouveau decorations. It also has dirty tables and disgusting toilets, so I didn't like it.

Metro back to the hotel.

Tuesday 14th August
9am breakfast. The boys had Champagne with their breakfast. They eat loads.

Left hotel about 11 am. Drove south towards Lisbon.

Arrived in Lisbon and booked into another Sheraton.

I sat in the lounge with the boys, looking out across Lisbon, while they drank beers. Husband went swimming with Bea. Some food arrived in the lounge, and we debated how angry Husband would be if we ate some before dinner. We agreed we'd all eat some and not tell him; we were just tucking in when he arrived! Felt guilty.

Got metro to old part of the city. Went to a burger and lobster place.

Wednesday 15th August
I went into breakfast on my own (very scary). I took a book. It was a very nice breakfast, and they put coffee pots on the table, which was better than having to wait to be served. Slight problem when I went to the buffet, and then had one of those 'car park moments' – no idea where my table was. Wandered around, pretending I fancied a stroll, then spotted my book and went back to the table.

I went for a walk, to try and find the prison we could see from the lounge. (Husband and Jay stayed at the hotel and went for a swim.) I got lost, so Bea had to guide me home.

Dinner at a Pizza Hut near the hotel, which was actually rather nice; especially the sangria.

Thursday 16th August
We agreed a time to meet to go sight-seeing.

We walked from the metro through the old part of the city to the castle. Jay didn't buy a fridge magnet. I didn't buy a cork cushion. We did however, find a queue. We weren't sure what it was for, but we're British, we joined it. It turned out to be a queue for the castle, so all good.

The castle had great views of the city, and very long lines for the washrooms.

We walked along cobbled streets, trying not to slip.

Ate lunch at Comidas de Santiago. They brought us bread, olives and fishcakes when we sat down. We then looked at the menu, and saw that these were charged for, and would have added €20 to the bill, so asked for them to be removed.

Went back to the hotel. Family went in the pool, and I Googled 'postboxes in Porto'. It turns out that the one where we posted our cork cards *is* a real one after all.

Dinner back in the city centre. Bea said that there aren't many people in Lisbon. We caught the metro during rush-hour and found them all. The metro station has saying written on the walls and ceilings, and strange gargoyles. We recharge our tickets (*bilh*) with extra journeys (*tickets*).

We walked through Arco da Rua Augusta (a big archway) to Paça do Comercio (a big square) where we saw a little beach. We had dinner in a nice Italian. The waiter (Portuguese) said he preferred us to speak in English as it was easier to understand than our bad Portuguese. Oh! We ordered a starter platter, which was huge, and sangria.

Friday 17th August
On a clear day, you can see Sintra from Lisbon. Husband suggested that we spent a day there, but a quick perusal of his guidebook, and we all declined, as it looked boring.

At breakfast, Emm said his Portuguese friend had said we should *definitely* visit Sintra, and he'd checked on the internet, and it looked really interesting. He showed us exciting pictures of deep wells you could walk down, and fairy castles, and we all decided to go. Husband said very little.

Most online reports about Sintra said you shouldn't drive, as there is nowhere to park and the walk to the palace is very steep. However, most online reports were written by tour companies, who earn their living transporting people to the palace, so we ignored them and drove.

Parking in Sintra was something of a challenge, because although there was a massive car-park (where a person could lose their car for several days) there were not many spaces. As people returned to their cars, a man rushed to stand in the space, and his friend then guided arriving cars to that space and charged a fee. We managed to avoid both scammers and a fee, by following a returning parked pedestrian, and then parking in their spot.

Bea then led us down lots of hills, and then up the same hills, to Quinta da Regaleira. This had very pretty grottos and follies, and way too many tourists. The best thing was the Tower of Initiation, which was the deep well we'd seen in pictures. It looked better in the pictures than in real life.

I wore practical clothes/shoes for the trip. Only Emm, who was also wearing 'practical clothes' would be in photographs with me. However, as our next task was to walk up a mountain, I was quite pleased I had worn my big trainers. We walked up (a lot of up) a narrow cobbled road, diving into bushes to avoid the coaches which filled the whole space, and tuk-tuks whizzing down, so you hoped the 10 year old driving had good brakes. I think these are the people who wrote those reports.

We reached the palace, and more long queues. There were queues to buy tickets, then queues to enter the grounds, followed by a super-long queue to enter the actual palace. To increase the challenge further, there were two queues to buy tickets – one to a ticket office and one to a machine.

Quick family discussion to decide strategy (not my genes) then family split; satellite group going to machine queue, main group staying in line for ticket office. Can life get more exciting? (If you prefer a less exciting trip, you can save time and buy tickets online at home.)

The castle was amazing. Ferdinand II built it as a summer palace for the royal family. He commissioned Eschwege, a German architect who was well travelled and wanted to incorporate lots of different elements. It has parts of Islamic influence, and Medieval elements. He said he wanted it to be like an opera – and it sort of is. It was completed in 1854. The last queen of Portugal, Queen Amelia, spent her last night here before she fled to Brazil. It really is amazing – sort of Taj Mahal meets Disney.

However, there were too many people, and too many queues.

The inside of the palace was pretty, but with so many visitors it reminded me of the slow shuffle through the Vatican, and it wasn't as worth seeing. The best part is the outside.

There is lots more to do in the area, like the Castle of the Moors, and of course the palace gardens and Sintra itself. But we were tired by the time we'd seen inside the palace, so we returned to the hotel via about 25 different motorways (car has a weird SatNav).

We rested at the hotel for about 3½ minutes, then went back into Lisbon. Jay bought a fridge magnet, then found a better one, so bought that too. I bought a cork cushion cover for way more money than I'd planned.

We ate in *Figu's*. Husband and Jay shared a 'seafood rice', which was a sort of paella with massive prawns and half lobsters. It looked fun. The boys drank 1L beers, so everything looked fun to them.

A nice day, if somewhat exhausting.

Saturday 18th August
Breakfast. Boys only 10 minutes late.

We did a quick trip to the supermarket. Bought a range of breads and crisps and plastic looking cheese slices. My bread rolls have a use-by date of next year, so I'm not convinced they have much that's natural in them.

Left the Sheraton 11:30. The resort in the Algarve only had a P.O. box address, so Husband looked on their website and entered the town name – *Praia da Falesia* – into the SatNav. All seemed fine.

After driving for about an hour, the SatNav directed us off the motorway. Jay checked, and said he thought it was probably avoiding the traffic queues which were ahead. The roads grew smaller and smaller. When we were directed down an unpaved road, we began to suspect something was wrong. Could the SatNav have been tampered with by a gang of criminals, who were waiting to rob and kill wealthy tourists they had led to remote Portugal?

No. There is another Praia da Falesia, a farm, in the middle of nowhere.

We found a very long route back to the correct motorway (some of the roads needed tarmac, but Husband didn't comment). We passed several trees, which we worked out were cork trees, as all the lower bark had been removed.

We stopped at services for petrol and washrooms (not food). There were many queues. Husband had to queue before he could fill with petrol, then fill the car, then queue again to pay. This took 20 minutes, which meant the people 3 cars behind had an hour's wait. Crazy system.

We found Pine Cliffs Resort in Algarve. Had rather more trouble finding reception. Drove 47 loops of the resort. It looks very lovely, with white buildings and fountains and beautiful gardens. Eventually we found the reception. Husband was fairly grumpy and completely adamant that none of us should accompany him to the reception desk. We were given the keys to our villa/flat.

We are staying in Pine Cliffs Residences, which is a little flat with hotel services. We have 3 bedrooms, 3 bathrooms, a lounge/dining room, and a kitchen/utility room. They clean and change the towels and replenish the toiletries, just like in a hotel room. It's pretty. Unfortunately, it also has quite a lot of ants.

Family went to one of the swimming pools, Husband and I went to the Intermarche to buy food for lunches. And ant powder.

The resort has several restaurants, but they were very expensive (we were quoted €40 per person). A short walk away, there are several restaurants and a supermarket, so we used those. They were much cheaper, and still nice – in many ways they were better, as the resort is full of English people, and it was nice to eat in places that Portuguese tourists ate.

We had dinner in *Ristorante Pizzeria S. Martino* – a nice Italian restaurant with a good selection of pizzas. I had a nice gnocchi dinner, followed by a horrible marshmallow ice-cream (which tasted of bubble-gum).

Sunday 19th August
Breakfast. It felt slightly more 'mass produced' than the Sheraton (but new hotels always feel less nice than the previous ones initially). It had a very good selection, and loads of fresh fruit. We ate under a canopy, looking out to the grounds. It's all very pretty. The coffee was a bit rough.

We went to the beach. Very easy to get lost here. Pine Cliffs is at the top of a cliff (clue in the name) and there's a lift down to sun loungers and a towel collection place.

We attempted to swim, but the sea was *so* rough. I never managed to get beyond the breakers, and I drank a lot of sea water during the attempt. It tasted nasty (in case you're wondering). Also had bit of an issue with swimsuit elastic.

Lunch in villa. Husband made coffee; while I gave everyone lunch, cleared away lunch, did 5 loads of washing and spring-cleaned the house. But it was nice coffee.

I read and slept, with many interruptions from maintenance men who don't read 'please do not disturb' signs; while family went to the pool.

Dinner in *Ristorante O Antonio* on the road outside the resort. Very pleasant.

Walked back to villa and played 'Unstable Unicorns' (Emm's card game) which was surprisingly fun, even when sober.

Monday 20th August

The veranda is full of dead ants (I'm not sure why they decided to cross the ant powder line).

We drove to a cork factory. Had a (quite long) lesson about how cork is harvested and manufactured. Very interesting (if long). We then had a tour of the factory. I liked seeing all the machines, and how the whole process worked. The boys spent the time devising new machines, that could replace the people and speed up production.

Sandwich lunch at the villa.

Dinner at *Restaurant Adega TiCosta* – another one from the road outside the resort. There was quite a long wait for the food, but the meals were really nice. Husband and Jay shared a fish stew thing, which they raved over. Husband then told us we should all have chocolate mousse for dessert, as it's a local speciality. Bea and I had coconut ice-cream, but the others had mousse. It was nice, but very rich.

Played 'Unstable Unicorns' again. I won, again. It is a game of much skill and mental prowess.

Tuesday 21st August
Breakfast uneventful.

Walked along the beach towards the town. The sea was much calmer, though very cold. Had a quick swim. It's a nice family beach, several children had large inflatables (and worried parents).

Bea and Emm stayed by the pool.

Husband and I went to the supermarket. Not a very nice job, as it's small and hot with too many people and nowhere to park. I bought some sardines for Mum (she likes sardines on toast, and sardines are very Portuguese!)

Cleaner arrived when we had lunch. They always seem to come at inconvenient times, and they take ages. The supplies they replenish seems to be fairly random.

Dinner at *'Stews and More'* in Albufeira. Very tasty little hotpots, with brilliant puddings.

Wednesday 22nd August

Drove to the west coast. Emm told us there are interesting geological features, due to the cliffs being pushed up by converging plates. It was a long drive.

We found a cove – but it was very full, and we were searching for 'secluded'.

Drove to next cove. Found a car park (full). Walked 15 minutes (in midday sun) through olive groves and fig trees (pretty). Saw a medieval fort (which some oink had written graffiti on). Found cove – it was very hot – and very full. Waves crashing onto beach, topless girls, dogs playing, absolutely no shade from the very hot sun.

Walked back to the car. Lunch at *Alandra*, which Jay found (impressively) on his phone when we were 3 minutes away. It was nice, with lots of frog ornaments, clean washrooms, and omelettes. While we ate, Jay did a very thorough phone-case clean out (he had dropped it in the sand). Family then had an in depth discussion about the multi-layered, very expensive, phone-case. I guess it used up the time.

Drove to another cove. As we drew nearer, we could see the mist rolling in from the sea, like a great cloud billowing into the valley. When we reached the cove, it was completely misty, we couldn't see the edges of the cove or out to sea beyond the breakers. Was rather cool. There was a surf school, and the line of wet-suit clad surfers waiting in a line out to sea, just visible in the mist, were like malevolent sharks.

There were lots of surfers on the beach – all suntanned and muscle-bound. I read Joanna Trollope, Bea sunbathed (the mist was clearing by this point). A woman walked along the beach, asking everyone if they would like to buy a "bottle of iced wee". We decided we didn't.

Drove back to the resort. Changed and showered then walked back to the pizza place. I had a very nice lasagne.

Thursday 23rd August

Breakfast. It is such a good breakfast. I have pancakes and fruit and yogurt. Jay tried the porridge. Husband had salmon and fried stuff.

Drove to some shops so Jay could buy an Algarve fridge magnet for his set. Successful.

Afternoon on the beach.

The hotel provides bathroom toiletries. The body lotion and hair conditioner look identical. I am hoping body lotion is good for hair.

After dinner, we played the unicorn game again. I won.

Friday 24th August
Breakfast was nice, as usual.

We went to Alte, a pretty village on the side of a hill. Away from the sea breeze, it was incredibly hot. We wandered around, looking at a donkey in a shed, a church, and a statue in a river, where the women used to do their washing. A man tried to sell Husband some suncream, but he refused, so the man cycled away.

We ate ice-creams, then drove back to Pine Trees.

On the way back, we spotted a large Intermarche, and Bea was keen to buy avocados to make guacamole, so we stopped.

After lunch, the family went to the beach. Husband realised that the man trying to sell him suncream had actually being trying to return our suncream, which Jay had left on top of our car. So much I could have said to both of them...

Saturday 25th August
Breakfast: Husband gave everyone champagne, and we had a toast.

Packed. I forgot to take the sugar out of the microwave (it was put there so the ants didn't find it). We packed the unopened wine – Husband always buys a bottle of wine on holiday. We left the villa clean, but with drifts of ant powder across all the doorways.

Drove to Faro airport. Returned the rental car. We were met by a very nice taxi driver, in a very nice big Merc. He was Spanish.

We drove down, through Spain, to the border with Gibraltar.

At the Gibraltar border, we switched taxis (because the Spanish won't drive taxis into Gibraltar). The new driver was very jolly, and told us lots of facts about Gibraltar. On the way to the hotel (*The Rock Hotel*) we drove across the airport runway. It has a sort of zebra-crossing, and before a plane can land, they stop all the traffic and sweep the runway. If there's a game in the nearby stadium, it has to be paused, in case the ball goes onto the runway. How funny!

I really liked Gibraltar. It's like England of 100 years ago. Our hotel is very spacious, with balconies overlooking the port.

Dinner at Wagamamas. It was a nice evening.

Sunday 26th August 2018
Breakfast at 9am Gibraltar time (an hour earlier). It was nice, but not as good as previous hotels. It did feel very "English" though, with all the things you would expect to see at a B&B – even the sausages were English. Which is a bit odd, as I assume everything has to be shipped in.

We caught a cable car to the top of the rock (because the people who are scared of cable cars were in the minority and therefore ignored). There were brilliant views, and I think I could see Africa across the sea (but that might just be dodgy geography).

There were also quite a lot of monkeys. We had looked online beforehand, so knew that they were likely to try and steal any bags that looked exciting, and a struggle with a determined monkey might result in a bite, which would have been bit of a negative. Husband agreed to carry a backpack, and we put all our smaller bags in there. We did see one woman being leapt upon by a monkey which did try to steal her bag, so I didn't feel entirely safe. I don't really like monkeys in the wild (there were lots in Delhi too). They look at you with very calculating eyes, like people but with absolutely no restraints at all. They also move very fast. There was one monkey that came to pose on a post, so everyone was taking photos, then with one smooth leap he had left his position was right amongst all the tourists, in what felt quite a threatening way.

Some people were putting their young children very close to a monkey, and taking photos, but this felt very unsafe to me. It was especially worrying when we had to pass a mother monkey and her baby on a narrow path, with a big male sitting next to them, watching us with his yellow eyes.

However, we didn't get attacked, and all was fine, and it was very interesting to see them.

We went into the siege caves, and saw lots of military stuff. Really, you needed to be someone who enjoys caves to appreciate this. Or military stuff.

We walked down to the town (further than you might think, and very steep in places). Had lunch in a pub, which was exactly like an English pub, complete with revolting toilets, but due to being in Portugal for a while, it felt like a novelty.

Bea went to the pool, and we set off for a walk across Gibraltar. This involved lots of steep hills, and lots of hot sun. We saw more monkeys. It was a nice walk, as you can almost always see the sea below you. Gibraltar feels like an island. We walked to Europa Point, then caught a bus back to the hotel.

We ate dinner at *Grouchos*. I think this is not part of the chain of *Grouchos* in the UK, but it was still excellent, with huge steaks. Husband spent a lot of time evaluating the cooking technique of the man next to us in the kitchen galley. I am hoping for good things next time he barbecues.

Monday 27th August 2018
After breakfast, we all piled into a taxi and drove to Gibraltar airport. As we could practically see the airport from the hotel, there was a move to maybe not get there the usual 16 hours before the flight that Husband likes. However, we also discovered

that if the weather isn't exactly right, planes detour and land in Malaga – which means all the passengers from Gibraltar then have to be bussed to Malaga – so we were keen to not be late. There was, I think a compromise (though we didn't exactly have to rush through the airport).

One very exciting aspect of Gibraltar airport is the price of alcohol in the DutyFree shop. There were quick online searches about import tax, and a few choice bottles were added to our luggage. I didn't even know it was possible to buy vodka bottles that big!

The airport is small, more like a bus station really (which I guess, given the number of times passengers are bussed to Malaga, is not inappropriate). We could go outside, and watch them stop the traffic and sweep the runway, ready for incoming flights. It was quite exciting to watch our own flight land.

When it was time to board, we walked out, across the tarmac, to our plane. As it took off, I tried hard not to think about the length of the runway, and the deep blue sea waiting at the end. Then we were up, Gibraltar was falling away below us, and another, very happy, holiday was over.

Thank you for reading my holiday diaries, I hope you enjoyed them. Please tell someone else about them.

You can read more of my writing on my weekly blog:
anneethompson.com

You can find my novels in bookshops and Amazon.

Also by Anne E. Thompson

Fiction
Hidden Faces
Invisible Jane
Counting Stars
JOANNA
Clara – A Good Psychopath?
Ploughing Through Rainbows

Non-Fiction
How to Have a Brain Tumour

Printed in Poland
by Amazon Fulfillment
Poland Sp. z o.o., Wrocław